Empathy and Ideology

Rand McNally Series in the Organization Sciences

Empathy and Ideology
Aspects of Administrative Innovation

Edited by

Charles Press
Michigan State University

Alan Arian
Tel Aviv University

Rand McNally & Company   Chicago

Rand McNally Series in the Organization Sciences
Robert T. Golembiewski, *Editor*

Abrahamson, *The Professional in the Organization*
Cornog, *EDP Systems in Public Management*
Golembiewski, *Organizing Men and Power*
Golembiewski and Gibson, *Managerial Behavior and Organization Demands*
Press and Arian, *Empathy and Ideology*

Preface

The original contributions collected in this volume were commissioned as part of a report to the Metropolitan Fund of Detroit, Michigan, made by the Institute for Community Development of Michigan State University. The report was part of a study design for a National Institute for Public Affairs project which was to determine the kinds of knowledges useful to public administrators. The purpose of the project was to suggest what kinds of university training would be appropriate for administrators at midcareer. The procedure we followed was one of seeking contributions from members of a number of disciplines.

In editing this book, we were aided by many. Allen A. Hyman, as Research Coordinator for the Metropolitan Fund, provided us the encouragement and cooperation of his organization in completing the manuscript. At Wayne State University, we received help from Norman Wengert, Chairman of the Department of Political Science and Project Director, and Robert McNeill of the Department of Political Science, who analyzed the feasibility of the project.

Duane L. Gibson, Director of the Institute for Community Development, and Charles R. Adrian, Chairman of the Department of Political Science, both of Michigan State University, were ready consultants in intellectual and technical matters. The secretarial staff of the Institute, and especially Almeda Ritter, Patricia Lane, and Fleurett Bodell, deserve our thanks for their devotion to this project during a long, hot summer.

C. P.
A. A.

East Lansing, Michigan
August, 1965

Contents

IV Values, Ideology and Innovation

I   Introduction

Chapter 1
Empathy and Ideology: Aspects of Administrative Innovation

Charles Press

Department of Political Science
Michigan State University

Alan Arian

Department of Political Science
Tel Aviv University

The study of bureaucratic organizations, to a greater degree perhaps than the study of other fields of knowledge, has been closely associated with applied administration. Practitioners have encouraged scholars to examine administrative processes and prescribe "correct" procedures and many scholars have over the years responded to this invitation.

The reason for the close relationship between theory and practice is easily understood. Bureaucratic organization is one of the important ways in which modern man hopes to control his physical and human environment. Accurate insights into the administrative process can often provide immediate advantage to those who apply them.

Thus, the historical development of the study of administration can be viewed as a process whereby the top level administrator has been furnished with special knowledges to aid him in coping with the problems of organization in complex societies. We distinguish four kinds of knowledges: technical skills, the legal structure of authority, interpersonal relations within organizations, and the societal values, norms and ideology. The last is an element in the administrative process increasingly recognized for its importance. It is a theme that appears at significant points in a number of the essays that follow and one we shall develop in more detail in our review of the kinds of knowledges that have been imparted to administrators and the interrelationships among them.

I

Application of complex methods of authority allocation in organizations dates back to early civilizations. Notions of hierarchical division of duties and privileges were developed for military conquest as well as for civilian activities that required unusual cooperative efforts, e.g., the building and administration of the water works system of Egypt or the construction of the Great Wall of China. But whether the Chinese, Persian, Roman, or some other civilization discovered and perfected such procedures is less important for our purposes than that conscious attempts were made in the late nineteenth century to specify precisely what the techniques of scalar organization might be. Max Weber provided one of the first and most complete explications of bureaucratic organization and also called attention to the interrelationship between such hierarchical organization and organizational norms. His work had little impact in America at that time. Independently from Weber, leaders of the scientific management movement prescribed a rigid set of administrative principles of organization that they believed were applicable to all organizations at all times. Over the next two generations, American scholars elaborated this theory of bureaucratic structure and applied it to many kinds of organizations.[1] Functional organization with neatly designed hierarchies having single heads, "proper" span of control and staff agencies were recommended by administrative reorganizers for local, state and national governments and private corporations both in America and abroad.

The practioners of scientific management in their time and motion study activities also developed practices for peak operation for many technical skills required of line workers. Studies involving bricklaying procedures, for example, produced marked increases in production, and the same kinds of techniques were applied to routine processes within organizations, such as the routing of communications or the preparation of forms.

The knowledges just discussed stressed organizational efficiency by increasing the technical competences of administrators and

---

[1]See for example Luther Gulick and Lyndall Urwick, *Papers on the Science of Administration* (New York: Institute of Public Administration, 1937).

workers by establishing clear-cut and rational patterns of authority. But it was found that some skills could not be routinized through time and motion study; the so-called universal principles of organization were subjected to skeptical scrutiny: Herbert Simon's critical appraisal of them as a scientific body of knowledge and Alfred P. Sloan's partial disregard of them in the building of the world's largest private organization, General Motors, in the 1920's, are examples.[2]

The improvement of technical skills and an unambiguous structure of legal rights was found to be only a part of the science of administration. These knowledges must be used in conjunction with other knowledges that we shall discuss next. That there is still a tendency to emphasize the technical and legal organizational dimensions at the expense of other knowledges is attested to by the belief on the part of many leaders of the developing nations that quick establishment of rationalized bureaucratic structures based on the Weberian model will provide solutions to all social and economic problems. LaPalombara argues that this assumption appears to be incorrect.

II

The challenge to the dominant role of legal authority and technical knowledges in the study of administration came from two sources. Both stressed the importance of social interactions and interpersonal relations within bureaucratic organization. One was an academic study made by Harvard University professors at the Hawthorne plant of Western Electric in Chicago in the late 1920's.[3] The researchers hoped to demonstrate that production would rise after they made common-sense improvements in features of the working environment, such as improved lighting. They ultimately discovered, however, that production was related to interpersonal factors and that administrative participants were more than inert instruments of top-level manipulators. A second source of insight came from a practioner having the gift of a reflective mind. Chester

[2]Herbert Simon, *Administrative Behavior, A Study of Decision-Making Process in Administrative Organization* (New York: Macmillan, 1947); Alfred P. Sloan, *My Years at General Motors* (New York: MacFadden, 1964).

[3]F. L. Roethlisberger and William Dickson, *Management and the Worker* (Cambridge: Harvard Univ. Press, 1941); Elton Mayo, *The Social Problems of an Industrial Civilization* (Cambridge: Harvard Univ. Press, 1945) and *The Human Problems of an Industrial Civilization* (Boston: Graduate School of Business Administration, Harvard Univ., 1946).

I. Barnard, a telephone company executive, conceived of organization as a network of interpersonal relations with communications systems being of primary significance.[4] His writings influenced the subsequent work of Simon and other students of organizations.

Following World War II, much administrative research began with the insight that informal social interactions are a crucial aspect of administration environment. Social interaction was related to authority structure, organizational goals and productivity, though sometimes in the process of adding to the knowledge of human relations these factors were seriously understressed.

Students of group dynamics emphasized the importance of interpersonal relations within organizations and conducted experiments to test the effects of different supervisory methods on production. Game theorists attempted to develop more rational means of decision making for top level administrators, building on the knowledge of human interaction among participants. Students of communication stressed the control aspects of the interaction process. Other scholars attempted the more ambitious project begun by Barnard of developing a theory of organizations that takes account of the role of human interaction and communications in achieving specific organizational goals within a bureaucratic authority structure. All of these scholars borrowed heavily from the insights of social psychology and stressed the significance of administrative participants having accurate knowledge about the feelings, thoughts and behaviors of others within bureaucratic organizations. This psychological process is technically called "empathic accuracy" and is one crucial to all administration. Special attention is paid to it in a number of the essays that follow.

The essays in this book which deal with this aspect of interpersonal relations in administration are written from the standpoint of the top level administrator or policy-maker seeking to implement organizational goals. They make these points regarding the relationship between empathic accuracy and administration: Empathy is a process common to all but the psychopath and closed minded. While empathy and empathic accuracy are not the same, to some degree both the tendency to empathize and improvement in empathic accuracy can be learned. Empathizing may lead to a reassessment of one's own norms of behavior.

Smith points out that by utilizing techniques, such as role playing and discussion group analysis, even the most insensitive can be

---

[4]Chester I. Barnard, *The Functions of the Executive* (Cambridge: Harvard Univ. Press, 1938).

made aware of the needs of others and others' reactions to their own actions. Zander and Gamson both agree that techniques can be learned, but Zander stresses that the student and his colleagues must desire to improve the process of group interactions before his (the student's) knowledge will be of value to the organization; Gamson suggests that game theory is only a technique for rationally implementing values — it can be learned, but the values and goals which motivate the actor are outside the province of the theory. Berlo cites conditions under which empathic accuracy is improved. It is clear from Bruck's contribution that empathy is related to innovation and change in ways that are not as yet known. Finally, LaPalombara characterizes the interrelationships between the administrator in the developing nations and empathy. He suggests that the relevance of empathic accuracy be judged in terms of the crisis to be faced and the culture and history of the nation facing the crisis. All of these authors find the process of empathy primary in understanding those interpersonal processes for goal achievement within organization that we call administration.

III

Underlying many of the essays in this volume is an assumption that the values, norms and ideology of society are important conditioners of administrative behavior. Modern students of administration, of course, follow Weber in emphasizing the importance of organizational values and norms for understanding the administrative process, but less attention has been paid to the relation of these to the values of the whole society. Implicitly it seems to be assumed that in the long run organizational values can continue successfully at odds with societal values. We suggest this assumption needs critical scrutiny.

We have been struck by the frequency with which the theme of conflict between organizational and societal values reappeared in these essays. Especially in discussions of human relations and empathic accuracy do the essayists face this problem of the relation between societal values and ideology and organizations. Technical skills and empathy and even the values of his organizational unit are seemingly not enough to guide the action of the administrator in a transitional, developing nation. Game theory without a clear recognition of the societal values accepted by the players may lead to monstrous behavior which would prove irrational in terms of the long-range goals of the actor and his organization. Metropolitan administration in America is stagnated by organizational ideologies inappropriate to the goals of the whole society. Even the successful application of group dynamics knowledge requires identification with the goals of the organization and of the society. The point is the old one that administrative units do not act in isolation, but within a cultural environment. It appears that an awareness of societal values and ideology constitute an additional knowledge required of the top-level administrator.

By way of definition, we designate values as those sentiments, or ethical principles regarded as ultimate. Such values cannot be criticized concerning their appropriateness. A society as a whole may affirm certain values as its implicit assumptions, but so, too, do all of the myriad of organizations within that society. Commonly, however, administrative units tend to affirm only some of the same values found in the larger society. Their values may be in partial conflict with those of the society.

Norms are derived from the ultimate values as rules of conduct applicable under specified conditions. Students recognize that the distinction between norms and values is often a fuzzy one in practice.[5] The distinction rests on the assumption that it can be demonstrated that the norm is a rule of conduct derived from an ultimate principle. Despite this vagueness in definition, scholars have found the distinction a useful one for reasons that we shall note in a moment.

Ideology is a set of interrelated norms. We define ideology as a system of ideas which is normative in nature in the sense that it depicts and justifies an ideal, is based (implicitly or explicitly) on assumptions concerning the nature of man and social reality, and is action-oriented. Ideology becomes the code of action based on the norms of a society or individual influenced by the conditions of reality.

Societal values, norms, and ideologies vary from place to place and from situation to situation. Even within a society institutional, organizational, and individual values, norms, and ideologies may differ. But if the administrator is to be effective in his efforts, he must attempt to forge an ideology which will synthesize the values and norms of his organization and society.[6] The result of this synthesis we have termed the "appropriate" ideology.

[5]See the discussion by Judith Blake and Kingsley Davis, "Norms, Values, and Sanctions," in Robert E. L. Faris, ed., *Handbook of Modern Sociology* (Chicago: Rand McNally, 1964), pp. 456-84.

[6]For a discussion of the distinction between "institution" and "organization" and the relationship between the administrative unit and the role of the individual administrator, see Robert J. Pranger, "The Clinical Approach to Organization Theory," *Midwest Journal of Political Science*, IX (August, 1965), 215-34.

We shall term appropriate an ideology of administration which, if followed by an administrator, yields a high probability of achieving both organizational and societal goals. (We purposely do not include individual goals because it would then appear that organizational and even social activity is all self-oriented.)

We are well aware that when we introduce the notion of an appropriate ideology for administrators we are on dangerous ground. We are not certain that there is always an empirical referent for the term. But we have encountered this underlying theme so often in the essays assembled here that we feel that the concept should be introduced and our own preliminary formulation be presented. Rather than being a definitive statement, this introduction to the idea of appropriate and inappropriate ideologies is an invitation to and a challenge for further and more complete work based on this concept.

We are also aware that some will object to the use of societal values, norms, and ideology as a standard. To them it will seem to encourage a Machiavellian chameleonism among administrators to speak of an appropriate ideology. Others will say that the standard should be chosen from a wider community — Western civilization or perhaps the international order. Sibley in his essay assumes the standard is an unchangeable one — namely, a kind of natural law. Nevertheless, we prefer the societal standard because it provides the researcher a ready empirical referent. Perhaps some day and perhaps for some practices even today the appropriate ideology is based on the values of the international society or community. But for the most part, cultural and societal variations are the most prominent characteristic of "universal" values.

The usefulness of the distinction between ultimate values, norms, and ideology is that it permits one to observe that differing, and even contradictory, modes of conduct may be derived from from the same ultimate values. The witch doctor and the psychiatrist may both espouse the values of mental health but their ideology and conduct differ. A witch doctor's actions are based on what he considers an ideology appropriate to the problem situation. So, too, are a psychiatrist's.

The source of the varying modes of behavior derived from the same societal values often lies in differing experiences. When individuals face new problems and new conditions and in the process gain new insights, they form new norms and ideologies with which they hope to explain and thus control their environment. The norms and ideologies that gain widespread acceptance within society, we suggest, are those based upon the experiences of its leadership group. New elites, as they move to positions of power alter the societal ideology. This new ideology then becomes that of the society's and remains so until new experiences and knowledges bring forward other elites to challenge those in power. Thus we would anticipate that, in a developing nation, old values will be maintained but will be clothed in new ideological forms. Such appears to have been the experience in Japan as its traditional forms were changed under the impact of Western ideas and society.

There are two pitfalls which we have tried to avoid in our formulation of an appropriate ideology. First, we recognize that there may be more than one such ideology at any given time or in any given situation. We do not yet know how to indicate appropriateness of an ideology except by a process of elimination, but we are confident that with added attention to the problem certain guidelines can be drawn.

Second, we want to explicitly avoid the pitfall of implying that once a seemingly appropriate ideology is isolated, all organizational and administrative units must immediately pay obeisance to the new code. In the long run, we would suppose that the goals and ideology of a specific organization will usually be somewhat in harmony with societal values and even with the societal ideology as well. If not, we assume that an organization with an ideology inappropriate in a society at a given moment will either alter its own ideology to conform with society's, will find itself less and less effective in the total society, or, in extreme cases, will have its ideology adopted as the societal ideology.

We are not suggesting that organizations, administrations or administrators "step in time." We simply feel that there may be more and less appropriate ideologies and an administrator who would be effective would do well to be aware of such differences. We are not suggesting that the administrator adopt the societal ideology as his own; rather, we think that he and his organization should attempt to recognize that he must operate within the framework of a societal ideology. This formulation is consistent with the tension between organizational and societal ideologies sometimes encountered in a democracy. It is more than a call to be aware of the "public interest"; it calls upon the organization and the administrator to be aware of the relationship between their actions and societal values.

Can there be honest differences concerning which ideology is appropriate under specific conditions? Of course. But, again, it is possibly easier to indicate ideologies which are clearly inappropriate than to point to an appropriate one. For example, Long sees the realization of American goals blocked because too many of the country's local administrators hold ideologies reflecting the values of subgroupings or suborganizations within the society. These are ideologies more appropriate to a rural rather than a metropolitan environment though. Now administrators holding such views are apparently incorrect in analyzing the conditions they face, and we may speak of them as holding an ideology inappropriate for modern society. In the same way, as La Palombara suggests, an inappropriate ideology may thwart the administrator in a developing nation and prevent him from properly applying technical, organizational, or human relations skills to pressing problems. Or it may be that his "modern" ideology is too much at variance with traditional values to succeed. Arian examines the ideology of the kibbutz in Israel and Press of administrators in metropolitan subunits from this perspective.

Innovation, in our framework, is provided by the administrator who adopts for his own an appropriate ideology and has the requisite other knowledges to achieve his goals. In most societies, institutions, or organizations, there is a lag between objective reality as seen by those claiming special expertise and the accepted ideology of the moment. Closing the gap—reducing the lag—is the work of the innovator.

Most innovation, then, will not be grandiose and all-encompassing. Most innovation will be small and gradual; both Krislov and Gamson discuss this as "incrementalism." If the gap between an appropriate ideology and what subgroupings practice is great—as Long would have us believe is the case today in local government in the United States—the innovator must apply himself to a large and difficult task. If the gap between the accepted ideology and the appropriate ideology is small—as LaPalombara infers may be the case in a developing country facing only one basic crisis—the need for innovation is less intensely felt. Indeed, if the appropriate and accepted ideologies are identical, the innovator would still be the one who tended to operate in terms of the appropriate ideology.

Our definition of innovation does not depart from normal usage as much as it might appear at first glance. This is so because of the change in the objective realities facing a society and the consequent necessity for change in the ideology appropriate to attain the societal values. Innovation, generally associated with change and creativity, retains these elements when understood in our terms. Used in the manner in which we have employed the term, we are able to retain its basic meaning while emphasizing that innovation, too, is relative in accordance with the society and the era in which the actor finds himself.

IV

Our formulation is immediately vulnerable to two types of attack. First, it may be argued that labelling an ideology by its appropriateness can only occur after-the-fact. Second, our idea of appropriateness falls into the same traps of oversimplification and elusiveness as do the "national interest" writers in foreign policy or the "general will" and "public philosophy" adherents in political thought. To the first criticism, we would reply that if, after exhaustive historical studies the applicability of the concept were indicated, the concept could also be used in a predictive sense. In answer to the second, we would respond that that criticism ignores "the residual meaning which is inherent in the concept itself."[7] That is, while it might be true that we can never define precisely what an appropriate ideology is, often we can indicate what it is *not*. Obviously, this is more easily done at the extremes of the continuum. In the middle ranges of the continuum, where most of the important distinctions in real life must be made, we are not now ready to specify which ideology is appropriate and which is not. Our inability to do so at this time, however, is something quite different from admitting the impossibility of the endeavor.

We are convinced that the science of administration will be enhanced if the relative nature of the specific knowledges requisite to successful administration be granted. The profession has slowly come to realize that different situations and cultures may demand different technical and organizational skills and different human relations techniques. If the study of values and ideology could leave the counting stage (how many individuals feel this way about this value, how strongly do they hold that view) the gains for the science of administration would be great. We must take that first faltering step of attempting to determine scientifically what type of ideology has been successful in managing what type of crisis at what stage of economic, social, and political development. We hope that the notion of an appropriate ideology represents that first step.

V

We have pointed out that students of administration have thus far isolated four kinds of knowledges having special relevance to the functioning of top and middle-level administrators: requisite

---

[7]Hans Morgenthau, "Another 'Great Debate': The National Interest of the United States," *American Political Science Review*, XLVI (December, 1952), 972.

technical skills, an understanding of the hierarchical structure of authority, empathic accuracy in relations within organization, and an ideology appropriate to societal goals in the situation faced. Other knowledges may subsequently be found to be of importance, but research thus far points to the special significance of these four.[8]

For our purposes, we view these four knowledges as belonging either to a behavioral dimension or to a valuational dimension. As depicted in Figure I, the behavioral dimension is composed of technical skills, knowledge of bureaucratic organization, and empathic accuracy. As we shall see in a moment, all three of these

VALUATIONAL DIMENSION
(appropriate ideology)
"what"

BEHAVIORAL DIMENSION
(technical skills,
organization, empathic
accuracy)
"how"

	+	
+	A (++)	B (−+) −
	C (+−)	D (−−)
	−	

FIGURE I. Knowledges needed by the administrator and types of administrators produced by acquiring these knowledges (+) or not acquiring these knowledges (−).

knowledges contain a goal-influencing component; nevertheless, these three knowledges are "skills" in the normal sense of that word. All of them are techniques or methods of behavior; all answer the question, "How is it to be done?" Comprising one dimension, these knowledges will obviously affect one another in this formulation. It is conceivable that an empathically accurate person may be rather weak in the technical skills required of an administrator. His place on the behavior continuum would be lowered accordingly. The continuum does not propose to represent a precise position for an individual administrator; rather, it is used to give a feeling of relative position in relation to others on the continuum.

Our discussion of appropriate ideology introduced the valuational dimension into the framework. Here we are concerned with the action to be taken in order to achieve organizational goals without paralyzing conflict with the societal values; we are interested in the answer to the "What is to be done?" question. This dimension involves the policy which is to be followed in realizing

[8]For a discussion relevant to the educational needs of top administrators see John J. Corson and R. Shale Paul, *Men Near the Top, Filling Key Posts in the Federal Service* (Baltimore: The Johns Hopkins Press, 1966) especially chaps. 6 and 7.

the value-goal. Without this valuational dimension, movement is random; with it, movement is goal-oriented. While we as individuals may not agree with the goal or the ideology, it should be possible to determine objectively whether or not that ideology is appropriate, *given* the goal to be achieved and the societal values. Employing the valuational dimension allows us to abandon the universal criteria previously used to measure administration and administrators and introduces a relative, situational factor to the comparison of administrators.

If we could assume that we could precisely determine a person's position on the two continuua, we could make some judgment about his effectiveness as an administrator in a society holding values emphasizing development and modernization. As LaPalombara suggests, all societies today are in such a transitional stage, but in some, societal values support modernization and in some they do not. In some, as Sibley points out, the modernizing trend is now less upsetting than in others.

The hypothetical administrator in the A quadrant of Figure I is characterized as possessing substantive knowledge as well as the appropriate ideology. He not only knows how to do his job, he also knows what to do. He is the effective innovator. The administrator in quadrant D is a "botch-up." Not only does he lack direction, he could not be effective even if direction were provided. Administrators B and C are less capable than administrator A. They lack skills and appropriate ideology, respectively.

While Figure I presents a convenient method of characterizing administrators and of distinguishing between the behavioral and valuational dimensions of administrative training, we must be aware that the knowledges represented by the continuum are interrelated. The four knowledges—technical and bureaucratic skills, empathic accuracy and appropriate ideology—are similar in that they are all situationally relative; that is, their significance is determined by the situation faced by the society and the organization. We cannot compare the level of technical skills necessary for an administrator of the twentieth century with those required of an administrator of an earlier century. The revolution in electronics, to name the most obvious recent change, precludes this kind of comparison. Empathic accuracy is also relative: The "other" which the administrator perceives will vary from situation to situation and from society to society. In crisis times and in unstable societies high levels of accuracy may be needed; in quieter times and in more stable societies administrators may simply muddle through. We have already noted in respect to ideology that what may be appropriate in some societies may be inappropriate in others.

The issue of how versed in the four knowledges an administrator should be in a specific society is a perplexing one. For the problems of managing a modern technical society we assume, with qualification, that the development of all administrative knowledges is cumulatively desirable much as we have visualized it in Figure I. Extensive training in technical skills, administrative organization, and empathic accuracy supplement and reinforce each other and encourage finding an appropriate ideology for society's quest for modern development. But our acceptance of the assumption that the more of the four knowledges the administrator acquires the better administrator he is must be qualified. There are probably built-in psychological devices that in most situations serve to prevent overdevelopment of one or the other knowledge. An administrator with highly developed technical skills and highly developed empathic accuracy might well find himself paralyzed in a situation demanding action. He so successfully estimates the thoughts and feelings of others and he is so expert in recognizing technical difficulties that he may be frozen by the realization of (1) how his action will be received by "others" and (2) the obstacles in the path of complete success in fulfilling the plan. The paralysis, we would suggest, is largely mitigated by the overriding ideological dimension. The administrator may find action possible in the name of organizational values or of the societal goal or the "cause." He may be insulated from paralysis by societal mechanisms which allow him to act in the name of a higher good: one of these mechanisms is ideology.

We have seen that the valuational dimension serves to liberate the administrator who might otherwise be paralyzed by overdevelopment of the behavioral dimension. This feedback from ideology to both training in skills and empathy is well-documented by social-psychologists and psychiatrists. As Bruck points out, most persons usually perceive only what they wish to perceive given their values and attitudinal predispositions. Values, norms, and ideologies act as gatekeepers or information blinders that limit one's ability to develop certain technical skills and empathic accuracy, especially in unfamiliar situations.

There is also a feedback process from skills and empathic accuracy to the ideology. The behavioral dimension has certain effects upon the valuational dimension which have often been overlooked in the literature. Technical skills are rarely "neutral."

They imply an overall goal or norm component which shapes the development of the administrator's ideology. On the surface, training for technical skills appears to indicate only a means of doing something. But the goal of action is also implied in the training. For example, a specialist can be so highly trained that he will be ineffective doing work which he deems to be beneath his professional level. Consider the plight of the trained highway engineer who is assigned to build dirt roads or even two lane open access highways. He is likely to be frustrated and rebellious or incapacitated. Thus experts become champions for what they regard as optimum standards, often, it may be noted, without clear consideration of the feasibility of these standards. A trained person consciously or unconsciously sets goals because he desires to exercise his skills in ways he considers proper. Training of specialists has clear implications for ideology—the societal values to be achieved are subtly influenced by the act of training.

In the case of the highway engineer, the societal ideology was inappropriate to utilize the levels of technical knowledges achieved. There are other cases when incongruence between skill level and ideology lead to situations which are potentially disastrous for the society. Generally, maximal application of technical skills depends on an appropriate societal ideology and varies, accordingly, from situation to situation. But it is less clear that an increase in skills is necessarily helpful when a modernizing ideology is inappropriate for solving problems in terms of a society's values. Then conflict among knowledges leads to chaos that perhaps can only be avoided by imposition of a new societal ideology in harmony with the increase of technical knowledges and empathic skills or a suppression of further increase in knowledges. At least this is the conclusion reached in some new nations. Thus Ataturk modernized Turkey by imposing a new ideological system. The same process was followed in the Soviet Union and is now tried in China. In a prosperous democracy, the disharmony among knowledges may be alleviated by gradualism. American city administrators facing racial crises can perhaps more adequately alleviate their problems through a questioning of societal ideology rather than perfecting further riot control techniques. The technical proficiency of police dogs may exacerbate rather than solve the problems since the ideological component implied by the technique is too clear to be misinterpreted.

Just as the overdevelopment of technical skills may be detrimental to a society, the development of bureaucratic principles may be undesirable for certain societies. A developing society, facing the crises of identity and penetration of which LaPalombara writes, may reduce its capacity to manage the crises if bureaucratic norms are followed. While acquiring knowledge of administrative organization and procedures, goal orientations are also acquired. This may be one of the obstacles to effective action handicapping a developing nation using the Weberian model of rationalized administration which falters when facing crises.

In the same way, modern sociologists have argued that the development of human relations expertise through training in sensitivity or what we have called development of empathic accuracy has ideological and goal-directed implications. The strictures against "the organization man" and the other-directed personality point out that continuous calculations of the motivations of others may have what the observers consider undesirable ideological implications.

VI

We have analyzed the knowledges which appear to be necessary for effective administration. We have noted that the study of administration passed through an "organization without people" phase. Subsequently, perhaps, the profession overreacted by concentrating on "people without organization." The value component of the society in which the administrator practices is an area of research which thus far has been neglected. In discussing the appropriate administrative ideology we attempted to provide a framework in which study could concern itself with "purposive people within organizations."

The essays which follow bring together the insights and findings of diverse disciplines to the knowledges required by administrators within the organization and broader society. The topics the essays cover represent some of the fields which have truly been innovative in extending the horizons of knowledge in the social sciences. In detail, each contributor introduces his own speciality and then explores those points which are relevant to our topic. In broader perspective, there is a unity in their essays: After considering the generalities which hold for the administrator in interaction with others, the essayists imply that the valuational dimension of norms and ideology is of basic significance but largely unexplored. In this introductory essay, we want to make their implicit appeal explicit:

Systematic study of the relationships between ideology and behavior is sorely needed. What we have called an appropriate ideology must be tested with the tools of social science; the process and function of "innovation" must be explicated. These advances will aid mightily in the on-going attempt to understand and improve public administration.

II Innovation

Chapter 2

A Review of Social and Psychological Factors Associated with Creativity and Innovation

Max Bruck

School of Social Work
Michigan State University

Even a cursory examination of the recent literature of the social-psychological field provides convincing evidence of the rapidly growing interest in creativity and innovation. Guilford's presidential address to the American Psychological Association on creativity stimulated a dramatic upsurge of systematic investigation of the problem.[1] Why such a mounting interest in creativity and innovation? Man's history is replete with events that reflect his seeking of the new and the unexplored, with his seeking of at least some change in his views, tools, and experience, and with his striving to discover and obtain whatever will enhance his security. As Green observed: Some men, however, "in every time and place are more curious than their fellows, more dissatisfied with at least something that is part of their common world—a tool, an idea, perhaps a religious system."[2] The men who are consciously motivated to

---

[1]Joseph Rossman, *Industrial Creativity* (New Hyde Park, N. Y.: University Books, 1964), p. xii, reported that, of some 121,000 titles which appeared in *Psychological Abstracts* from 1927 to 1960, he found only 186 titles which definitely bore on the subject of creativity. Since then there has been a marked increase in research projects in the field of creative imagination. According to Rossman the Creative Education Foundation of the University of Buffalo, in a compendium of research on creative imagination (1958), listed 30 research studies concerned with the identification and development of creative ability. The second compendium published in 1960 reported 27 additional published studies and 26 current research projects. In 1955 the Industrial Research Institute published a "Bibliography on Creativity" which lists 1,919 items. Mildred Benton, "Creativity in Research and Inventions in the Physical Sciences," published by the U.S. Naval Research Laboratory, lists 1,359 items. Numerous other references in the form of books and articles have appeared in the sociological and psychological journals and in the literature pertinent to the management field.

[2]Arnold W. Green, *Sociology* (New York: McGraw-Hill, 1965), p. 165.

affect change and to succeed are the innovators. Often they borrow technical and cultural elements from other societies; less often, they invent these. Such men have been variously described as "wishing for new experience," or as being "impelled by the curiosity drive," or as seeking adventure. These are static terms, however, which do not convey the dynamic essence of the process which compels them. Creativity is at once one of the most highly valued human qualities and one of the most illusive.

The literature in the management field reveals a strong interest in the creative (innovative) process and an equally strong desire to foster creative ability. The $10 billion spent on research and development in the United States in 1960 and the projected increase to about $21 billion by 1970 for the same purpose would support this view. The significance of new product development is such that the business organization is dependent upon it not only for growth, but for its very existence. "In a competitive situation . . . from one-fifth to one-half of the present business may derive from products which did not even exist ten years ago."[3] The creation of multi-billion dollar research and development activity has propelled research, development, and engineering into the category of big business, and growth in this area has been phenomenal.

For the purpose of this chapter "creativity" and "innovation" will be treated as being synonomous. Rogers defined innovation as "an idea perceived as new by the individual."[4] Barnett defined innovation as "any thought, behavior, or thing that is new because it is qualitatively different from existing forms."[5] Haefel defined the creative process as "a new combination formed from pieces already in the mind by symbolic manipulation during dissociated thought."[6] Rogers made a distinction between innovators and inventors: Innovators *adopt* new ideas but they do not necessarily invent them. Inventors are the individuals who *create* new ideas. Innovators may also be inventors, and inventors may also be innovators. Thus, while they may overlap, the two roles of "innovator" and "inventor" are not necessarily the same.[7]

In spite of this definitional distinction, for the purpose of this chapter the innovational and the creative process alike will refer to the ability, in Taylor's (1959) view, "to mold experience into new

---

[3]John W. Haefele, *Creativity and Innovation* (New York: Reinhold, 1962), p. 178.
[4]Everett M. Rogers, *Diffusion of Innovations* (New York: The Free Press of Glencoe, 1962), p. 19.
[5]Homer G. Barnett, *Innovation* (New York: McGraw-Hill, 1953), p. 7.
[6]Haefele, *op. cit.*, p. 7.
[7]Rogers, *op. cit.*, pp. 195-96.

and different organizations, the ability to perceive the environment plastically, and to communicate the resulting unique experience to others."[8] Such a view of the innovative and creative process appears compatible with the general usage of the concepts in the sociological and psychological literature, and efforts toward redefinition of these two words would not serve a useful purpose at this time.

Two Approaches to Analyzing Innovation

There are two interrelated approaches to the analysis of innovation: the psychological and the cultural.

Sociological theories stress "social forces"—the given combination of circumstances which, if not producing innovators, is at least supposed to facilitate the manifestation of their individual abilities—to explain social change.[9] Thus, economic pressures plus the already available accumulation of technical knowledge are seen as central to the discovery of mechanical and scientific devices. With regard to nontechnological innovation Green stated that "The forces enabling leadership to be assumed, to take certain directions, must be present in the fields of politics, religion, and reform movements." He continued, however, "still, the personality, ego drives, abilities, and ambitions of individual dynamic leaders would appear in some measure to affect what they accomplish."[10] Barnett argued in a similar vein: A culture cannot be said to experience a need, for "culture" is an abstraction and never needed anything. Only an individual is capable of experiencing a need, and, as such, it becomes a highly personal experience existing in the psychological configuration of the individual. The mental content may be socially defined, and its substance may be in major part influenced by tradition. But the way the content is treated, apprehended, modified, and recorded is inevitably dictated by the unique configuration of characteristics comprising the individual.[11]

Innovators as Deviants

Menzel reported that every innovator is not necessarily a deviant from local norms as it is possible that the norms in some social

---

[8]I. A. Taylor, "The Nature of the Creative Process," in P. Smith, ed., *Creativity* (New York: Hastings House, 1959), pp. 51-82.
[9]Green, *op. cit.*, p. 635.
[10]*Ibid.*, p. 636.
[11]Barnett, *op. cit.*, p. 152.

systems favor innovativeness.[12] It is reasonable to assume that the degree to which the innovator is perceived as deviant would be influenced by the norms of the social system as these relate to innovativeness. In studying the deviancy of innovators, Rogers investigated the perception of the innovators by other group members in the innovators' social system and the innovators view of themselves in relation to the norms of their social group. He found that innovators *are* deviants and are perceived as deviants by other members of their group and that they generally tend to perceive themselves as deviant from the norms of their social system. Rogers qualified his findings, however, by cautioning that the degree to which innovators are perceived as deviant from their membership group is a function of the extent to which the norms of the membership group are traditional or modern. The more traditional the social system's norms tend to be, the more are the innovators seen as deviant. This finding conforms to the conclusion of other investigators reported by him in his summarization of the literature.[13]

In addition, the position of the respondent in the social structure of adopter categories also determines the respondent's view of the innovator. For example, the greater similarity in the social characteristics between the innovator and the early adopter may contribute to the greater degree of familiarity between the early adopter respondent and the innovator. As a consequence, the relatively early adopter may tend to regard the innovator more favorably than do the later adopters.[14]

Who are the men who invent or transmit the atomic reactors and the gasoline engine, who lead social reform movements, who initiate political and religious movements, or who are the leaders in business and techology, military strategy, or administration? There are many studies concerning the psychosocial characteristics of the innovator. Two points of view are expressed. Terman's studies of gifted children, for example, found the gifted student to be healthier than average, more attractive personally, better coordinated, and, in general, enjoying a richer and fuller life.[15] These findings contradict the stereotypes held by many people of the

[12]Herbert Menzel, "Innovation, Integration and Marginality: A Survey of Physicians," in Rogers, *op. cit.*, p. 197.
[13]*Ibid.*, pp. 199-201, 196-207.
[14]*Ibid.*, p. 201.
[15]L. M. Terman *et al.*, "Mental and Physical Traits of a Thousand Gifted Children," *Genetic Studies of Genius*, I (Stanford: Stanford Univ. Press, 1925), in Jacob W. Getzels and Philip W. Jackson, *Creativity and Intelligence* (New York: Wiley, 1962), p. 1.

innovator, the gifted, and the creative person. Popular conceptions included such a person as being long-haired, wild-eyed, dreamy, impractical, isolated from life, queer, physically inadequate, awkward, bespeckled, unattractive, asocial, and rejected by most people.

Barnett, an anthropologist, observed that the acceptors of culture innovation and change were viewed as the maladjusted, the socially incompetent, the dissatisfied, and the frustrated. Innovators and their acceptors were seen by him "as most likely to be impersonal friends, the reluctant participants, and if they have the courage, the chronic dissenters and escapers. They are truly marginal individuals."[16] In investigating characteristics of highly creative scientists Roe was impressed by the frequency and often rather serious psychological and social problems experienced by those in her sample. She speculated that these very emotional problems may be the mainspring of the powerful impetus such people have to succeed in their professions.[17]

Support for Roe's hypothesis may be derived from Kleiner and Parker's review of laboratory experiments of levels of aspiration and achievement of normal and neurotic subjects. The evidence points to a tendency for emotionally disturbed subjects either to over- or under-aspire compared with those who make a better adjustment. The dominant tendency in these studies, however, is for over-aspiring in the maladjusted groups. Two lines of reasoning were advanced: Neurotic individuals have high anxiety and high fear of failure compared to the better adjusted subjects. They attempt to dissolve anxiety by selecting a task that is so easy that they cannot fail, or which is so difficult that failure would be no cause for self-blame. An alternative explanation is that the high level of anxiety experienced by maladjusted subjects prevents them from accurately evaluating their own abilities relative to the realistic difficulties in reaching certain goals. Other studies reported by Kleiner and Parker relate the level of aspiration to a personality type. The results do not always confirm the findings that maladjusted subjects select either very high or very low levels of aspiration, but that the maladjusted group only selected (relatively) extreme aspirations after a failure situation.[18]

[16]Homer G. Barnett, "Personal Conflicts and Culture Change," *Social Forces*, XX, 110 (1941), 160-71, 380.

[17]Anne Roe, *The Making of a Scientist* (New York: Dodd, Mead, 1953).

[18]Robert J. Kleiner and Seymour Parker, "Goal-Striving, Social Status, and Mental Disorder: A Research Review," *American Sociological Review*, XXVIII, 2 (April, 1963), 200-201.

On the other hand, Carl Rogers and Maslow pointed to low need for defensiveness and its counterpart, "openness to new experience" or "self-actualization," among other factors, as the primary motivational forces for creativity.[19] It would appear that innovators *are* "different" in some important respects.

Psychological Differences Between Innovators and Noninnovators

How do innovators differ psychologically from others?

Rossman sought to identify the characteristics of inventors by asking 710 successful inventors to specify the requisite characteristics of a successful inventor. Perseverance, imagination, knowledge and memory, and originality were greatly stressed. This coincided markedly with the frequency of characteristics mentioned by the 78 directors of research who were queried about the cognitive qualities of research workers and inventors.[20] Analytical capacity, perseverance, originality, imagination, training, and education were mentioned most frequently.

In a similar study in which Van Zelst and Kerr related self-descriptions to a productivity criterion, it was found that production scientists described themselves as more original, imaginative, curious, enthusiastic, and impulsive and as less contented and conventional.[21] Stein reported that creative subjects regarded themselves as assertive and authoritative, while less creative subjects regarded themselves as acquiescent and submissive.[22] MacKinnon reported that the highly creative emphasized their inventiveness, independence, individuality, enthusiasm, determination, and industry, while the less creative stressed virtue, good character, rationality, and concern for others. He suggested that the highly creative are able to speak frankly in a more unusual way about themselves because they are more self-accepting than their less creative colleagues.[23]

---

[19]Carl R. Rogers, "Toward a Theory of Creativity," in H. H. Anderson, ed., *Creativity and Its Cultivation* (New York: Harper, 1959), p. 69-82; A. H. Maslow, "Creativity in Self-Actualizing People," in *ibid.*, pp. 83-95.
[20]Rossman, *op. cit.*, pp. 40-41.
[21]R. H. Van Zelst and W. A. Kerr, "Personality Self Assessment of Scientific and Technical Personnel," *Journal of Applied Psychology*, XXXVIII (1954), 145-47.
[22]M. I. Stein, "A Transactional Approach to Creativity," in C. Taylor, ed., *The 1955 University of Utah Research Conference on the Identification of Creative Scientific Talent* (Salt Lake City: Univ. of Utah Press, 1956), pp. 171-81.
[23]D. W. MacKinnon, "The Study of Creativity in Architects," in *Conference on the Creative Process* (Berkeley: Institute of Personality Assessment and Research, Univ. of California, 1961), Chs. 1, 5.

Chambers investigated certain differences in personality and biographical factors between mature scientists who are highly creative research men and those who are much less creative.[24] The creative person emerged as a dominant, strongly motivated, persistent, and energetic individualist who is self-propelled and whose interests are channeled away from social and civic activities and are directed toward his own individual research problem. He shows no perference for, or little interest in, religion. The less creative scientist is predominantly concerned with opportunities to combine teaching and administrative duties with research. The creative scientist is not overly concerned with other persons' views or with obtaining approval for his work. He does not depend on direction from external sources but acts on his own with little regard for convention or current fashion. He is also prepared to face the consequences of his unconventional behavior.

In investigating one dimension of the innovator's group relationships — his reference group — Rogers utilized a cosmopolite scale developed to measure differences in the geographical location of the innovator's reference groups. He found that the farm innovator's group relationships are likely to be spread over a much wider geographical area than the noninnovator's and that the innovator's reference group is external rather than related to his community of residence. He also concluded that the innovator *is* different from the average farmer, he is much more cosmopolite than the other farmers and, as such, he does not fit smoothly into the social relationships of the local community.[25]

Responses from a sample of 99 farm innovators indicated that they held a wider perspective and traveled to learn about new farm ideas and that they obtained psychological support from reference groups of like-minded innovating individuals from outside their county and state while many of their close-by neighbors held them in disrespect and ridicule. This finding anticipates the later discussion (see p. 31) of the particular psychological constellation of characteristics and formative life experiences that enables the innovator to sustain the many variants of hostility that he tends to evoke from less innovative individuals. Rogers concluded that

> innovators are impervious to this group pressure (from
> their neighbors)...the present evidence suggests that
> this group pressure may be outweighed by the group
> support for their ideas innovators received from another

[24]J. A. Chambers, "Relating Personality and Biographical Factors to Scientific Inquiry," *Psychological Monographs*, LXXVIII No. 7 (1964), 1-20.
[25]Rogers, *op. cit.*, pp. 203-4.

source. . . . their neighbors are relatively unimportant to them (as a reference group and therefore as a security source) . . . innovators belong to a cosmopolite clique whose norms favor innovativeness. These reference groups provide consensual validation for the innovator to give him psychological support with which to combat criticism from his local social system.[26]

Innovators of unsuccessful innovations as well as of ideas not recommended by experts and scientists also tend to be evaluated by peers as being somewhat deviant, and this also is their own self-conception. Innovators of recommended ideas also generally discern carefully between economic and noneconomic innovations. It should be observed that a similar relative freedom from dependence on community-of-residence norms was found by Menzel and Ben David to be true of the physicians, bacteriologists, and neuro-psychiatrists who were the first to introduce scientific innovations into their practice.[27]

Generally younger in years, venturesome and willing to take risks, openminded toward new ideas and enthusiastic to try them, more highly educated and thereby able to assimilate and manipulate complex technical information, sustained by sources of more accurate information, and possessing an intelligence that is relatively fast in its ability to conceptualize new ideas in reference to their own situation — these are among the earmarks of the innovator, and they sharply differentiate him from the laggard.

The Contribution of Psychoanalysis

We have seen that anthropologists, sociologists, and psychologists have all been concerned with the phenomenon of innovation. Since current researchers and writers on creativity in the social and psychological literature explicitly or implicitly are increasingly coming to view the issue within the psychoanalytic frame of reference, it is appropriate to review briefly some of its formulations as these relate to creativity. Freud unequivocally conceived of creativity as a continuation of the spontaneous curiosity-motivated play of childhood. He saw the source of creativity in the intra-psychic conflicts raging in the unconscious which could lead to either

[26]*Ibid.*, pp. 204-5.
[27]Herbert Menzel, "Innovations, Integration and Marginality: A Survey of Physicians," *American Sociological Review*, XXV (1960), pp. 704-13; Joseph Ben David, "Roles and Innovations in Medicine," *American Journal of Sociology*, LXV (1960), pp. 557-68.

neurosis or creativity. The creative act was seen as an adaptive solution to neurotic conflict.

At the risk of overquoting from Freud, the following passage from his writing is reproduced because it points up with particular clarity his conception of creative imaginativeness:

> ... The untiring pleasure in questioning observed in little children demonstrates their curiosity, which is puzzling to the grown-up, as long as he does not understand that all these questions are only circumlocutions, that they cannot come to an end, because the child wishes to substitute for them only one question which the child still does not put. When the child grows older and gains more understanding, this manifestation of curiosity suddenly disappears. But psychoanalytic investigation gives us a full explanation, in that it teaches us that many, perhaps most, children, at least the gifted ones, go through a period beginning with the third year, which may be designated as the period of *infantile sexual investigation*. ...

> If the period of infantile sexual investigation comes to an end through an impetus of energetic sexual repression, the early association with sexual interest may result in three different possibilities for the future fate of the investigation impulse. The investigation either shares the fate of the sexuality; the curiosity henceforth remains inhibited and the free activity may become narrowed for life. This is especially favored shortly thereafter by education and powerful religious inhibitions. ... In a second type the intellectual development is sufficiently strong to withstand the sexual repression pulling at it. Sometimes, after the disappearance of the infantile sexual investigation, it offers its support to the old association in order to elude sexual repression, and the suppressed sexual investigation comes back from the unconscious as compulsive reasoning. It is naturally distorted and not free, but forceful enough to sexualize even thought itself and to accentuate the intellectual operations with the pleasure and anxiety of the actual sexual processes. ...

> By virtue of a special disposition the third, which is the most rare and most perfect type, escapes the inhibitions of thought and the compulsive reasoning. Also here sexual repression takes place, but it does not succeed in evincing a partial impulse of the sexual pleasure in the unconscious; instead the libido withdraws from the fate of the repression by being sublimated from the outset into curiosity, and by reinforcing the powerful investigation impulse. Here, too, the investigation becomes to some extent compulsive

and substitutive of the sexual activity, but owing to the absolutely different psychic process behind it (sublimation in place of emergence from the unconscious) the character of the neurosis fails to express itself; the subjection to the original complexes of the infantile sexual investigation disappears, and the impulse can freely put itself in the service of intellectual interest. . . .[28]

In an excellent summarization of the Freudian approach to creative activity, Getzels and Jackson stated the following:

The major issues in the Freudian approach to creative activity may perhaps be outlined most simply as follows. (1) Creativity has its genesis in conflict, and unconscious forces motivating the creative 'solution' are parallel to the unconscious forces motivating the neurotic 'solution'; (2) the psychic function and effect of creative behavior is the discharge of pent-up emotion resulting from conflict until a tolerable level is reached; (3) creative thought derives from the elaboration of the 'freely rising' fantasies and ideas related to day-dreaming and childhood play; (4) the creative person accepts these 'freely rising' ideas, the noncreative person suppresses them; (5) it is when the unconscious processes become, so to speak, egosyntonic that we have the occasion for 'achievements of special perfection'; (6) the role of childhood experience in creative production is emphasized, creative behavior being seen as 'a continuation and substitute for the play of childhood.'[29]

More recent neo-analytic writers disagree with Freud's emphasis on the unconscious as the source of creativity and place the genesis of the creative act on the freedom of preconscious forces. Kubie viewed the preconscious processes as having "the highest degree of freedom of any psychological process. The contribution of preconscious processes to creativity depends upon their freedom in gathering, assembling, comparing, and reshuffling of ideas."[30] Both the conscious and unconscious processes are said to act in such a way as to rigidify the preconscious processes and thus render even the most potentially gifted person uncreative. Domination of the preconscious by conscious forces leads to the constriction of the creative forces; domination by unconscious forces leads to confusion. The essential quality of the creative person is seen to lie in his

---

[28]S. Freud, *Leonardo da Vinci: A Study in Psychosexuality* (New York: Random House, 1947), pp. 46-50, as quoted in Getzels and Jackson, *op. cit.*, Ch. 3, pp. 92-23.
[29]Getzels and Jackson, *op. cit.*, p. 106.
[30]L. S. Kubie, *Neurotic Distortion of the Creative Process* (Lawrence: Univ. of Kansas Press, 1958), p. 47, as quoted in Getzels and Jackson, *op. cit.*, p. 106.

ability to allow preconscious material readily to achieve conscious expression in the service of the ego.[31]

Psychosocial Characteristics of High Intelligence and High Creativity

One of the most systematic inquiries to date into high creative ability in adolescents and its relationship to high intelligence was undertaken by Getzels and Jackson.[32] Carefully comparing adolescents who were high in creativity but not as high in intelligence (as measured by standard intelligence tests) with adolescents who ranked high in intelligence but not as high in creative ability, the authors pointed out that creative ability and high intelligence are by no means synonomous. Evaluation of the heavily relied on intelligence tests has not kept pace with advances in theories of cognition, learning, and problem-solving and has retarded progress in comprehending the creative child. Study of the creative child has clearly demonstrated that currently conceived intelligence tests simply do not adequately sample qualities associated with creative thinking. In reality, it appears that test behavior on presently utilized intelligence tests bears little relationship to performance on creativity tasks.

Getzels and Jackson approached the decisive issue of advancing the understanding of all forms of cognition and human excellence and of the forces that bring them about by examining the adolescents within the broad context of school performance, achievement needs, and perception by teachers. Basing their evaluation of scholastic achievement on the verbal and numerical achievement measures that together comprise standardized achievement tests, the authors discovered the first of their highly provocative findings: "(1) A relatively low relationship between the IQ metric and measures of creativity, at least at the IQ level of the subjects included in the study, and (2) perhaps more significantly and surely more unexpectedly, despite the 23-point difference in IQ, the equal superiority of the high IQ and the high creativity groups in scholastic performance as measured by standardized achievement tests."[33]

Replication of this study with eight different samples supported these findings with only the parochial and rural schools contradicting the results. The reader is cautioned that no implication of

---

[31]Getzels and Jackson, *op. cit.*, p. 106.
[32]*Ibid.*
[33]*Ibid.*, p. 29.

irrelevance of IQ metric to creative imagination was intended but what was stressed was that, at the high average level of intelligence and above, "the two are sufficiently independent to warrant differentiation."[34]

Rokeach's insights into differences in cognitive behavior between open- and close-minded subjects contributes considerable understanding to these findings. Rokeach speculated (supported by his research) that the closed (and noncreative) person finds it more difficult to distinguish between information received about the world and what the source wants him to believe and do about it. On the other hand, the open-minded (creative) person, governed less by irrational forces and more by "self-actualizing" forces, is better able to resist pressures exerted by external sources and is freer to evaluate independently information on its own merits and to act in accordance with the inner structural requirements of the situation.[35]

Closed-minded subjects did about as well as open-minded subjects in synthesizing material into the problem solution so long as the problem-solving task was not a psychologically new or novel one as determined by their previous experience. Ehrlich's finding that dogmatism is inversely related to the degree of learning and that the relationship between dogmatism and learning is independent of academic aptitude further confirms Rokeach's findings.[36]

Significant differences in attitude toward the problem and in problem-solving behavior became apparent when the experimental group was confronted with a psychologically new task, i.e., one with which neither the open- nor the close-minded groups had had previous experience. When compared with the open-minded group, the close-minded group experienced significantly greater difficulty in integrating new ideas into their belief systems and in forming new conceptual and perceptual systems. Closed subjects were not as "willing to go along" with the new experimental situation. They had greater difficulty in accepting and remembering new ideas, and they tended to reject the problem, or sought to make it over in their more familiar but not revelant frames of reference.

Postman's and Brunner's findings are of particular relevance here. They demonstrated quite clearly that the dynamics of personality and the dynamics of perceiving are interdependent. Personal values and expectations of reality act as joint and active governors

---

[34]*Ibid.*, pp. 23-25, 26.

[35]Milton Rokeach, *The Open and Closed Mind* (New York: Basic Books, 1960), pp. 182-223, 58.

[36]Howard J. Ehrlich, "Dogmatism and Learning," *Journal of Abnormal and Social Psychology*, LXII, 1 (1961), 148-49.

of selectivity of perception and remembering, imagining and problem-solving. Stimulus objects in accord with the individual's value system were perceived more easily while stimulus percepts incongruent or threatening to the individuals's value system were resisted or rejected.[37]

Rokeach observed that differences in integrating new experiences and modification of existing beliefs "requires an openness to experience, a capacity to entertain new systems that are in one way or another in opposition to every day systems. It is essentially in this respect that those with open systems are seen to differ from those with closed systems." Anticipating the later discussion of some explanatory factors to account for such clear-cut differences in problem-solving behavior in open- and closed-minded subjects, the magnitude and nature of anxiety appear to mark an important distinction between them. According to Rokeach, "differences between them (persons who are open and closed in their belief system) can be accounted for by assuming that an enduring state of threat in the personality (and related to childhood experience) is one condition giving rise to closed belief systems. . . . the correlations between closed belief systems and anxiety are always positive and factorially the same." As a consequence closed persons find new experiences and unfamiliar stimuli more threatening, and it is this quality and not intellectual inferiority that seems to account for the difference in cognitive functioning.[38]

The closed subject's greater rejection of the experimental task may be interpreted as an effort to protect the configuration of self-conceptions vital for the maintenance of inner consonance. These findings point up the interplay of cognition, emotion, thought, attitude, and formative life experiences in influencing problem-solving behavior. Furthermore, a person's problem-solving behavior, once it assumes its particular style, becomes a relatively enduring system within his personality and may be predictive for a creative and innovative and noninnovative approach to reality.[39]

Getzels and Jackson's investigation deserves further comment: In view of equally good achievement despite a 23-point difference in IQ and in view of no earlier measured difference in achievement motivation, perceptions of the research population were compared.

---

[37]Leo Postman *et al.*, "Personal Values as Selective Factors in Perception," *Journal of Abnormal and Social Psychology*, XLIII (1948), 142-54; Jerome Bruner, "Personality Dynamics and the Process of Perceiving," in Robert R. Blake and Glenn V. Ramsey, eds., *Perception* (New York: Ronald Press, 1951).
[38]Rokeach, *op. cit.*, pp. 222, 403, 211.
[39]*Ibid.*, p. 376.

Again the findings were clear-cut and highly provocative: "The high IQ group stands out as being more desirable (to the teachers) than the average student, the high creativity group does not," in spite of the fact that his scholastic performance is the same.[40] Again replications of the study by others consistently confirmed the results.

Two explanations were offered to clarify this curious phenomena. One, not especially satisfactory, was related to the so-called halo effect that would accrue to a child when the teacher discovers his high-intelligence quotient. The other explanation was that the teacher's preference for the high-IQ students "is in the nature of the students themselves — their personal values and attitudes, their fantasies, and their long-term aspirations."[41]

Exploration of the values, fantasies, and aspirations of the high-intelligence and high-creative groups revealed clear-cut and striking differences between them. The high-creative group, unlike the the high-IQ group, was simply not committed to the same success-oriented values as their teachers.[42] The findings leave no doubt that both groups were equally aware of the objects, ideas, and behavior that lead to conventional success that are valued by their teachers. The high-IQ group adopted these as its own while the high-creative group did not prefer these qualities for themselves, even ridiculed them and seemed not to care that they differed themselves in this respect. These findings may explain the teacher's favoring the high-IQ group over the high-creative group: The greater conformity of the high-IQ group to their values may evoke greater mutual empathic identification between the teacher and the group, while the high-creative group, with their greater independence of, and difference from, the teacher's value system may be enigmatic and dissonant to the teacher and may arouse her disapproval and antipathy.

In examining the content of verbal and nonverbal imaginative productions (fantasy) and the stuff out of which they were fashioned (substance), the investigators reported "the high creative adolescents were significantly higher than the high IQ adolescents in stimulus-free themes, unexpected endings, humor, incongruities, and playfulness, and showed a marked tendency towards more violence in their stories."[43] In general, the high creatives tended to playfully abandon themselves to the stimulus with relatively

---

[40]Getzels and Jackson, *op. cit.*, p. 30.

[41]*Ibid.*, p. 32.

[42]*Ibid.*, pp. 135-37.

[43]*Ibid.*, p. 38.

greater ease, liveliness, humor, and zest. They utilized the stimulus and the instruction as a "launching pad" to go off into their idiosyncratic directions without feeling constrained by internalized disapproval or by the fear of disapproval from external referents. They engaged with the task for the sheer pleasure of it, and their productions reflected a greater measure of exuberance, a freedom to express themselves, and an inner locus of evaluation.

The greater degree of self-acceptance that tended to be true of the creative person[44] was also found to be true of the high-creative and high-IQ groups. The high-creative adolescent, in contrast to his high-IQ counterpart, appeared to be much more "in tune" with himself, was decidedly more open to new experiences, and at the same time could safely experience his own emotions and thoughts without inappropriate repressive and isolating strategies. As a consequence, the imaginative productions of the high-creative group were woven not only of humor and fun, but also of the bizarre, angry, violent, and shocking[45] which would be unlikely to be so openly present if their defensiveness were high.

The imaginative productions of the high-IQ group were marked by "obedience to the stimulus." In addition, their depersonalization of the stimulus gave their production a superficial quality that was suggestive of a strong and pervasive reliance on defensive strategies. Their responses were constrained by fear of offending external authority referents. They appeared much more concerned with conforming to the expected and "giving the right answer."[46] There was a concomitant literal interpretation of the stimulus, much more preoccupation with detail, greater measure of earnestness, and a much greater exclusion of aggression and all of its variants from the imaginative content.

In view of the findings drawn from the analysis of the free response activities of the high-creative and high-IQ adolescent groups, Kubie's formulation of creative thinking involving the dynamic interplay of the preconscious between conscious and unconscious processes deserves reproducing:

> In between (the conscious and the unconscious processes) come the preconscious functions with their automatic and subtle recordings of multiple perceptions, their automatic recall, their multiple analogic and overlapping linkages, and their direct connections to the autonomic

---

[44]M. I. Stein, "A Transactional Approach to Creativity," in C. Taylor, op. cit., pp. 171-81.
[45]Getzels and Jackson, op. cit., pp. 37-56.
[46]Ibid., pp. 37-56.

processes which underlie affective states. The rich play of preconscious operations occurs freely in states of abstraction, in sleep, in dreams, and as we write, paint, or allow our thoughts to flow in the non-selected paths of free association.

Preconscious processes are assailed from both sides. From one side they are nagged and prodded into rigid and distorted symbols by unconscious drives which are oriented away from reality and which consist of rigid compromise formations, lacking in fluid inventiveness. From the other side they are driven by literal conscious purpose, checked and corrected by conscious retrospective critique. The uniqueness of creativity, i.e., its capacity to find and put together something new, depends on the extent to which preconscious functions can operate freely between these two ubiquitous concurrent and oppressive prison wardens.[47]

The findings related to the high-IQ and high-creative groups confirm both the Freudian and non-Freudian hypothesis of creativity being at least partially expressive of "regression in the service of the ego," that is, of being expressive of a continuation and substitution for the play of childhood.

It is almost as if the creative adolescents experience a special delight in playful intellectual activity for its own sake. They involve themselves in the game-like task not because their teacher will like them for it, or because of the anticipated better grade, but seemingly because of the intrinsic pleasure that accompanies their use of fantasy. This delight in imaginative functioning—even in seemingly profitless situations—strikes us as reminiscent of the young child's joy in exploring the world and testing his intellectual powers in make believe and in acting "as if." It may be an exaggeration to say that our highly creative students evinced an ability to regress to more primary process perceptions of their world and to experience the quality of affect that accompanies a child's discoveries. But there can be little doubt that both in style and content their free productions more often reflected the uninhibited spirit of play than the stringency to do well on a task by reproducing a familiar, safe, and correct "reality."[48]

The enriching play of preconscious process upon conscious operations and the "playfulness" of the high creatives, when com-

[47]Kubie, *op. cit.*, pp. 50-51, as quoted in Getzels and Jackson, *op. cit.*, p. 97.
[48]Getzels and Jackson, *op. cit.*, p. 110.

pared with the high IQs, was also apparent in the biographies and in the range of occupational choices reported earlier. In making reference to the abundance of humor and playfulness but also to the presence of sharp violence and aggression interwoven with jest and joke directed at conventional custom and institutions, it does appear that the highly creative, when compared with his noncreative counterpart, tends to view the world with a particular affective intensity. The highly creative person, much more so than the high-IQ person, is more truely open to the range of his affective experience, both from within and from without. He tends to feel and feel more deeply and pervasively and completely the humor, but also the grotesque, the fears, and the violence from which his world of fantasy is fashioned. He tends much more than his noncreative counterpart to feel greater social concern for, and insight into, himself and others. Again, his creativity is such that it facilitates an ingenuity in problem-solving that is original as well as adaptive to the inner requirements of the reality situation. He can truly see new and different forms where others see only the tried and the familiar.

Mydean's finding that highly creative subjects chosen from the "top rank" of diverse fields of art utilized primary process significantly more than the noncreative group is very relevant to understanding the differences in the behavior of the experimental group. Primary and secondary processes were adequately integrated, and their (Rorschach) imaginative productions did not appear to provoke or increase anxiety in highly creative persons. Their imaginative thinking, when compared with the noncreative group, was marked by controlled regression and not by symptomatic loss of control. The creative group also employed significantly less repression than the noncreative group. Mydean observed that the creative group was markedly more "inner directed and not easily swayed by outside reactions and opinions."[49]

A passage from Guilford is highly relevant:

> In tests of convergent thinking there is almost always one conclusion or answer that is regarded as unique, and thinking is to be channeled or controlled in the direction of that answer.... In divergent thinking, on the other hand, there is much searching about or going off in various directions.... Divergent thinking...(is) characterized...as being less goal-bound. There is freedom to

---

[49]G. Mydean, "Interpretation and Evaluation of Certain Personality Characteristics Involved in Creative Production," *Perceptual and Motor Skills*, IX (1959), 139-58, 156. Monograph Supplement 3.

go off in different directions. . . . Rejecting the old solution and striking out in some new direction is necessary, and the resourceful organism will more probably succeed.[50]

Getzels and Jackson summarized as follows: "Obviously in these terms our IQ adolescents tend to favor 'convergent' modes of thinking and our high creativity adolescents to favor 'divergent' modes of thinking."[51]

The discussion of convergent and divergent thinking is reminiscent of Rokeach's astute insights into the cognitive and emotional behavioral differences between open- and closed-minded individuals. The closed-minded person is characterized by a relatively greater degree of psychological compartmentalization and isolation between systems of thinking and feeling which is designed to satisfy the individual's need to see himself as consistent with external authority.[52] Rokeach's formulation relates to Guilford's factors of convergent and divergent thinking, and both are highly relevant in comprehending the task behavior of the high-creative and high-IQ experimental groups.

Insight into the ultimate career goals and aspirations of the two groups, as represented by their occupational and career choices, revealed differences both in the *quantity* and *quality* of occupational selections. Based on reports from the subjects in the study group, the choice of high creatives, when compared with the high-IQ group, reflected a greater range and greater "eccentricity" or unconventionality of career choices. Examples of "unconventional" career choices of the parents of high-creative students were veterinary medicine, entertainer, "law or music," "teaching or art," writing, and dancing. Their choices reflected an independence from the teacher's judgment of successful career selections and a divergence from the expected by local norms. Seventy-five per cent of the parents of the high-IQ adolescents expressed an interest in but five career categories: engineering and architecture, science, medicine, law and teaching. None of these mentioned "writing or dancing."[53] The career aspirations of the high IQs reflected their adherence to conventional career choices and were in agreement with their teacher's standards. These findings were

---

[50]J. P. Guilford, "A Revised Structure of Intellect," Report No. 19, Psychological Laboratory (Los Angeles: Univ. of Southern California, April, 1957), pp. 6, 7, 9, as quoted in Getzels and Jackson, *op. cit.*, pp. 54-55.
[51]Getzels and Jackson, *op. cit.*, p. 51.
[52]Rokeach, *op. cit.*
[53]Getzels and Jackson, *op. cit.*, pp. 56-57, 58.

supported by data obtained from questionnaires given to parents of children who had expressed interest in some career.

In view of the systematic differences found in the study of cognitive and other personality dimensions between high-creative and high-IQ adolescents, the question of whether these distinctions were related in systematic ways to differences in family environment was explored. Information was gathered through "free response" interviews with parents, and psychological questionnaires which required parents to respond to certain specific questions. The authors concluded: "It appears that we are dealing not only with two different types of children, but possibly with two different types of parents."[54]

The parents of the high IQs were more anxious about "the dangers of the world" and more frequently recalled insecurities in their own background. The family style was more "child-centered," and the parents were more watchful and directive, were more worried, and were more critical of their children's behavior, their academic performance, their progress in school, and their friends. They implicitly or explicitly exerted significantly greater pressure on their children to conform to such standardized and immediately visible "virtues" as good manners, cleanliness, studiousness, and intellectualism.

In contrast, the parents of the high-creatives focused on such qualities as the child's "openness to new experience," his "values," his interests, and his enthusiasm for life—qualities that represent divergence from stereotyped meanings and adherence to convention. "The overall impression of the high IQ family is that it is one in which individual divergence is limited and risks minimized, and the overall impression of the high creativity family is that it is one in which individual divergence is permitted and risks are accepted.[55]

Role of Anxiety in Relation to Creativity and Noncreativity

In the preceding sections an attempt was made to present some of the characteristics of the cognitive, social, and psychological qualities that have been found to be related to creativity and innovativeness and noninnovativeness. Recall that creativity and innovativeness were related to a particular cognitive and social-psychological

---

[54]*Ibid.*, pp. 61-75.
[55]*Ibid.*, pp. 75-76.

style that enabled the individual to create new and different organizations out of existing forms. Evidence has been presented that clearly demonstrated the intimate relationship between creative thinking and such qualities as "inner directiveness," openness to internal experience, ability to receive information from both the inside and the outside and to deal with it rationally, and independence from irrelevant internal or external interferences.[56]

It is now necessary to examine more closely some of the dynamics of creative-imaginative and noncreative persons. Evaluation of the differences between the high-creative and high-IQ groups and their family environments discussed in the preceding section warrants the hypothesis that the important distinction between them can be explained by differences in the magnitude and the nature of anxiety that is present in parents and children.

Clinicians, of course, consider anxiety a major motivational force in the organization of personality. Perlman stated, "the functions of the ego – to perceive, to protect or adapt, mobilize and to act – are heavily affected by emotional or environmental conditions."[57] Most theorists agree that anxiety is a central determinant in activating and maintaining the ego's self-protective functions. It follows that a person's perception and the nature of his adaptive behavior are materially influenced by his anxiety. The cumulative effect of an individual's anxiety may be to narrow his perceptions and prevent him from achieving a dispassionate assessment of the nature of the problem-solving task.[58]

Rokeach's theory of personality constructs of high and low dogmatism as related to open- and closed-mindedness offers a framework that further clarifies the nature of the creative and the innovative process. That anxiety affects learning and adaptability

---

[56]Rokeach, op. cit., p. 57, described such internal interferences ("irrelevant internal pressures") as unrelated habits, beliefs, and perceptual cues, irrational ego motives, power needs, the need for self-aggrandizement, the need to allay anxiety, and so forth. He described external interferences ("irrelevant external pressures") as pressures of reward and punishment arising from external authority, for example, as exerted by parents, peers, other authority figures, reference groups, social and institutional norms, and cultural norms.

[57]Helen H. Perlman, Social Casework: A Problem Solving Process (Chicago: Univ. of Chicago Press, 1957), p. 85.

[58]Thomas M. French, "Reality and the Unconscious," Psychoanalytic Quarterly, VI, 2 (April, 1937), 23-61. His concept of the "ego span" expanding or retracting depending on its strength and the pressure impinging upon it is an essential formulation contributing to the understanding of the relationship between anxiety and "perceptual defense." Likewise, E. C. Tolman, "Cognitive Maps in Rats and Men," Psychological Review, LV (1948), 189-208, has discussed the possibility that "anxiety acts to narrow the individual's cognitive map."

has been well documented. Taylor and Spence and Montague showed differences between high- and low-anxiety groups which favored the low-anxiety group on social learning tasks especially when many responses were present.[59] Bruck demonstrated the effect of anxiety in undermining the competence of social casework-ers to adapt to the problem-solving task with their clients.[60] Experimental data has shown that anxiety retards learning and increases rigidity in problem-solving.[61]

Since high anxiety and high dogmatism and closed-mindedness are closely related three studies will be cited which concern them-selves specifically with dogmatism, learning, and innovativeness. Powell found that closed-minded (high-dogmatic) subjects were less able than their open-minded counterparts to perceive a mes-sage independent from its source.[62] Andrews reported that au-thority exerts a differential effect on learning and performance. Closed-minded subjects showed a greater tendency to follow the reinforcement of authority even when the reinforcement was an irrelevant one for solving the problem. Her hypothesis was sup-ported: Open-minded persons have a greater tendency to formulate problems in terms of their structure and objective attributes and thus less willingly follow blindly the experimenter's reinforcement without searching for an internal logic.[63] Jamias and Troldahl ex-plored the effects of dogmatism on the adoption of innovations by farm operators. The investigators tested and confirmed that (1) highly dogmatic farm operators have a lower rate of adoption than less dogmatic persons, and (2) the strength of the "value for innova-

---

[59]Janet Taylor and K. N. Spence, "The Relationship of Anxiety Level to Performance in Social Learning," *Journal of Experimental Psychology*, XLIV (1952), 61-64; E. K. Montague, "The Role of Anxiety in Serial Rate Learning," *Journal of Experimental Psychology*, XLX (January-June, 1953), 91-96.
[60]Max Bruck, "The Relationship Between Anxiety, Self Awareness, and Self Con-cept and Student Competence in Casework," *Social Casework*, XLIV, 3 (March, 1963), 125-31.
[61]For evidence of retarded learning, see Seymour B. Sarason *et al.*, *Anxiety in Elementary School Children* (New York: Wiley, 1960), p. 2; E. K. Montague, "Discrimination with Awareness," *American Journal of Psychology*, LII (1932), 562-78. For increased rigidity in problem-solving, see E. L. Cowen, "The Influence of Varying Degrees of Stress on Problem Solving Rigidity," *Journal of Abnormal Psychology*, XLVII (1952), 512-20; B. M. Ross *et al.*, "Effects of Personal, Impersonal and Physical Stress upon Cognitive Behavior in Card Sorting," *Journal of Abnormal and Social Psychology*, XLVII (1952), 546-52.
[62]F. Powell, "Open and Close-Mindedness and the Ability to Differentiate Between Source and Message," unpublished master's thesis, Michigan State Univ., East Lansing, 1961.
[63]Martha G. Andrews, "Discrimination Learning in Open and Close Minded Sub-jects," unpublished master's thesis, Michigan State Univ., East Lansing, 1962.

tiveness" in a social system influences the adoption rate of highly dogmatic farm operators, but has relatively little influence on low dogmatic persons.[64]

The persistent finding of a very significant relationship between high anxiety on the one hand and the descriptions of the behavioral styles and family environments of closed-mindedness, authoritarianism, prejudiced, and high-IQ, noncreative subjects strongly suggests that all these may be considered conjointly with the generally accepted psychoanalytic framework of personality constructs related to the obsessive-compulsive character structure.[65] Reflect for a moment upon the typical personality patterns of the obsessive-compulsive person. He is characteristically unimaginative, devoted to hard work, very orderly and perfectionistic, gives a disproportionate measure of attention to detail and minutea, and relies essentially on intellectual pursuits. Achievement is valued above pleasure, and his overriding need is to be respected and admired. It is almost impossible for him to be emotionally spontaneous, to "let go" and have fun. The lives of such people are generally devoid of zest, humor, and excitement. Instead, their frugality, overcontrol, inflexibility, rigidity, and reliance on "routine" are cardinal features of the personality style. They are generally very "moral" persons and highly scrupulous. Although significant inconsistencies usually pervade their behavior, these are often not recognized or they are well rationalized.

Compare these characteristics with Rokeach's personality constructs of high and low dogmatism related to open- and closed-mindedness, with the studies of authoritarian and prejudiced personalities, and with Getzels and Jackson's findings of characteristics of the high-IQ group and it becomes strikingly apparent that we may be dealing with one and the same personality configuration of which the characteristics just mentioned are but variants of a particular cluster of qualities that are products of remarkably similar family environments, especially parent-child relationships.

Although the study of creativity and innovativeness was not the major concern, Adorno did offer the observation that the ethnically unprejudiced person in our culture tends to be more creative and

---

[64]Juan F. Jamias and Verling C. Troldahl, "Dogmatism, Tradition and General Innovativeness," unpublished paper, Michigan State Univ., East Lansing, 1965.
[65]For closed-mindedness, see Rokeach, op. cit.; for authoritarianism, see T. W. Adorno et al., The Authoritarian Personality (New York: Harper, 1950); for prejudice, see Else Frenkel-Brunswick, "Personality Theory and Perception," in R. R. Blake and G. V. Ramsey, eds., Perception: An Approach to Personality (New York: Ronald Press, 1951); and for high-IQ, noncreative subjects, see Getzels and Jackson, op. cit.

imaginative than his prejudiced counterpart and that he is characterized by a fuller integration of his personality.[66] For this reason it is well worthwhile to supplement and expand somewhat Getzels and Jackson's description of the family environments of their experimental group in order to make them still more explicit.

A summarized and composite picture presents a relatively harsh and threatening home discipline that above all demands the child's passive submission to parental authority.[67] The image of the parent assumes for the child an ominous, forbidding, and often distant quality. The parents are dominated by much status anxiety which forces them to conform to an externalized value system. The socially accepted becomes what is necessary in achieving conventional success. "Love," such as it is, is highly conditional upon the child being "good" and submitting to parental coercion. Above all, the parents demand of the child an almost immediate abandonment of his assertiveness and independence, especially in relation to themselves, and an instant obliteration of any visible impulses not acceptable to them. Owing to the immaturity of the child, he cannot comprehend the values of the parents. His urgent need to preserve whatever security he obtains forces him to be obedient, and he eventually tends to conform with the rigorously imposed demands. Later on he will try just as hard to adhere to society's laws and customs with the same inflexibility with which he earlier obeyed his parents.

During his earlier formative years the mother's unrelenting insistence on impulse control and obedience stimulates in the child an acute feeling of victimization, hurt pride, and a provocation of open or disguised violent defiant rage which tends to spread over his entire behavior. Just as predictably this leads to collision with his mother's punishment and threats of punishment and with her particular proclivity for making her disobedient child feel guilty and for requiring her forgiveness through expiatory behavior in order to again feel loved. The urgency of his security needs eventually forces him to "split off" and repress his defiant rage over which he subsequently must maintain a vigilant guardedness.

What the obsessive-compulsively organized personality fears above all is loss of control over his dissociated and "ego alien" impulses. It is precisely for this reason that the controlled "regression of the ego" and the intra-psychic fluidity that is the mainspring for creative and innovative behavior is almost inconceivable to the

---

[66]Adorno, *op. cit.*, p. 389.
[67]Adorno, *op. cit.*; Silvano Arieti, ed., *American Handbook of Psychiatry* (New York: Basic Books, 1959), I, 324-43.

compulsive person. "Letting go," "taking a chance," experiencing impulses and fantasies tend to be equated with loss of control with disastrous consequences to self and others. Remember that the early rigorously and impatiently imposed demands excited the child's massive and violent defiance. Impulses and wishes that were forced under repression too early, too severely, too suddenly retain their primitive, unneutralized strength and insistence for gratification through discharge. Abrupt and sudden repression hinders the integration of the parental demands into the personality system, and, while the process further complicates the child's incomprehensibility of the parents' demands, it also undermines the mastery of such demands.

The obstinate, rebellious, defiant, and explosively angry but also fearful and guilt ridden child lives on threateningly in the body of the adult. The maintenance of a constant perceptual vigilance to guard against the breakthrough of basically unmodified and unruly impulses is an ever-present necessity lest controls will be unexpectedly overcome. Lack of integration of impulses into the personality system leads to a surface conformity which expresses itself in a stereotyped approach, empty of genuine effect in almost all areas of life.

The early automization of the child's defense strategy (under strong pressure of loss of security and strong fears of punishment) forces it to become overly strong and rigid. It is this development that may account for Rokeach's thinking of a person's belief system as "possessing . . . enduring properties. . . ."[68] The need to maintain the precarious balance between impulses which lurk everywhere compel the compulsive person, the highly dogmatic person, the authoritarian person, the prejudicial person, and the high-IQ, noncreative person to take "natural" recourse to ready-made cliches in place of spontaneous behavior. "Whatever the topic may be, statements . . . stand out by their comparative lack of imagination, of spontaneity and originality and by a certain constrictive character." They maintain "a simple, firm, often stereotypical, cognitive structure . . . their relative lack of individuation is compensated for by taking over conventional cliches and values."[69]

A very significant difference between high- and low-prejudiced subjects was found in their capacity for introspection. The greater creativity, imagination, and ability for empathy of the low-prejudiced person was distinctly related to the tendency toward intro-

---

[68]Rokeach, op. cit., p. 44.
[69]Adorno, op. cit., pp. 389, 480.

spection, as well as a readiness toward gaining insights into psychological and social mechanisms.[70]

Patterns of family relationships in low-prejudiced families differed mostly in degree of emphasis placed upon the various factors just discussed.[71] One of the most important differences between high- and low-prejudiced families was that less obedience was expected of the children in low-prejudiced families. Parents had fewer status needs and showed less anxiety with respect to conformity and were more tolerant toward deviations from socially accepted behavior. They preferred to provide guidance, support, and help for the child in mastering his impulse life instead of condemning. Socialization of impulses was in this way facilitated. More unconditional affection and greater richness and liberation of emotional life were observed. There was less obedience to custom and convention and less conformity to the various external authority referents. Children felt more independent of their parents as well as of external authority representations, and they had greater freedom in making their own decisions.[72]

Some Concluding Thoughts

The present state of research on creativity, innovativeness, and open-mindedness on the one hand and high IQ, noninnovativeness, and closed-mindedness on the other does not permit firm generalizations. But some tentative observations bearing on these characteristics are justified.

First, currently available research findings point to distinct and systematic differences between high-IQ and highly creative persons toward problem-solving with respect to motivation, cognitive style, and psychosocial dimensions. Differences between the two groups also correspond to distinct and systematic differences in their family environments and in their formative life experiences. Until recently high intelligence was held as being synonymous with high creativity and high innovative capacity. What has become apparent, however, is that the IQ metric, as derived from the traditionally constructed intelligence tests, fails to sample a sufficiently wide variety of behavior which would be expressive of all mental abilities and cognitive processes involved in situations

---

[70]*Ibid.*, p. 466.
[71]Observe the striking similarity between Getzels and Jackson's findings and Adorno's results, as reported previously.
[72]Adorno, *op. cit.*, pp. 387-88.

other than conventional academic learning capacity and classroom achievement. To predict for creativity and innovativeness in problem-solving in the academic world as well as in other situations will require first of all a still sharper identification of motivational, cognitive, and psychosocial properties that stand in a causal relationship to creative thinking specific to given problem-solving tasks, as well as broadening the base of available evaluation methods to make assessment more meaningful.

Second, the currently available evidence points up in clear-cut fashion that creative and innovative and noninnovative problem-solving behavior is dynamically and inextricably intertwined with the psychosocial dynamics of the total personality. Above a certain intelligence level differences between these two groups are not related to the intellectual superiority of one group over the other, but appear connected to the amount and nature of enduring anxiety (threat) experienced. There is abundant evidence that anxiety leads to the contraction of the cognitive span and thereby narrows the range of perceiving, remembering, imagining, and problem-solving in the dual interest of filtering out threats to the configuration of self-conceptions vital for the maintenance of inner consonance as well as to maintain maximum comprehension of reality. The nature of such threats and their psychosocial determinants need to be better understood in order to more selectively and systematically identify and nurture abilities relevant to creativity and innovativeness.

Review of current research on creativity and innovativeness suggests that the closed-minded person, the prejudiced person, the authoritarian character, and the high-IQ, noncreative person may be considered conjointly with the psychoanalytic conception of the obsessive-compulsive character structure. Indeed, there is reason to venture the hypothesis that closed-mindedness, prejudice, authoritarianism, and high IQ, noncreativeness may be only different expressions of a more fundamental obsessive-compulsive character unity. Common properties in family environment and formative life experiences, especially in the quality of parent-child relations, as reported in the social-psychological literature give further support to this hypothesis.

With so much emphasis on the functional relationship between motivations and cognitive and emotional dimensions in creative and innovative and noninnovative problem-solving behavior, it is possible that the effects of the situationally induced threats on problem-solving behavior may be overlooked. Data from such diverse sources as the study of the effect of threat on dogmatization of the Catholic Church, the investigations of factors contributing to the resistance of production workers in a manufacturing corporation to the necessary changes in methods and job assignments, and experiments in classroom creativity[73] provide ample evidence that the situation itself can materially effect problem-solving behavior. Major characteristics of educational programs designed to foster an open, skeptical, active, and critical view toward information and opinions may already be identified. We may begin by implementing the precepts formulated many years ago by John Dewey and the progressive education movement calculated to automize the "scientific method" approach to the solving of problems. Further research has delineated the roles in creative and innovative imaginativeness of such factors as ways of encouraging and rewarding unusual, provocative, and original ideas and questions, opportunities for fostering and nurturing creative thinking and behavior and the producing of original ideas in both teachers and students.

The essential problem, as stated succinctly and cogently by Wiesner, is that of

> ... devising an educational process which will allow the development of easy competence in rigorous methods of reasoning; the amassing of the large collections of facts and theories that constitute current knowledge; and the inculcation of habits for efficient use of available ideas and facts, without the simultaneous establishment of inhibitions and intellectual rigidities that limit the free and imaginative use of research (or in other work) of all the skill and knowledge that have been acquired.[74]

Fortunately, there is growing appreciation for the need to foster a climate that would encourage and reward creative thinking. Our very survival may depend on our accepting the creative challenge.

---

[73]For data from the Catholic Church, see Rokeach, *op. cit.*, pp. 376-90; for resistance of production workers, see Lester Coch and John R. P. French, Jr., "Overcoming Resistance to Change," in G. E. Swanson, T. M. Newcomb, and E. L. Hartley, eds., *Readings in Social Psychology* (New York: Holt, 1952), pp. 474-90; and for experiments in classroom activity, see E. P. Torrance, *Rewarding Creative Behavior: Experiments in Classroom Creativity* (Englewood Cliffs, N. J., Prentice-Hall, 1965).
[74]Jerome B. Wiesner, "Education for Creativity in the Sciences," *Daedalus*, XCIV, 3 (Summer, 1965), 530.

Chapter 3
Organizational Theory: Freedom and Constraint in a Large-Scale Bureaucracy

Samuel Krislov

Department of Political Science
University of Minnesota

I

Modern writing on bureaucracy tends to paraphrase Rousseau: "Man is born free, but is everywhere enmeshed in red tape." The concern expressed by the early Marx for the absence of self-identity on the part of the worker is today expressed as a dangerous tendency toward conformity by the middle-level bureaucrat, the "organization man." Criticism of egalitarian conformism voiced as early as de Tocqueville, fear of psychological constraint upon self-realization which found its classic formulation in Freud, prediction of the dire effects of a growing technological society upon the individual's power to control his own environment derived directly or indirectly from Marx—all of these divergent, and hitherto generally regarded as opposing, strands have in recent years been combined into a general synthesis and advanced as a critique of large-scale organizations and a society based upon such structures.[1]

This synthesis either in diluted or in variant form has been repeatedly stressed in best-selling volumes and echoed in lectures and on political platforms—as often under the guise of conservatism

---

°In the preparation of this discussion, the author has drawn from a study on compliance, supported in part by the Society for the Psychological Study of Social Issues and the small grants program of the National Institute of Mental Health, neither of whom are responsible for any views, conclusions or errors herein.
[1]Herbert Marcuse, *One-Dimensional Man* (Boston: Beacon Press, 1964), is almost the epitome of this particular blend.

as under the label of ultra-liberalism—reflecting a general and seminal concern shared by thinking men of all ideological commitments. How much freedom is indeed compatible with large-scale organizations is hardly a trivial question. If one concluded, for example, that our society were sliding inevitably toward the controlled antiseptic societies of *1984* or *Brave New World,* the answer of "better dead than Red" or its opposite would seem to be rather a matter of indifference. The structure and character of the society whose nature we imprint upon our children and grandchildren looms as one of the last intimations of immortality left in a doubting world.

Almost invariably answers to the question of the effect of expansive bureaucracy upon freedom purport to rest upon more or less rigorous deductions from organizational theory. On the whole, however, such efforts seem rather forced. For organizational theory as such remains to this day largely a body of a prioristic notions generally derivable from neo-utilitarian propositions with rather undefined and unexplored relationships to the realities of the world.

In spite of Herbert Simon's harsh but justifiable indictment of his predecessors as having left a legacy of "administrative theory through proverb," the current state of organizational analysis is only very slightly more advanced.[2] Today there exists a body of relatively integrated propositions, yet on the whole these are unverified even in part. Other propositions are synthetic theoretical formulations derived from bodies of empirical research; yet, as Golembiewski perceptively noticed, such formulations all too often accept at face value conceptual labels whose authors really were referring to different or overlapping phenomena.[3] Thus, the conclusion derived from the cumulation of such studies does not truly reflect what had been treated in the original. The result is that organizational theory may have progressed in recent years, but largely from the proverb to the axiom stage.

Perhaps the best proof of this relatively glacial improvement is the history of Simon's own attitude toward the basic assumptions underlying his *Administrative Behavior*. Simon originally treated rational decision-making as the selection, from among all possible alternatives and their foreseeable consequences, of that alternative which maximized the decision-makers values and goals. By the

---

[2]Herbert Simon, *Administrative Behavior* (New York: Macmillan, 1947), Ch. 2.
[3]Robert Golembiewski, book review, *Midwest Journal of Political Science,* III, (November, 1959), 404-7.

time of the second edition of his book, Simon was convinced that this was hardly a description of any actual decision procedure. Rather, he suggested in a preface, from salient alternatives a reasonably successful or most rewarding solution is analyzed, a "satisfying" rather than a "maximizing" solution is accepted. Subsequently, Charles Lindblom was to develop a similar viewpoint explicitly arguing not only that decision-makers work that way but that they are justified in so doing. This particular approach Lindbolm was to dub "incrementalism." Simon, thus, is in the interesting position of being both Lindblom's chief opponent and his John the Baptist.[4]

This lack of concreteness remains rather characteristic of organizational theory. So, for example, on the specific point which is the subject of this essay, it could easily be argued that large-scale organization augments as well as diminishes the possibility of individual freedom. It is on the one hand plausible and consistent to argue that the bigger the organization the more imperative are the requirements of careful delineation and specialization of roles and positions; it is equally plausible to note that large bureaucracies can permit considerably more deviation and still meet crucial needs, that there is in toto more "give" in the total structure.

But if organization theory is clearly not in a position to definitively answer the question of the effects of increasing size of bureaucracies upon freedom — and it is not clear that it should ever be able to do so in any scientific sense — neither is it without any guidance on the matter. The richness of current organizational research and the nature of general thinking about large-scale structures remain neither uniform in quality nor comprehensive in coverage. Some of the answers are Delphic; still others are nonexistent. But particularly in the last generation, some evidence of promising lines of thought have opened up the possibilities for at least beginning to analyze the future.

II

The first question on the alleged conflict between individual aspiration and organizational need is indeed even more basic. Is

---

[4] See "Introduction," in Herbert Simon, *Administrative Behavior* (2nd. ed.; New York: Macmillan, 1957); as well as Herbert and Peter Simon, "Trial and Error Search in Solving Difficult Problems," *Behavioral Science*, VII (October, 1962), 425-29; and Charles Lindblom, "The Science of Muddling Through," *Public Administration Review*, XXIX, 2 (Spring, 1959), 79ff., as well as his later writings expanding on the theme.

there, in fact, any incompatibility between them at all? Is such conflict a reality, or is it merely an updated version of romantic notions about the corruption of the noble savage by a decadent society? If organization in bureaucracy is, as writers since Weber suggest, the integration of rational purpose, why should it not enhance instead of diminish the range of choice available to individuals?

The closest approximation to an unequivocal answer has over the years emanated from the pen of Chris Argyris. In an argument that has become almost his trademark, Argyris postulated a fundamental discrepancy between the needs of the mature personality—a notion which is not totally devoid of some romantic trappings—and large-scale organization. To Argyris, the latter tends to require that its individual members suffer:

1. minimal control over their workaday world;
2. passivity, dependence, and subordination;
3. a short time perspective;
4. perfection of esteem for the frequent use of a few "skin surface" shallow abilities; and
5. production under conditions leading to psychological failure.

But Argyris also indicated that those deprivations can be intelligently controlled though never totally eliminated.[5]

In a statement that is both less highly individualized and more persuasive, Philip Selznick merely stressed the "recalcitrance of the tools of action." The "tools" of the organization are individuals, and their goals may, and inevitably at some point will, differ from those of the organization and the leadership which implements its purpose. He suggested five types of behavior that are particularly likely to be interdicted by the organization, that is to say where deviation can not be readily permitted. These include (1) behavior affecting the organization's external environment and security; (2) those actions which affect the stability of lines of authority within the organization and therefore constitute a threat to the organizational structure itself; (3) behavior which threatens the stability of informal power relations within the organization; (4) behavior which challenges legitimacy of operating procedures; and (5) behavior endangering the consensus with respect to the meaning and role of the organization. These he called the "derived imperatives" for the maintenance of organization, and these imperatives imply

---

[5]Chris Argyris, *Personality and Organization* (New York: Harper, 1957), p. 66.

that behavior threatening to the inherent stability and organizational integrity will in fact be met with reprisal.[6]

Selznick's formulation seems inescapable. Conflicts between individual goals and organization goals must at times occur, and, should they occur in areas fundamental to the maintenance of the organization, the freedom of the individual to oppose relentlessly will at some point or other be curtailed. Even in an anarchist society presumably at some point in time some extreme sort of antisocial behavior would be met with ostracism or minimal reprimand designed to compel adherence to basic norms or arrangements. It is merely a difference of where the line would be drawn.

It seems to follow, then, that the type of organization and the number of organizational imperatives that interdict deviation will be more significant in determining the degree to which idiosyncrasy may be tolerated than size itself. In essence, this is the argument of Karl Wittfogel's *Oriental Despotism,* although Wittfogel intended the thrust of the argument to be delivered in rather a different direction.[7] Totalitarian states, it follows from Wittfogel's argument, come about because of the inclusiveness of purpose that dictates the structure of the organization. In societies aimed at achieving a single major goal, conformity is necessarily demanded in pursuing this overweening purpose. Thus, Wittfogel postulated the model of totalitarianism to be the "hydraulic society," but the argument would seem to be quite general in its application to all truly unipurpose structures. Approaching the problem from quite an opposite vantage point, Goffman's inquiries into "total institutions" suggest the same thing—that it is the nature of the goal rather than the size that is the most obvious formulator of decisive characteristics of an institution and that, surprisingly, such arrangements as the army and a small nursing home have a great deal in common.[8]

The scope of the claims made for the organization is a principal determinant of the degree to which idiosyncrasy can be tolerated in a structure. This is true not only with regard to the necessity for maintenance of the structure itself, but also with regard to the external relations of the structure with others and the necessity for perpetuation of uniform roles and patterns. Thus, the Federal

[6]Philip Selznick, "Foundations of the Theory of Organization," *American Sociological Review,* XIII (1948), 25-35 (Bobbs Merrill Reprint Series, S-255). I am here following Christian Bay's imputation of a dynamic force in Selznick. See Bay, *The Structure of Freedom* (New York: Atheneum, 1955), p. 291n.

[7]Karl Wittfogel, *Oriental Despotism* (New Haven: Yale Univ. Press, 1957).

[8]Erving Goffman, "The Characteristics of Total Institutions," in A. Etzioni, ed., *Complex Organizations: A Sociological Reader* (New York: Holt, 1961), pp. 312-341.

governmental bureaucracy finds it necessary to number meticulously every single door—even those of janitors' closets and water closets—in order to maintain careful continuity and accountability to a general public which can both laugh at and demand such precision. Changes in personnel are not supposed to be reflected in any wide deviation in the pose assumed by the organization toward the general public. The scope of service to the public is not defined in terms of any single criterion—say, the sale of electric power or a textbook—but rather in terms of an all-pervasive "service to the community." Where the scope is both so general and so vague, deviations of any kind are possible sources of criticism and constitute failures of the organization. Therefore, standardization of very minute relations is more typical of a civil service bureaucracy than even of a comparably sized business bureaucracy with its more well-defined set of purposes. In this sense, the Von Hayek argument on the dangers of politization of economic relations would seem to have some validity.[9]

Organizations, thus, can be categorized as varying in scope and type of conformity required. The scope of the demand varies as the domain or organizational purpose is seen as expanding or contracting. The threshold of required conformity also varies as the nature, size, and structure of the organization alters.

Probably the sum total of all constraint, but certainly of its visible and consciously experienced component, varies depending upon the means available for securing organizational continuity and integrity. The pervasiveness of legitimating factors, the skill and adroitness of the leaders, and the ease of communication are all active substitutes for a cruder form of securing necessary compliant behavior.

The level of technique in an organizational sense is thus a key variable in the understanding of the psychological experience of freedom and constraint on the part of individual actors. But it also is a component of the reality. Thus, a Russian military unit in World War II with weak communication arrangements necessarily prescribed in redundant fashion many types of behavior that could conceivably cause confusion or conflict with strategical objectives; on the other hand, adaptive direction and flexibility on such matters was possible in comparable American units.

Innovation and skill both of a mechanical and procedural nature can be effectively utilized to minimize incursion of organizational

---

[9]Fredrick von Hayek, *The Constitution of Liberty* (Chicago: Univ. of Chicago Press, 1960), pp. 231-32, is perhaps the clearest statement of this position.

needs upon individualized and idiosyncratic behavior. It is perhaps generally true that organizational development reflects a human desire to control and even standardize the environment and minimize the risks of an uncertain future; it may even be, as has been argued, that the progressive unraveling of complex problems tends to generate larger units of action with wider scope of organizational effort. But there is also developing skill in the pinpointing of organizational demand to meet its necessary protective goals. Thus, a prime component of organizational technique is the ability to demand only crucial compliant behavior, rather than compliance for its own sake.

Instead of a linear development toward all-encompassing monoliths, there seems to be a cyclical and evolutionary tendency with regard to organizations. A race can be seen as generally taking place between the level of technological and human skills available for decision-making, including the securing of compliance on the one hand and the magnitude of the problems, engendered, inter alia, by such factors as size of organization, on the other. Holding organizational techniques constant at any level of skill development, it seems plausible to suggest a movement based upon size of organization as follows:

1. A stage of "underpopulated" organizational size where requisites of conformity are in fact extremely high, but are largely determined by the needs of the situation and are viewed by the participants as inevitable, or are enforced by immediate social pressures;

2. A stage of "balance" where organizational needs quite easily are accommodated as are also idiosyncratic requirements;

3. A stage of relative "over-population" where conformity is required in order to avoid conflict and the overburdening of communication channels, where personal bargaining is at a minimum and coercion is enforced through more overt personalized behavior.

A similar cycle could probably be postulated with regard to the types of problems handled through an organization, although historically there probably is no linear development toward an increase of such problems.

Additionally, the *mode* of relations between the organization and its constituent members will vary. Christian Bay suggested that

the degree of coerciveness of organizations depends on
at least these variables:

(a) the degree of involuntariness of the membership status:
(b) the power of the organization, or the sanctions available to its actual leaders (this variable is likely to correlate highly with the former one);
(c) the degree to which organizational goals deviate from important individual goals, thus tending to provoke deviation in individual behavior; and
(d) the extent to which individual deviation is perceived as a threat to the imperatives of organizational continuity.[10]

Such factors as available alternatives to both the organization and to the individual, proferred inducements, and other bargaining elements more or less subsumable under Bay's categories could (and probably should) be added. Further, it should be noted that Bay's categories gloss over a two-dimensional aspect of his own conditions of coerciveness. Not only are there the "objective realities" involved in his preconditions of power, but there is also the psychological perception of these realities on the part of both decision-makers and the participants involved. This added dimension relates not only to the preconditions of coerciveness, but also is at the heart of the definition of what is compliance on the one hand and what is coercion on the other. "What is or is not compliance belongs in the realm not of 'objective reality' but rather is defined by what is acceptable." Thus ". . . the zone of compliance will vary based upon social perception."[11]

But these patterns still allow for considerable variation in individual role-playing with respect to whether leaders on the one hand or individuals on the other pursue either group goals or individual aspiration. Following Weber, writers on bureaucracy have largely assumed an autonomy of organization development based on societal trends, ignoring individual variations. Indeed, any developing sociology of organizations must largely follow this path. We are interested in general patterns and only secondarily in the deviants, and even with regard to these we seek understanding in terms of encompassing generalizations.

Yet, historically speaking, individual purposes triumph when apparently they should fail. The bumblebee continues to fly in apparent contradiction to the laws of aerodynamics. The Bolshevik conspirators and their triumph remains "the scandal of Marxism," basically unexplained by the most convincing elements in Commu-

---

[10]Bay, op. cit., p. 291.
[11]Samuel Krislov, "The Perimeters of Power" (unpublished paper, American Political Science Association, September, 1963), p. 11.

nist theory. And the success of the Communists, and even more strikingly the Nazis, in subordinating, controlling, and replacing members of a recalcitrant bureaucracy, as Fredric Burin pointed out, suggests the need for the incorporation of such notions of intensity of purpose into any comprehensive scheme of bureaucratic analysis.[12] That the ruthlessness and savagery of the Nazi take-over, which quite willingly sacrificed bureaucratic efficiency where necessary, brooked no opposition and succeeded — in part simply because its leaders acted in defiance of general operating principles — is one sample of the possibilities of personalism as an explanation in organizational development and the limitation of other theoretical variables.

It would also be remiss to analyze any organization as insulated from its social environment. Most organizations are shaped by the broader society in content and form, in structure and style. A restrictive society will not foster within it an overwhelming number of permissive organizations, and conversely a permissive society will create pressures that minimize coercion within its sub-structures. Some limitation of this principle surely exists. In every society there are variations of degrees of freedom and Etzioni suggested brilliantly that some organizations, in order to be successful, must take on certain forms of action regardless of the society in which they exist.[13] Nonetheless, even those will reflect some emphasis of culture patterns.

At the same time the organization also creates demands of its own and shapes its external environment. Modern technological structures, for example, require certain types of skills and radiate demands that in turn create organizations satisfying these needs. The rise of educational structures in our society, for example, has been largely a history of catering to the demands of an industrial civilization. The type of people who are needed in order to meet the needs of these skills requires tolerance of at least certain kinds of nonregimented behavior. For example, it has been pointed out that, with conspicious exceptions like the Bell Telephone laboratories, the more tightly regulated business operations have been running a very distant second to the more flexible Academy in producing basic research. The type of structures needed to train these people and the flexible market arrangements that facilitate geographic and social mobility lead all of these secondary institutions to create an

[12]Fredric S. Burin, "Bureaucracy and National Socialism," R. K. Merton *et al.*, eds., *Reader in Bureaucracy* (Glencoe, Ill.: The Free Press, 1947), pp. 33-47.
[13]Amitai Etzioni, *A Comparative Analysis of Complex Organizations* (Glencoe, Ill.: The Free Press, 1961).

atmosphere and social patterns that militate against the social control generally found within the organizations that originally made the demands.

Oddly enough, this analysis is clearly understood and emphasized in discussions about the Soviet Union. Commentators well over a decade ago correctly predicted that some relaxation of social control was necessary in order to meet Soviet scientific and technological aspirations. Oddly, many of these same commentators apply a different logic when analyzing their own society, relying upon superficial indicators and ephemeral fads and fashions rather than deeper social analysis. That same method, the application of broad organization theory findings to our society, provides no unequivocal support for expectations of any sharp reversal of the pattern of American liberty. On the contrary, it suggests a continuation.

III

The impact of organizational pressure upon the individual, no matter what that quantum may be, is hardly uniform in its consequences from person to person. There seems ample evidence of wide variation in a tendency to comply with authoritative requests from era to era, from country to country, between social strata in the same country, and by sheer personality traits within the same strata. The classic resistor in the Korean prison camps who explained his refusal to cooperate with the Chinese with the simple "I'm stubborn" contrasts through time with the others whose desire to be accepted caused them to shift their opinions with the wind.

As Asch's experiments with perception of the length of lines in social groups indicate, many individuals will easily deny the reality of their senses when under social pressure while others will "call them as I see them, sir."[14] In trying to assess the impact of any program of "broadening horizons," these differences in tendencies to accept restrictions must first be assessed.

Culture

Some of the more extreme formulations linking national culture with tendencies to conform, which were current right after World

---

[14]Solomon Asch, "Opinions and Social Pressure," in A. Rubenstein and C. Haberstroh, eds., *Some Theories of Organization* (Homewood, Ill.: Dorsey Press, 1960), pp. 242-49.

War II, have been on the whole discredited. Nonetheless, some relationship is quite obviously established. Verba, for example, pointed out that differences in overall social structure and general cultural patterns are reflected in differences in the family units in differing societies, not only in a static sense but in an active sense of inducing change.[15] Such penetration of even this relatively isolated sanctuary by the political system is paralleled throughout the society. Lerner pointed out that within the same culture different social forces may induce differing cultural patterns with consequent effects on conformity. Thus, in a single society under transition sharp differences between "moderns" and "traditionals" in accepting authority can prevail. The "traditional" who lacks the empathy to imagine himself in a role of authority is doomed to an acceptance of the role of dependence or childish opposition. While some of Lerner's emphasis has been questioned, *The Passing of Traditional Society* suggests an abyss between different cultures in their attitudes toward idiosyncratic innovation.[16]

And Wittfogel's highly suggestive work, *Oriental Despotism*, with ramifications for all aspects of social knowledge, emphasizes the great differences in acceptance of authority in various societies; it further suggests a simple and useful index of such permissible deviation in the posture required of subordinates before a superior in the social hierarchy. Thus, at one extreme prostration—a position of humiliation and complete helplessness—suggests one type of legal order, and at the other a democratic, "forthright" man-to-man stance breeds quite a different relationship.[17]

Social Structure and Vulnerability

Both social mythology and historical evidence suggest the peculiar vulnerability of rising, but not firmly rooted, groups in society. These "strainers," as Southerners are said to describe upwardly mobile middle-class people, have been noted for conformity to both custom and abstract values; Ranulf indeed traced the rise of legal punishment to middle-class moralism.[18] Weber pointed out

---

[15]Sidney Verba, *Small Groups and Political Behavior* (Princeton: Princeton Univ. Press, 1961), p. 55.

[16]Daniel Lerner, *The Passing of Traditional Society* (Glencoe, Ill.: The Free Press, 1958). For a different view that is nonetheless related, see Lucian W. Pye, *Politics, Personality and Nation-Building* (New Haven: Yale Univ. Press, 1962).

[17]Wittfogel, *op. cit.*, pp. 152-54.

[18]Svend Ranulf, *Moral Indignation and Middle-Class Psychology* (New York: Schocken Books, 1964).

that historically a centralizing monarch or despot has utilized the services of such relatively rootless groups in an effort to overthrow entrenched elites. Among other groups that have been relied upon for such efforts are the clergy, lawyers, literati, intellectuals, and in many societies foreigners and minority groups.[19] The extreme of this as Wittfogel suggested, with his usual eye for the revealing case, has been the reliance of monarchs upon eunuchs.[20] The arriviste who has to preserve social or other capital is always in a position where he can be threatened with loss of what he has patiently and only barely accumulated.

Organizational Structure and Vulnerability

Closely related in concept and operation is the position of the striving trainee and lower executive within an organization. These middle-strata men have much the same position within an organization as the members of the upwardly mobile middle-class in society generally, and the same psychological mechanisms are generally operative. Particularly vulnerable in an organization are staff members whose authority must be channeled through a line executive. Their status, their power, is constantly under threat of disappearance should there be a change in the line structure. Dalton found in the plant studied in *Men Who Manage* that staff members insisted upon a daily shave and a weekly haircut. "The staff ostracized the rare member who did not measure up. One competent and cooperative individual who shaved only every other day, rarely got a haircut, suspended the knot of his tie far below his unbuttoned collar, and wore the required white shirt beyond the one day limit was shunned and heckled until he quit his job."[21] Moore and Levy found that engineers had a greater fear of failure than line executives.[22]

Argyris suggested that the lower down on the social structure one proceeds in an organization the more vulnerable the individual is to pressures. However, evidence from both popular and more analytic literature indicates that those at the bottom of the pyramid enjoy certain license to misbehave, with restrictions tightly limited to

---

[19]Max Weber, "Politics as a Vocation," in H. H. Gerth and C. W. Mills, eds., *From Max Weber: Essays in Sociology* (New York: Oxford Univ. Press, 1946), p. 92.
[20]Wittfogel, *op. cit.*, pp. 354-58.
[21]Melville Dalton, *Men Who Manage* (New York: Wiley, 1959), p. 93.
[22]Harriet Moore and Sidney J. Levy, "Artful Contrivers: A Study of Engineers," *Personnel*, XXVIII (1951), 148-53.

their specifically assigned functions. As one rises up the ladder, there are pressures for general and diffuse conformity until one reaches a level of integration and security arrived at by formal position or by the accumulation of "idiosyncracy credits."[23] The greater one's aspiration and the more one wishes to rise to the top the greater the pressure for conformity until the period of security arrives.

Gross emphasizes that increase of size can easily be accommodated with relatively small levels of hierarchy interposed.[24] The consequences of doubling or quadrupling or multiplying by even larger numbers are in quick fashion astronomical. With only six subordinates to a man, a five-level hierarchy can accommodate roughly 50,000 people. Seven levels of hierarchy can accommodate an army of 1,500,000. Proliferation of subordinates will, of course, increase the numbers involved. Increasing size, then, does have the effect of reducing "room at the top." It likely leads to more competition, greater conflict, and the need for stronger controls. Certainly it requires much more formalization of procedures and operations in order to carry out the same functions at the same level of efficiency.

Market Conditions and Compliance

The most recent volume by Blau emphasizes even more explicitly than its predecessors the classic Bernard-Simon-March approach of exchange of surpluses and utilities in organizations. Compliance is thus one of the utilities which can balance the scales of individual and organizational exchange of surpluses to their mutual advantage. An individual who has comparatively little to offer to the organization may find that he has little choice but to accept the wishes of the organization. The greater the attractiveness of the organization to the individual the less bargaining power he has with regard to deviation. An individual who is overpaid for his work and would have to move into a less attractive position should he leave the organization is thus relatively disadvantaged with regard to power. To capture an enemy one may over-reward him and thus make him vulnerable. If many others can substitute in the position, the incumbent has less power to resist demands from the organization. On the other hand, if another structure would

---

[23]Peter Blau and W. R. Scott, *Formal Organizations* (San Francisco: Chandler, 1962), pp. 99, 106.
[24]Bertram Gross, *The Managing of Organizations* (New York: The Free Press of Glencoe, 1964), p. 375.

find his talents valuable, an individual finds his power to deviate enhanced. Blau made much of the principle of "least interest"; as in the love relationship, the person who has greater psychological need for the relationship is, in fact, in a weaker bargaining position.[25] On the other hand, an individual in an organization who feels secure and integrated is more likely to be an innovator. Thus, doctors who were held in high esteem by their colleagues were the quickest to utilize new developments where they thought they were worthy.[26]

But the pattern of innovation in large-scale organizations has not been extensively studied. There would appear to be many contradictions and strains in the role structure in such organizations, particularly on this point. On the one hand, innovation must be primarily the function of the upper strata of middle-class executives. Their likelihood of rising or failing must be tied to some degree of success of their own innovations. Temptation for them to stress change is also clear-cut, for such changes often will provide opportunities for alteration of power relationships within the organization. This point is well documented in an excellent study of the widespread ramifications of innovation in philosophy or outlook in Richard McCleary's study of prison management.[27]

At the same time, the position of these executives within the organization is such as to make innovation extremely risky. Deutsch pointed out that the number of decisions in which such middle-range executives participate is relatively small, and therefore the record of success or failure may be largely fortuitous; indeed, it can be mathematically demonstrated, as Deutsch did, that at least some of the highest ranking management people under such conditions of choice and decision-making would be people of bad judgement who are unusually lucky.[28] The reverse situation will, of course, also occur.

The forces that pull in opposite directions, however, may actually be functional. The penalties of failure and the social strains that discourage self-confidence may tend to reduce what would otherwise be an excessive encouragement of innovation on the part of such executives.

---

[25]Peter Blau, *Exchange and Power in Social Life* (New York: Wiley, 1965), esp. pp. 119-20, 78.

[26]Elihu Katz and Paul Lazarsfeld, *Personal Influence* (Glencoe, Ill.: The Free Press, 1955), pp. 218, 220.

[27]Richard McCleery, *Policy Change in Prison Management* (East Lansing: Governmental Research Bureau, Michigan State Univ., 1957).

[28]Karl Deutsch and William G. Madow, "A Note on the Appearance of Wisdom in Large Bureaucratic Organizations," *Behavioral Science*, VI (1961), 72ff.

Much has been made of the contradiction between the requirement that the trainee or middle-level aspirant be a conformist in all kinds of behavior (often radiating out to a requirement that he select, train, and control a "corporation-type" wife), yet that he prove to be an innovator and develop new functions, even styles, for the organization once he reaches the point of power. While on paper it would appear that such a caterpillar-butterfly metamorphosis of personality is unlikely, it has not yet been demonstrated that it is impossible or even improbable. Without discussing the relevance of this phenomenon, Blau, for example, pointed out cogently and eloquently a similar paradox with regard to power-seeking. Thus, the person who wishes to accumulate power must first disrupt the organization and then later reunite it; therefore, the conduct which is functional to his reaching power is dysfunctional to his conduct afterwards. Whether individuals have the capacity to adjust to these changing functional requirements must, of course, be a personal variable and a rather important one.[29]

Blau suggested that the rewards for people in elite positions in an organization constitutes essentially payment for willingness to withstand great amounts of uncertainty. The people who seek such positions are in fact those who find such uncertainty either personally rewarding or a matter of indifference. Again, there is a certain contradiction in structural position and the degree of uncertainty in organization. As Blau himself pointed out, the higher up in an organization one goes, the more one can "spread the risks," that is, make statistical estimates of the probability of one outcome or another and hedge against unfavorable predictions. People at lower executive lines must make decisions which do not have this built-in component of insurance.[30]

Type of Organization and Appeals to Conformity

In a brilliant tour de force, Etzioni argued that organizations work best when there is a congruence between the type of organization and the type of appeals and rewards utilized within the structure.[31] Thus, normative organizations, such as educational and charitable structures, use moral persuasion as the major means of securing compliance on the part of their constituents; utilitarian organiza-

---

[29]Blau, *op. cit.*, pp. 203-5.
[30]*Ibid.*, pp. 217-18.
[31]Etzioni, *A Comparative Analysis, op. cit.*

tions are most efficient when they reward with money or other tangibles; coercive organizations, such as prisons, ultimately require a kind of force. Where other modes of appeal are used an incongruence or instability results. In practice, most organizations are mixed, partaking of all three types of function and therefore requiring a peculiar mix of appeals and rewards. The degree to which organizational leaders will be able to achieve this mix will, of course, vary. It therefore follows from Etzioni's discussion that compliance may be more or less imperfectly secured depending upon the skill of the top policy-makers in utilizing and timing their appeals. Herbert Kaufman, for example, showed that in so diffuse an organization as the Forest Service control of and conformity to vital aspects of the program are maintained through careful training and indoctrination and precise statements of rules and regulations as well as close accounting procedures. The factors that should theoretically produce erosion of control policies have been to an amazing degree countered.[32]

Personality Traits and Reactions to Authority

At the present stage of theory and research, in the social sciences at least, individual variation is not reducible to or subsumable under the heading of cultural patterns. While individual reaction to authority does vary in societal and sociological terms and can be ultimately traced to "modal characteristics" or "modal personality" found generally dispersed throughout a society, individual variations not accounted for by such concepts clearly also exist. It is hardly our concern at this point, either, whether these individual reactions can be traced to some sociological factor not previously discussed, such as relations with the father or the like. It is enough to know that such differences exist.

The most interesting discussion of such differences of personality in relation to bureaucracy is found in Victor Thompson's little book *Modern Organizations.* He discussed the new social disease of "bureausis" and developed different forms of it. Certain individuals he diagnosed as "bureaupaths," i.e., neurotic individuals who savor the luxury of formal regulation, authority, control, and avoidance of responsibility. He also characterized another type of behavior as "bureautic," i.e., a childish opposition to rationality and

---

[32]Herbert Kaufman, *The Forest Ranger* (Baltimore: Johns Hopkins Press, 1960).

efficiency for its own sake. All sorts of variations exist within this general behavior pattern.[33]

Evidence and theory would seem to indicate that individuals of lower middle-class origins who are rising in the social scale, who are also rising but not yet established within the organization, and who particularly value status and status achievement are the most vulnerable of all types to authoritarian seeking of compliance and conformity. Certain conclusions appear justifiable from this general pattern in addition to the statement of the pattern itself. It would appear that at this time, in American society, a number of individuals fitting just this type of description has reached such a vulnerable juncture. Indeed, it may very well be that, with the ethnic pluralism that crested during the Depression and in the post-World War II era, the height of just such a pattern of mobility occurred. It would then appear that the social critics discussed in the first pages of this chapter have mistaken a temporary phenomena (due to the pattern of immigration into the United States in the 1920's as well as the opening up of certain possibilities in American society in the 1930's and 1950's) for a broader, and inevitable, social pattern.

It would also appear that certain types of organizations create pressures and make claims which their memberships are more likely to be unable to resist. For example, civil servants generally would seem to fit uniquely, again, the pattern of persons most susceptible to conformist pressure; governmental structures are also just the type of structures that can create the greatest amount of such pressure. The mitigating factor in all of this has been the opposition of the general public to the creation of excessive overt governmental pressure. Yet, the pattern of conformity that is induced underneath the exterior of protection of individuality may be a greater reality than the veneer.

It should also be noted that where organizations may have strategies for securing compliance and conformity, so may the individuals have strategies available to them for resistance and opposition. The general public is not hopeless in this situation. Certainly vis à vis its own governmental organizational expression, it may induce considerable deviation and control over efforts to secure certain types of compliance. The outcry over governmental secrecy, over the use of technological and other devices by the government to check on its employees — which could not be easily raised against private employers — is a sample of the type of control that the public can exert. Similarly, expressions of preferences for certain types of

---

[33]Victor Thompson, *Modern Organizations* (New York: Knopf, 1961), Ch. 8.

public servant and the like may act as a strategy for the general public. Some pressures may also be exerted against nongovernmental or semi-governmental structures through public criticism. If one accepts the notion that lack of conformism or freedom may be desirable even as against the needs of organizational efficiency and that this is a social cost that must be borne from time to time, then it follows that awareness of the causes and occasions of conformity is desirable and necessary for its alleviation. That is to say, if one accepts the view that the pressures of large-scale organizations toward conformism are inevitable, but that their success is hardly guaranteed, one can then move to the last question, which is the possibility of doing something about it.

IV

Fatalistic identification of an alleged "wave of the future" has a tone of hard-headed cynicism and scientific precision; in contrast, hopeful notes and suggested incrementalist improvements tend to sound fuzzy and utopian. Yet, such sweeping forecasts as Burnham's *Managerial Revolution* have not only been proven false; by and large they misunderstand the nature of scientific prediction and confuse it with mere soothsaying.[34] Time has demonstrated, for example, that Burnham. misunderstood the psychology of the technocrat, underestimated his loyalty to the catchwords "stewardship" and "ownership," as well as overstated his independence and self-assertiveness. But science, in fact, goes farther and emphasizes the impossibility of incorporation into pure theory all of the variables of the situation; indeed, it stresses the practical inevitability that on the technological level some factors will be misunderstood, limiting the possibilities of probing into the long-range future. Thus, the physicist will predict the action of bodies in a complete vacuum but, as Marion Levy pointed out, will not predict when a leaf dropped from a building will reach the ground.

An understanding of the limits of science and projected historical inevitability is in fact a liberating notion. Such an approach suggests the limitations of current formulations, challenges the alleged "inevitability" which tends to be easily found and urged, and encourages the instrumental use of the few validated principles in the creation of new conditions toward emergent and creative goals. Science is essentially a body of knowledge based upon a series of deduced resultants, arrived at by a combination of theoretical

[34]James Burnham, *The Managerial Revolution* (New York: John Day, 1941).

statements and empirical observation, stated in the form of such resultants expected under hypothesized conditioning causes — "if x, then y."[35] Such knowledge can be utilized, it will quickly be seen, to avert or modify x, the causes, and therefore to avoid or to alter y, the resultant. That is to say, the relationship would still exist "if x, then y," but in the real world y in its undesirable form could be avoided. Such an effort, however, is hardly simple in nature, either in the effort or in achievement. The same problems that face any translation of theoretical statement into action in the real world — the transition from theory to technology — would plague us here, too. Not only may the theory or its interpretation be incorrect or incomplete, we may also stumble off into unchartered directions that will lead us by an unexpected route to the position we sought to avoid, or indeed into a worse one. Such real dangers — often impressed upon us by spokesmen of the Right — should not prevent us from exercizing human creativity with problems, any more than the cry of "inescapable paths" — currently usually emanating from the Left. We must at least attempt to make organizational life the servant of our society; any other course is in fact an active and not merely passive establishment of it as the master.

Mainly within the last quarter century, we have witnessed a revolution on the part of leaders of the largest industrial corporations with regard to the corporations' social responsibilities (charitable obligations, unemployment, and the like) internal structures (as witnessed by the development of corporate notions of internal "due process" and the establishment of review boards) and, finally and for our purposes most importantly, cultural flexibilities (not only the support of external institutions, but emphasis on broadening the background of their own officeholders and leaders). These alterations have taken place in sufficiently pluralistic — read contradictory and muddled — fashion to discount fears of corporation take-over of social functions on the one hand, or damage to the profit motive on the other. Nor has the pattern as yet pervasively infiltrated smaller business and other institutions.

What advantages, if any, have accrued or could accrue to the corporation by general extension of "broader vistas" to executives? While the motives of those who have been involved in developing this broader outlook are undoubtedly admixed with public relations

---

[35]A good succinct statement of the difference can be found in Mulford Sibley "The Limitations of Behavioralism," in James C. Charlesworth, ed., *The Limits of Behavioralism in Political Science*, Special Supplement, *Annals of the American Academy of Political and Social Science* (October, 1962), pp. 68-93.

and good will advantages as well as some "keeping-up-with-the-Joneses" corporate status-seeking, there is no doubt also that many advocates have viewed these as commercially and rationally desirable, with pay-offs in the crudest sense of efficiency and profit.

In an era in which technological change is the norm, provision for updated skills is becoming a standard quest at all levels. It is indeed a necessity. Management in particular bears a new and threatening burden not only of adjusting to change but also of sponsoring it. In spite of a great deal of talk to the contrary, American corporations have never emphasized recruitment from classically trained "amateurs" or generalists as have the British; in spite of many pious lectures to the contrary, they have increasingly demanded specialization even for trainee positions in the management struggle. Such specialized skills quickly need updating from time to time. Additionally, there is a felt gap between past training and the needs of a broader perspective for promotion to higher positions. As a general rule, even in the most specialized organization a higher position on the social ladder requires familiarity with more and broader types of information.[36] Such programs as executive training serve these functions — updating and broadening — but also augment the range of action afforded to any individual.

Psychologists have generally established the absence of a single generalized "intelligence" and the existence of a separable number of traits or factors; continuous absence of experience with some types of decision-making and some types of raw materials on the part of any individual under any operative conditions, will be reflected in an inability to cope with them. Perhaps more significant is the usual and gradual loss of yet another factor, the ability to learn and deal with new materials. What Bateson called duetero-learning[37] — learning to learn — has in our society been consigned largely to childhood. Americans have relied upon education for the young and have neglected it for the rest of life or relegated it to a form of recreation and masked retirement for the old. But the need for refurbishing old patterns and attitudes toward the learning process can be expected to become increasingly evident in mid-career.

Further, as Barnett pointed out, innovation is essentially not

---

[36]For a summary of the literature on this point, see Robert Dentler and Bernard Mackler, "Originality: Some Social and Personal Determinants," *Behavioral Science*, IX (1964), 1ff.

[37]Gregory Bateson, "Social Planning and the Concept of Deutero-learning," in Lyman Bryson, *et al.*, eds., *Science, Philosophy and Religion* (New York: Harper, 1942), pp. 81-97.

creation *ex nihilio,* but the combination of hitherto known elements in a unique pattern.[38] "The milk I take from 21 cows, but the butter I make is my own." It follows that the accretion of knowledge through technology and augmentation in knowledge of patterns of organization and information, in new evidence on communication patterns, make it likely on both empirical and theoretical grounds that innovation will be more and more the order of the day. That is to say, the accumulation of components of past innovations will lead to innovation.

It also follows that the greater knowledge and types of skills an individual has the more likely he is to contribute. Further, it should be emphasized that in Barnett's view the creative process is not limited to technological or cultural innovation but also includes advances in administrative technique. Indeed, as Barnard once argued, it may well take more ingenuity to implement and utilize a technological innovation than to develop it.[39] Thus, such programs may contribute materially to the advancement not only of the organization but of the society and not only of the individual but also of the organization.

One must be careful, however, not to over-state the case. We have here been discussing what intellectual growth might occur in individuals brought into contact with such a program at the mid-career stage. Any particular program, however, may or may not succeed with any given individual. Its relative success or failure will hinge upon the content of the program, the skill of the planners, and certainly the receptivity of the participants, to state merely the most obvious variables. Studies of the impact on the student of any course or indeed of the entire college years have emphasized that with a few exceptions there is a comparative lack of effect of any small segment of a person's life.

By the same token, little harm is likely to befall participants if they do not get out of the program what they wish. Argyris suggested that greater understanding of the process, greater mastery of the materials of daily life, will in fact lead to frustration for most persons.[40] The more mature individual will find the imposed conditions of organizational life more arduous and less acceptable. In this view, only the very elite of the elite should be encouraged to

---

[38]H. G. Barnett, *Innovation: The Basis of Cultural Change* (New York: McGraw-Hill, 1953).

[39]Chester I. Barnard, *The Functions of the Executive* (Cambridge: Harvard Univ. Press, 1956), pp. 237-38.

[40]Argyris, *op. cit.,* pp. 137ff.

develop "maturity." But this seems to rest upon the assumptions that the individuals will be totally unable to alter the conditions of their work, that organizational frustration is not only a necessary part of a bureaucratic life but is a constant necessity which cannot be seriously reduced or altered. Evidence in selective perception would seem to suggest that by and large those who would best utilize the information proferred by such broader perspectives would be most likely to absorb it. The degree to which individuals have already made efforts—perhaps futile—in the past to obtain such training and such information may be an index of the possibility of their effectively utilizing new materials.

For the bulk of those involved in such programs, the resultant should be increased ability to practice effective nonconformity; even from the standpoint of the organization such deviation involves the possibility of pay-off in approved innovation. Even officially sanctioned creativity necessarily involves deviation and thus could be successfully increased. Many facets of mid-career training should contribute to this. The increase in information available to the proposed innovator and his better appreciation of modes of innovation will be primary. At the same time such programs should facilitate the individual's sense of integration into the organization—a mood which tends to be a prerequisite for innovation. The contacts within the organization that he develops should both widen his horizons and improve his sense of identification, as well as provide him with information he could utilize in successfully implementing organizational change. He should have an awareness of potential opportunities, within the organization and without, for promotion or lateral transfer. Such things as these paradoxically increase the sense of integration and self-confidence which precedes most deviation.

At a minimum, such mid-career training will facilitate inter-organizational channel jumping—usually a desirable procedure. It may also facilitate inter-organizational understanding along the lines recently and on the whole impressively developed by the Defense and State departments.

But even more routine and standard tasks done through normal channels may take on new aspects. In the course of my current study of Equal Employment in the Federal service, for example, I came across such a development. The Kennedy Equal Employment orders emphasized not only corrective machinery to prevent discrimination but also encouraged "affirmative action" to overcome the cumulative effects of past discrimination and social patterns of discrimination.[41] The President's Committee, The Civil Service Commission, and other active elements in the picture emphasized the desirability of review of the records of minority employees for possible upgrading; to avoid the charge and reality of "reverse discrimination," such review was ordered on an intensified level for all employees. Personnel officers in many agencies have found considerable personal satisfaction in their achievements in upgrading under the new emphasis. Nominally such re-evaluation was within their purview at any time, and the new program in that sense afforded nothing that had not formerly been ordered. But the Equal Employment program suggested, glorified, and legitimized the function and made it a point of pride for the implementors as well as for the recipients. Such an investment of creativity into the routine ought to be a prime goal of any mid-career program. The military with their network of colleges and institutes, and the imputation of honorific standing as expressed in the mere invitation to attend them, could serve as the model for the mechanical aspect of the program.

On the whole, governmental service — the large-scale bureaucracy most accessible to public control and alteration — is the one most in need of such glamorizing. Rational updating of technology is less likely under political control than under the relatively strict cost accounting that prevails in comparable bureaucracies. The push for innovation is less likely to be felt from within the structures. In the Federal government, the very salience of the organization tends to bring it somewhat more up to date. The modernization of the Defense Department and the techniques, including budgeting and control, which attended it provides a model other Federal organizations must emulate. Local and state governments, on the other hand, may, and do, lag completely behind, depending upon the particular emphases and pressures of their locales. The attentions to programs and details are often not close enough, the caliber of personnel may not be high enough, the leadership may not be inspiring enough to even approximate maximum adaptation to modern conditions. Certainly the area of greatest variation in effectiveness, with the greatest potential for growth in all of our bureaucracies, lies in the realm of the public service at these levels.

Even within the Federal service Kilpatrick and his associates showed the public servant as feeling constrained in what he per-

[41]Samuel Krislov, "The Government as Employer," in Arthur Ross and Herbert Hill, *Employment, Race and Poverty* (New York: Harcourt, 1967) and Samuel Krislov, *The Negro in the Federal Service: The Quest for Equal Employment Opportunity*, (Minneapolis: Univ. of Minnesota Press, forthcoming).

sonally can do or undertake, lacking a sense of identification with the structure generally and having a relatively low morale.[42] Such images of the Federal services apparently have a firm base in reality — salary schedules at the upper levels and their relative inadequacy for example — but they also reflect a lack of the trappings of individuation and attention to the significance of the sense of self-importance; they result from lack of mechanisms to overcome the impersonalism of a large bureaucracy. Indications are that the problem is worse at the local levels.

If localism is to hold its own in our country, it must do so in large measure through the bringing of its administrative structures not only to the level of the Federal bureaucracy but actually to surpass it to compensate for the advantages of experience and centralized communication which the Federal government has. In the possibilities of developing a sense of creativity and individual accomplishment, the state governments seem to have many inherent advantages. If we are to once again invest local governmental structures with a sense of significance and accomplishment, we will have gone a long way toward meeting some of the desirable redress of balances in our governmental structure so long urged by experts and the public. The Federal government, though at the present ahead of the more localized levels, has only vaguely exploited the opportunity for a significant contribution in effective utilization of its employees. But the opportunity exists for significant contribution not only to democratic government but also to a free society, an opportunity that should not be left unexplored.

---

[42]Franklin Kilpatrick *et al.*, *The Image of the Federal Service* (Washington: Brookings, 1964).

Chapter 4

Public Administration and Political Change: A Theoretical Overview

Joseph LaPalombara

Department of Political Science
Yale University

Introduction

Slightly more than fifty years after the Western world traded the horse and buggy for the gasoline engine, Russian and American astronauts took their momentous "walks in space." Scientifically and technologically, a portion of mankind has reached a level of evolution undreamed of just a few decades ago. Such evolution was facilitated not merely by the availability of material resources but, perhaps above all, by the development of human skills in such vital areas as science, technology, communication, and human organization.[1]

Fiery speeches by Nkrumah or Sukarno, national economic plans in India and Venezuela, coups d'etat in Algeria and Vietnam, technical assistance programs in Egypt and Afganistan — all of these things attest to the intention of the "have-not" countries to make the leap to modernity. This desire for modernity — the "revolution

---

[1]The extent to which developing countries are also relatively deprived as to the availability of information is dramatically portrayed in Wilbur Schramm, *Mass Media and National Development* (Stanford: Stanford Univ. Press, 1965). On the meaning of information for problems of national economic and political development, see John T. Dorsey, Jr., "An Information-Energy Model," in Ferrel Heady and Sybil L. Stokes, eds., *Papers in Comparative Public Administration* (Ann Arbor: Univ. of Michigan Press, 1962), pp. 37-57. Management of large-scale, specialized enterprises has only in recent years been recognized in the West as an area requiring special training and attention. Schools of business and public administration as well as professions, such as city management or hospital administration, are of very recent vintage.

of rising expectations" as it is often called in the social sciences —
now encompasses all but a handful of the world's nation-states.[2]

A long roll call of studies illustrates the wide variety of impediments to the achievement of the kind of public administrative
apparatus, and public administrators, that would be most consonant
with rapid social, economic, and political development. Countries
like Vietnam and Burma alert us to the unhappy consequences of
difficult relationships existing among the politicians, military, and
civil administrators of developing countries.[3] A new nation like
Pakistan points up the great difficulties for administrative reform
that emerge from extreme conflict between a religious Muslim
elite, on the one hand, and a secular bureaucratic elite, on the other.[4]
Egypt provides a prime and disquieting example of the extent to
which administrative behavior associated with premodern eras can
survive both colonial attempts to effect change and later efforts to
create formal public administrative organizations patterned after
those of Western nations.[5] India, despite a central civil service that

---

[2]It now seems quite obvious that the perception of the so-called revolution of rising
expectations as a social groundswell inaccurately describes the developing countries. Technical assistance programs confirm what we have known all along about
the development of the West, namely, that deeply rooted social patterns are not
easily transformed by the promise of greater material well-being.

[3]Reports from United States technical assistance officials are replete with observa-
tions of this nature. For an interesting account of such problems by two men who
were intimately involved in one of the most ambitious of these programs, see
Robert Scigliano and Guy H. Fox, *Technical Assistance in Vietnam: The Michigan
State University Experience* (New York: Praeger, 1965), esp. Chs. 2,5. On Vietnam,
cf. Robert G. Scigliano, *South Vietnam: Nation Under Stress* (Boston: Houghton
Mifflin, 1964). For Burma, see Lucian Pye, *Politics, Personality and Nation Building*
(New Haven: Yale Univ. Press, 1962).

[4]In striking contrast, such impressive steps as India has taken toward certain kinds
of formal bureaucratic reform are said to be owing to the confluence of such elites
around the values of learning and intellectuality. See Ralph Braibanti, "Reflections
on Bureaucratic Reform in India," in Ralph Braibanti and Joseph J. Spengler, eds.,
Administration and Economic Development in India (Durham: Duke Univ. Press,
1963), pp. 3-68. This essay is also one of the best critiques in print of the relative
merits of United States Government financed technical assistance programs as
opposed to similar efforts made by private philanthropic foundations. Braibanti's
message is very clear: He does not believe that the United States Government—
with or without American university assistance—is very capable in the matter of
providing the answers for public administrative reform.

[5]This point is exhaustively documented in Morroe Berger, *Bureaucracy and Society
in Modern Egypt* (Princeton: Princeton Univ. Press, 1957), esp. Ch. 8. The reader
would be well rewarded to compare Berger's comments on the impact of British
colonial administration in Egypt with what Braibanti has to say about the British
impact in India. Berger alerts us, too, to the vital need for *not* approaching other
public administrative systems with "models" of bureaucracy derived from Western
experience.

has rightly been called one of the best in the world, demonstrates that the traditional village will not easily yield to intensive — and, in the case of the panchāyat program, ill-advised — administrative reform programs that run counter to centuries of established practice.[6] Uganda and Ghana provide striking examples of how previously existing structures of political and administrative authority and social differentiation will deeply influence a developing nation's capacity to effect change.[7]

Most of these works demonstrate that we now know much more about this problem than was true just a few short years ago; however, they would also indicate that we are still groping at the surface of the problem and that, moreover, much uncertainty exists regarding exactly what is meant when attempts are made to relate bureaucracy, or any other institutions, to the processes of development.

This chapter will provide an overview of the ways in which contemporary social science has attempted to deal with the processes and problems of "development" or "moderization" and particularly with that aspect of these processes that might logically be denominated political.

The Concept of Political Development

The Literature

Almost all of the working definitions or conceptions of political development have been more or less deeply influenced by the seminal writings of Max Weber and Talcott Parsons.[8] Weber's

---

[6]The important critique of the *panchāyati raj* is made by Hugh Tinker, "The Village in the Framework of Development," in Braibanti and Spengler, *op. cit.*, pp. 94-133. Cf., on the issue of social impediments to development, Robert O. Tilman, "The Influence of Caste on Indian Economic Development," *ibid.*, pp. 202-23.

[7]David E. Apter, *The Political Kingdom in Uganda* (Princeton: Princeton Univ. Press, 1962). Apter's work is a splendid antidote for arguments that all traditional institutions are hostile to or impede change. Apter's work in Ghana and Uganda demonstrates that one must probe in some detail the character of such traditional systems and that some traditional arrangements may actually facilitate social, economic, and political transformations.

[8]Interest in political development owes much to the pioneering efforts of Gabriel Almond as an individual scholar and as chairman for some years of the Social Science Research Council's Committee on Comparative Politics. Works of Almond that are particularly relevant to this problem, and which seek to face up to certain difficulties represented by his own earlier formulations, are: "A Functional Approach to Comparative Politics," in G. A. Almond and James S. Coleman, eds., *The Politics of the Developing Areas* (Princeton: Princeton Univ. Press, 1960), pp. 3-64; "Political Systems and Political Change," *The American Behavioral Scientist*, VI (June,

central influence lies in what he had to say about ideal-type authority systems associated with "traditional," "charismatic," and "legal-rational" societies. Parsons' impact derives in part from his model of society as consisting of related sectors having to do with integration, adaptation, pattern maintenance, and goal gratification and in part from his formulation of the so-called "pattern variables," a set of five dichotomous variables concerning which individuals and institutions must make choices before they act. Although Parsons, himself, has not identified particular patterns of choice with ideal-type societies, other social scientists have tended to associate one side of his dichotomy with "traditional" societies and political systems, the other with "modern" or "legal-rational" types. This association is greatly facilitated by the many points of congruence between the work of Weber and Parsons.[9] Broadly speaking,

---

1963), 3-10; "A Developmental Approach to Political Systems," *World Politics*, XVII (January, 1965), 183-214.

The matter of providing greater conceptual clarity to the notion of political development has in turn been explored by the editors of the SSRC Comparative Politics Committee's series of volumes on political development. See Lucian Pye, ed., *Communications and Political Development* (Princeton: Princeton Univ. Press, 1963), pp. 14-20; Joseph LaPalombara, ed., *Bureaucracy and Political Development* (Princeton: Princeton Univ. Press, 1963), pp. 9-14, 35-39; Robert E. Ward and Dankwart A. Rustow, eds., *Political Modernization in Japan and Turkey* (Princeton: Princeton Univ. Press, 1964), pp. 3-7; James S. Coleman, ed., *Education and Political Development* (Princeton: Princeton Univ. Press, 1965), pp. 13-32; Lucian Pye and Sidney Verba, eds., *Political Culture and Political Development* (Princeton: Princeton Univ. Press, 1965), pp. 3-13.

[9]H. H. Gerth and C. Wright Mills, eds., *From Max Weber: Essays in Sociology* (New York: Oxford Univ. Press, 1946); R. K. Merton *et al.*, eds., *Reader in Bureaucracy* (Glencoe, Ill.: The Free Press, 1952), pp. 18-27, 60-68, 92-100. Cf. R. Bendix, *Max Weber: An Intellectual Portrait* (Garden City: Doubleday, 1960); Alfred Diamant, "The Bureaucratic Model: Max Weber Rejected, Rediscovered, Reformed," in Heady and Stokes, *op. cit.*, pp. 59-96. See Talcott Parsons, the works cited in following paragraph and "Some Principal Characteristics of Industrial Societies," in C. E. Black, ed., *The Transformation of Russian Society* (Cambridge: Harvard Univ. Press, 1960), pp. 13-42; T. Parsons and N. J. Smelser, *Economy and Society* (Glencoe, Ill.: The Free Press, 1956).

The well-known "pattern variables" are: (1) ascription—achievement, (2) particularism—universalism, (3) diffuseness—specificity, (4) affectivity—affective neutrality, and (5) self-orientation—collectivity orientation. See T. Parsons and E. Shils, *Toward a General Theory of Action* (Cambridge: Harvard Univ. Press, 1959). These variables, as well as most other aspects of Parsons' general theory, are explored in detail in an excellent volume edited by Max Black, *The Social Theories of Talcott Parsons* (Englewood Cliffs, N. J.: Prentice-Hall, 1962). The essay by Black is a brilliantly lucid critique of the ambiguities in Parsons. His rendering of Parsons' central postulates in "plain English" (p. 279) will amuse some readers and provoke others. Black's conclusions about the pattern variables are terse: "It would be hard to imagine more distressing choices of technical terms for labeling the distinctions invoked. Apart from being barbarous neologisms, and correspondingly hard to remember, they have a pronounced tendency to suggest misleading or irrelevant associations." *Ibid.*, pp. 286-87.

views, notions, or "theories" of political development that derive from Weber or Parsons visualize three major types of societies and political systems—the "traditional," "transitional," and "modern."[10]

Following Weber's description, a "traditional" political system is one in which authority rests on tradition itself. Authority is exercised, and the governed follow their rulers, because the weight of history supports established patterns. Rulers in such systems are not accountable to their subjects; the established order enjoys an aura of sanctity; rules can change at the discretion of the rulers; precedent and perhaps "divine right" are invoked as justification for the exercise of political authority. In short, the legitimacy of such a system is grounded in habits unchanged over time.

In such systems, some scholars claim that one will find behavior dominated by the "underdeveloped" side of Parsons' pattern varia-bles. Thus, the sector of politics is said to be functionally diffuse, lacking specific or specialized structures for dealing with political matters or decisions. Politics is an intermittent phenomenon; it has not reached the point of political division of labor where one can readily identify political structures (e.g., bureaucracies, legisla-tures) or political roles (e.g., tax collectors, senators, judges).

Equally important in these systems are the facts that such politi-cally relevant roles as do exist (intermittent or otherwise) are based on ascription rather than achievement (e.g., one may inherit the job or get it because of age, status, sex) and that political decisions rest on particularistic rather than universalistic considerations (e.g., in reaching decisions, you favor your friends, family members, age peers, townsmen). Presumably, too, such traditional systems lack a sense of the collectivity and any strong identification with it. One's orientation is to one's self, and choices are made on primarily this basis. Finally, such systems lack discipline, affective feelings (of love or hate) dominate behavior and strongly influence the actions of rulers and ruled.

At the other extreme one finds "modern" systems which Weber described as the "legal-rational" ideal-type. The political system and the authority it exercises is based on written prescriptions and limitations, on the "rule of law." Authority is hierarchical; those

---

Parsons' acknowledgement of his intellectual debt to Max Weber and others is included in his concluding essay, "The Point of View of the Author," in Max Black, *op. cit.*, pp. 311-63.

[10]Needless to say, neither Weber nor Parsons can be held responsible for what they might or would judge to be misunderstandings of their theories or their misappli-cations. Perhaps the critical test of how important both men have been to the intel-lectual development of the West is the amount of controversy their work has engendered.

below who obey those above obey not the person but the office. Officeholders neither "own" nor inherit offices but reach them on the basis of carefully prescribed rules. Complex procedures exist for coping objectively and rationally with political problems and controversy. Legitimacy in such a system rests not on tradition but on social contractual agreement.

The "developed" side of the Parsonian pattern variables is ascribed to such systems. Here there exists a high degree of specilization of political labor. Political roles are functionally specific (there are judges for judging, lawmakers for legislating, police and soldiers for maintaining order, and security officers, tax collectors, and treasurers for gathering, husbanding, and disbursing public funds, etc.). Recruitment to political roles is based on achievement standards (e.g., any citizen who meets qualifications that are not ascriptive can be elected president, appointed as a judge, hired as a bureaucrat). Political decisions are based on universalistic criteria (e.g., the output of the system does not penalize persons because of, say, race or sex, does not reward them because of kinship or friendship). Presumably, action in such systems has a strong community as opposed to selfish orientation, and behavior is affectively neutral or disciplined rather than based on feelings of love or hate.

In between these two extreme types, there exists the "transitional" system. Within it, one finds a wide variety of mixtures of the characteristics we have associated with the traditional and the modern. However, we must note that for Weber the middle category was also an ideal-type (which he called "charismatic") to which he ascribed quite specific attributes of authority and patterns of administrative organization and behavior. Thus, a charismatic authority (i.e., political) system rests on the perceived superhuman, divine, mystical qualities of the leader. These attributes are not necessarily objectively identifiable as such in the leader, but he is believed by his followers to possess them. Charisma, then, is not so much a way of characterizing a political leader as it is of describing a leader-follower relationship, or of identifing the basis upon which the legitimacy of the political system rests. This charismatic relationship, rather than either tradition or legal-rational rules, describes the structure of authority and the basis on which the output of the system rests. Such a system is fragile in the sense that the leader may lose his charisma through perceived failures of his superhuman powers, or his death. Recognition of this danger will often cause the leader and his immediate lieutenants to "routinize" charisma through plebiscites or other devices on which continued legitimacy might be based.

Dissatisfaction with both Weberian ideal-types and with the pattern variables of Talcott Parsons has led to a number of efforts to provide other conceptions of development, even if the intellectual debt to important formulations of these scholars remains great. One of the most influential of recent writers is Gabriel Almond.

In an early formulation of his "functional" theory of political systems, Almond notes that use of the pattern variable dichotomies leads to great difficulties in our ability to comprehend "dual" or "mixed" systems.[11] Almond's first attempt to resolve this problem was to accept Weber's classical definition of a political system and then to suggest the salient functional characteristics of such systems.[12] These "functional requisites" are said to apply to any political system wherever it might be located in time and space. The functional requisites are then divided into an "input" and an "output" category.[13] On the input side, he lists the functional requisites of *political socialization* (the development of necessary allegiant feelings and attitudes among subjects), *political recruitment, interest articulation* (expression of demands for public policies), *interest aggregation* (combination, mediation of demands for public policy), and *political communication.* On the output side, Almond's functions of rule-making, rule application, and rule-adjudication are essentially those activities long associated with the legislative, executive-administrative, and judicial branches of government.

Almond's scheme has much to commend it. Instead of thinking of political systems in terms of concrete institutions (e.g., city councils, sheriffs, presidents, supreme courts, etc.), one is led to ask in what particular way, in any political system, the functional requisites are satisfied. Presumably, unless one made the mistake of assuming that a developed political system were equated with patterns of functional performance found, say, only in the United States or Great Britain, functional analysis would avoid the normative and culture-bound pitfall implicit in the notion that *only* Houses of Commons legislate or Supreme Courts adjudicate. Furthermore, the functional approach suggests what appear to be

---

[11]Almond and Coleman, *The Politics of the Developing Areas, op. cit.,* p. 22.

[12]"What we propose is that the political system is that system of interactions to be found in all independent societies which performs the functions of integration and adaptation (both internally and vis-a-vis other societies) by means of the employment, of more or less legitimate physical compulsion. . . .Legitimate force is the thread that runs through the inputs and outputs of the political system, giving it its special quality and salience and coherence as a system." *Ibid.,* p. 17.

[13]I am summarizing here from various portions of the essay. The interested reader should consult it for details which must be omitted for lack of space.

important dimensions along which differences among and changes within political systems could be measured. Ideally, one would construct a typology based on particular combinations or "profiles" of functional characteristics, and, if this were done, the problem of classifying dual or mixed systems would be in considerable measure resolved.

Almond's formulations resulted not only in a great deal of further theorizing but also in considerable field research designed to provide more information about the input side of the functional scheme. Thus, in an effort to associate certain patterns in society with what we already described as the input functions, we now have books dealing with the phenomena of interest articulation and aggregation, political socialization, and political communications.[14] Beyond this, two works have appeared which rest on another of Almond's insights, namely, that the dynamics of political systems are in considerable measure dependent on the nature of their "political cultures," that is, on the patterns of beliefs, feelings, identifications and evaluations that people have about political institutions and about political actors in their societies.[15]

Almond, of course, is not alone in the general attempt to bring greater conceptual and theoretical clarity to the idea of political change or development. Daniel Lerner, in a widely read and justly admired study, suggests that the central thread in political development is increasing political participation, and he pro-

---

[14]See, for example, the interest articulation and aggregation sections of the area studies in Almond and Coleman, *op. cit.* Cf. Myron Weiner, *The Politics of Scarcity* (Chicago: Univ. of Chicago Press, 1962); and Joseph LaPalombara, *Interest Groups in Italian Politics* (Princeton: Princeton Univ. Press, 1964). See, as an important example of the "identity crisis" (the person's search for meaning of self in relationship to the nation-state), Pye, *Politics, Personality and Nation Building, op. cit.* Also of importance in this regard is James S. Coleman, ed., *Education and Political Development, op. cit.* It should be noted that work on political socialization owes much to the pioneering study of Herbert Hyman, *Political Socialization* (Glencoe, Ill.: The Free Press, 1959). See Pye, ed., *Communications and Political Development, op. cit.* Communications, of course, is a phenomenon or structure that necessarily impinges on all other functions in a political system. However, it is vitally important to understand analytically its salience for political change, particularly in those currently developing countries that are in a sense prematurely exposed to the technology of mass communications. Again, the ground-breaking work of Wilbur Schramm in this area is of critical importance. In addition to the recent volume cited in note 1, see his edited volumes, *Mass Communications* (Urbana: Univ. of Illinois Press, 1944), and *The Process and Effects of Mass Communications* (Urbana: Univ. of Illinois Press, 1954).

[15]See G. A. Almond and Sidney Verba, *The Civic Culture* (Princeton: Princeton Univ. Press, 1963). Cf. Pye and Verba, *op. cit.*, and note particularly the concluding chapter in which Verba tries to spell out the beginnings of a theory of political culture.

vides a developmental construct whereby societies move from rural to urban configurations and increase literacy, which in turn increases media consumption, which in turn leads to increased political participation.[16] In describing the process of modernity, Lerner lays great stress on the need to develop *empathy* in traditional personalities. The idea here is that modernization is greatly impeded unless the spatial universe and frame of reference of the traditional person is broadened to the point where he can stand in the other man's shoes and see the world and his problems from that perspective.

David Apter offers an interesting scheme wherein he shows that attempts at change are usually efforts to modify the stratification system of a society. The principal foci for analysis in his model are, therefore, social stratification, political groups, and government. Apter has sought to apply this developmental scheme in some of his other published work.[17] David Easton, whose work has also strongly influenced thinking about political systems and their evolution, has worked with an input-output model of the political system and has tried to specify what kinds of factors on each side of this process would be necessary to keep a system in a state of equilibrium.[18] Everett Hagen, greatly dissatisfied with economic explanations of social change, develops a most provocative theory attempting to show that social changes are greatly dependent on the structure of personality and its transformations.[19] Closely allied to

[16]Daniel Lerner, *The Passing of Traditional Society* (Glencoe, Ill.: The Free Press, 1958), esp. pp. 43-75. Lerner's formulations also rest on generalizations about "traditional" and "modern" society and particularly on the role in development of the "empathic" personality, to which we will return in the next section of this paper.

[17]David E. Apter, "A Comparative Method for the Study of Politics," *The American Journal of Sociology*, LXIV (November, 1958), 221-37. See, also, his "The Role of Traditionalism in the Political Modernization of Ghana and Uganda," *World Politics*, XIII (October, 1960), 45-68. In his *The Political Kingdom in Uganda, op. cit.*, Apter elaborates and seeks to apply the basic model, though not always convincingly. His most recent and elaborate development of his ideas is found in *The Politics of Modernization* (Chicago: Univ. of Chicago Press, 1965).

[18]See David Easton, *The Political System* (New York: Knopf, 1953). Cf. "An Approach to the Analysis of Political Systems," *World Politics*, IX (April, 1957), 383-400. Easton later published a set of qualifications regarding equilibrium analysis as applied to politics which are fairly discouraging for those who wish to move from abstract conceptualization to empirical validation of theory. See his "Limits on the Equilibrium Model in Social Research," in H. Eulau *et al.*, eds., *Political Behavior* (Glencoe, Ill.: The Free Press, 1950), pp. 397-404.

[19]Everett E. Hagen, *On the Theory of Social Change* (Homewood, Ill.: Dorsey Press, 1962). Personality variables in development are also important in the work of Lerner, *op. cit.*, and Pye, *Politics, Personality and Nation Building, op. cit.*

Hagen's work are the writings of David McClelland who argues that development or modernization is closely tied to the achievement motive, or to the degree of "need achievement" present in a society.[20] Although the theoretical work of both Hagen and McClelland deals specifically with the problem of economic modernization, it has had considerable influence among those who have sought to apply some of their ideas to problems of political development. More recently, Samuel Huntington has reviewed much of the literature on development, has found it wanting, and has suggested a conception of political development that ties it to "the institutionalization of organizations and procedures." For any political system, he would measure the degree of institutionalization along such continua as adaptability-rigidity, complexity-simplicity, autonomy-subordination, and coherence-disunity. In addition he has attempted to distinguish between organizations and procedures in politics that are *mobilized* as opposed to institutionalized.[21]

We also have what we must loosely call a number of structural-functional formulations of development which may or may not include assumptions about the threefold typology of traditional, transitional and modern societies. Gabriel Almond's most recent statement of his theoretical ideas continues to describe the political system as a mechanical model involving input, output and conversion functions. He notes that in viewing the political system as it operates within its broader environment, one will be centrally concerned with its "capabilities." On the output side of such systems, he divides their "transactions" into (1) *extractions*, which may take the form of tribute, booty, taxes, or personal services, (2) *regulation of behavior*, which may take a variety of forms and affect the whole gamut of human behavior and relations, (3) *allocations or distributions* of goods and services, opportunities, honors, statuses, and the like, and finally (4) *symbolic outputs*, including affirmation of values, displays of political symbols, statements of policies and intents. These categories in turn are related to capability functions

---

[20]David C. McClelland, *The Achieving Society* (Princeton: Princeton Univ. Press, 1961), esp. Ch. 2. McClelland's work, of course, is closely related to Weber's *The Protestant Ethic and the Spirit of Capitalism*, trans. Talcott Parsons (New York: Scribner's, 1930).

[21]Samuel Huntington, "Political Development and Political Decay," *World Politics*, XVII (April, 1965), esp. 394-403. Huntington makes the important point that a concept of political development should permit reversibility or "political decay." Cf. C. E. Black, *The Dynamics of Modernization* (New York: Harper and Row, 1966), which is a provocative attempt to identify phases of "modernization" and to identify historically comparable periods of development for more than 130 nation-states.

that Almond labels "extractive," "regulative," "distributive," and "responsive."[22]

Similarly Apter continues to view political development in a structure-functional context which is based on work cited previously and which finds its most extensive treatment in his *The Political System in Uganda.* This volume is of particular interest to those who are concerned with the relationship between bureaucratic organization and national development.

Evaluation

In evaluating the various schemes proposed for understanding political development, we must keep four questions in mind.

1. Is the meaning of political development clear? Or, is a "developed" or "modern" political system too often measured by criteria more relevant to the economist or sociologist (i.e., per capita gross national product and literacy rates)?[23]

---

[22]Almond, "A Developmental Approach to Political Systems," *op. cit.* It should be noted that Almond means to relate this article to his earlier formulations and that he designates as a major change in his thinking the classification of functions into capabilities, conversion functions, and system maintenance and adaptation functions. He indicates that this article emerges from long-extended dialectics with himself, his students, and particularly with colleagues on the Committee on Comparative Politics. A somewhat related but nevertheless different conceptualization of political development is contained in the forthcoming concluding volume of the Committee's series. See Leonard Binder, James Coleman, Joseph LaPalombara, Myron Weiner, and Lucian Pye, *Crises of Political Development* (Princeton: Princeton Univ. Press, forthcoming).

[23]On the limitations of associating economic growth, as generally conceived by economists, with the presence or absence of economic barriers, see Hagen, *op. cit.,* Ch. 3. The work of S. M. Lipset both regarding the so-called economic requisites of democracy and the impact of economic affluence on an alleged decline of ideology is centrally relevant here. See, e.g., his *Political Man* (Garden City: Doubleday, 1959), esp. pp. 45-76, 403-17, and his "The Changing Class Structure of Contemporary European Politics," *Daedalus,* XCIII (Winter, 1964), 271-303. I have sought to provide a partial rebuttal to the "decline of ideology" thesis in my "Decline of Ideology: A Dissent and an Interpretation," *American Political Science Review,* LX (March, 1966), 5-16. The reader will also want to consult Lipset's pioneering study in political development, *The First New Nation* (New York: Basic Books, 1964).

By far the most questionable exercise in seeking to make political systems dependent on economic measures (many of them of dubious reliability for a great many polities) is Arthur S. Banks and Robert B. Textor, *A Cross-Policy Survey* (Cambridge: Harvard Univ. Press, 1963).

I am, of course, aware that what the political scientist may think are universally accepted definitions around which comparable data can be gathered in the field of economics are in fact highly ambiguous measures for the economists themselves. Measurements of gross national product and definitions of unemployment would be examples.

2. Is the definition of political development adopted so narrow, normatively based, or culture-bound as to exclude concrete political systems from analysis? Are "developed" political systems equated—implicitly or explicitly—with pluralistic democracies found in a few highly industrialized, relatively open social systems of the Western world, while systems which fall short of the Anglo-American model are considered "underdeveloped" or downright abberations?[24]

3. Is political development perceived as an inevitable, irreversible, unilinear process moving toward a predetermined or fixed-end state?[25] One example of this deeply-rooted intellectual formulation is the Marxian historical dialectic which postulates a final state of historical evolution. Another unilinear and fixed-end state assumption is contained in what appears to be the premature—and possibly wishful—conclusion that the Soviet Union may be evolving into a more liberal or democratic political system. It seems obvious enough that for some time into the future developmental theories

---

I should also note, however, that even if one could have complete confidence in the consistency of definition and comparable availability of data concerning economic variables, there are still important reasons for remaining skeptical about indoor-plumbing and birth-and-death-rate "theories" of *political* development. See Max Weber, *The Theory of Social and Economic Organization*, trans. A. M. Henderson and Talcott Parsons (New York: Oxford Univ. Press, 1947).

[24]To some extent, this defect is true of the important essay by Almond previously cited: *The Politics of the Developing Areas*. Similarly, see Edward Shils, *Political Development in the New States* (The Hague: Mouton, 1962). This problem can also be detected in Max F. Millikan and Donald L. M. Blackmer, eds., *The Emerging Nations* (Cambridge: Harvard Univ. Press, 1961), although the authors clearly attempt to separate economic, social, and political development and warn the reader that "while the process of modernization creates some of the preconditions for democracy, its emergence is by no means foreordained" (p. 42). Samuel Huntington also notes that most current definitions of political development associate the concept with democracy. He objects to this and provides his own review of shortcomings into attempts to define political development. See his "Political Development and Political Decay," *op. cit.*, pp. 386-93. Cf. C. Black, *op. cit.*, Ch. 5.

The central interest in a "theory" of democratic development is now made explicit in Almond and Verba, *op. cit.*, and in several of the SSRC volumes cited previously. Growing concern with empirical democratic theory owes much to the important work of Robert Dahl. See, for example, his *A Preface to Democratic Theory* (Chicago: Univ. of Chicago Press, 1956). More recently, a symposium edited by Dahl seeks to explore the varying impact of patterns of political opposition on the maintenance of stable pluralistic democracies. See R. A. Dahl, ed., *Political Oppositions in Western Democracies* (New Haven: Yale Univ. Press, 1965).

[25]See Walt W. Rostow, *The Stages of Economic Growth: A Non-Communist Manifesto* (Cambridge: Harvard Univ. Press, 1960), and, by the same author, "The Take-off into Self-Sustained Growth," *The Economic Journal*, LXVI (March, 1956), 25-48. But cf. the very important theory that denies many of Rostow's assumptions: Albert O. Hirschman, *The Strategy of Economic Development* (New Haven: Yale Univ. Press, 1958).

will have to leave the door open to formulations of multilinearity.[26]

4. Do writings on political development assume that development in human society is an indivisible and balanced process whereby economic, social, psychological, and political factors are inextricably bound together?[27]

This type of analysis carries with it two kinds of dubious conclusions: first, that democracy as a system cannot develop until certain economic or social preconditions are met and, second, that once such preconditions come into being political systems become less ideological, more liberal or democratic. The difficulties with such formulations are that the so-called correlations are often based on "poor" data, the association of economic and political variables is begged, and in any case, many empirical cases simply do not fit the formulation.

The Weberian model of ideal-types and the Parsonian pattern variables have been widely accepted as seeming to provide a felicitous method for analyzing political development. But these models have a number of serious intrinsic limitations.

The Typology is Deceptively Attractive Empirically. Because, as I have warned above, the differentiating characteristics of this typology are very gross, it is relatively easy to point to real political systems that seem to fall essentially into one or another of these categories. Much of what we know about "primitive" tribes, for example, seems to confirm the existence there of traditional patterns. Political roles are diffuse — it is difficult to know when someone is acting as judge, medicine man, educator, or hunter. Ascription and particularism seem to govern most facets of human behav-

---

[26]An important, and somewhat controversial, book pointing in this direction is Julian H. Steward, *Theory of Culture Change: The Methodology of Multilinear Evolution* (Urbana: Univ. of Illinois Press, 1955).
[27]Single works or symposia which seem to me to have brought us a much more "holistic" understanding of the development process, without manifesting extreme formulations of developmental interdependency, would include the following: Lipset, *The First New Nation*, op. cit.; Hagen, op. cit.; Almond and Verba, *The Civic Culture*, op. cit.; Pye and Verba, op. cit.; Ward and Rustow, op. cit.; Braibanti and Spengler, op. cit.; Apter, *The Political Kingdom in Uganda*, op. cit.; Pye, *Politics, Personality and Nation Building*, op. cit.; Myron Weiner, *The Politics of Scarcity*, op. cit.; Karl Deutsch, *The Nerves of Government: Models of Political Communications and Control* (New York: The Free Press of Glencoe, 1963); Daniel Lerner, *The Passing of Traditional Society* (Glencoe, Ill.: The Free Press, 1958); S. N. Eisenstadt, *The Political Systems of Empires* (New York: The Free Press of Glencoe, 1963). In a forthcoming volume in the SSRC series cited in note 9, Myron Weiner and I attempt to delineate both the dependent and independent character of political party systems in political development. See J. LaPalombara and Myron Weiner, eds., *Political Party and Political Development*, (Princeton: Princeton Univ. Press, 1966) introductory and concluding chapters.

ior. Traditional precedents have enormous power in regulating patterns of social interaction, and so on. Our knowledge of political evolution in the West seems to confirm these impressions; particularly as we reflect on such social or political systems as nomadic tribes, villages, feudal organizations, monarchies, and the like. We know, too, that political specialization—the development of differentiated and functionally specific political institutions and roles— spanned centuries and that standards of achievement and universalism in the operation of political systems are (with some striking exceptions) relatively recent and still imperfect accomplishments in the West.

Similarly, we can find a wide array of modern political systems that display many of the Weberian and Parsonian criteria previously listed. On most such criteria, these "modern" polities seemingly stand in stark contrast to the "traditional" or less developed matrices from which they emerged. The complex variety of political institutions and roles, the rules making for equality in everything from elections and judicial bodies to civil services and public education, the great stress on rationality in organization and behavior—all of these are characteristics that one can point to in a wide variety of contemporary societies to confirm the utility of the typology.

Finally, the rapid rate of transformation that characterizes the present century provides empirical examples of the "transitional systems." In the so-called developing areas, one can certainly find examples of charismatic leaders, even if this term is now used much more loosely than I suspect Weber intended. A Gandhi or a Nehru in India, a Nkrumah in Ghana, a Sukarno in Indonesia, an Ataturk in Turkey will confirm that charismatic leaders tend to emerge in times of rapid transition. A Diem in Vietnam or a Ben Bella in Algeria will suggest exactly how fragile an authority system based on charisma may be. Reports from these societies also tell us in considerable detail what wide and often perplexing juxtapositions of traditional and modern institutions and behavior these systems reveal.

The Typology Seems to Conform to Economic Development. A second reason for the attractiveness of the typology is that it fortifies notions that economic and political development go hand in hand. Traditional systems are (with a few important exceptions) strikingly backward economically; modern political systems (again with some striking exceptions) seem to be those that are highly urbanized and industrialized and which have reached a stage of self-sustaining economic growth. Indeed, the side of the Parsonian dichotomies that is associated with political modernity seems to be required by modern economic organization and, presumably, either spills over to the political sphere or indeed necessitates that the political system take on such characteristics as a precondition for economic growth.

The Typology Suggests a Broad Pattern of Similar Political Development. The attractiveness of the typology on this ground is self-evident. It appeals both to those who are drawn to the idea of unilinear growth toward a fixed-end state and to those who are searching for consistent dimensions along which development can be gauged.

The Typology is a Useful Checklist. Finally, the typology is attractive to social scientists, and particularly to political scientists, because it provides an apparently useful list of factors or dimensions that one will want to explore, both in assessing where along the path to modernity a given political system may be and in identifying what aspects of the system are in greatest need of change in order to hurry development along.

The use of such a typology of political development is open to a number of objections, some of which I have noted above as well as others that might be added. The most serious of these, in my view, is that all empirical systems are in fact mixed, dual, or "amalgamate" systems. Although Weber himself was aware that his ideal-type did not correspond to empirical reality, one notes with distressing frequency work which is based either on the assumption that such correspondence exists or which includes suggestions or formulae designed to bring the modern system into existence. It is true that ideal-typical formulations are to be judged not by reality tests but, rather, by their utility in helping us better to understand systemic qualities, their interrelationships, and their susceptibility to transformation. I would nevertheless suggest that if, in fact, all political systems are mixed as to the kinds of dimensions we have discussed here, ideal-typical descriptions or typologies based on patterns of this mixture would probably better serve the political scientist who is interested in development.

In most of the literature on political development an important tendency can be discerned, namely, that structure-functionalism seems to be preferred over ideal-type constructions. A search for combinations of structures and behavior that one can use in typological construction, and in demonstrating the interpendence of social, economic, psychological, and political variables, has gained ascendency. In this sense, the broad functional approach has helped us to overcome the limitations of analyses using ideal-types which were often too far removed from empirical conditions to be useful, too lacking in dynamic quality to suggest why particular patterns of political or administrative organization occured in the first place and how such patterns might be changed.[28]

Models involving structural-functional analysis have also been widely and severely criticized. Some of the attacks rest on arguments that such models fall prey to some of the same difficulties which befall analyses using ideal-types. Beyond this, critics claim that the basis for choosing a particular list of functional requisites (rather than some other list) is never justified in theory or logic, the nature of the alleged interrelationship and interdependence among functional categories is never convincingly specified, and there is nothing in the scheme that identifies what would be the dynamics of change or development in political systems.[29]

Public Administration and Development

The Literature

Much of the conceptual and theoretical evolution I have described above can also be found in the field of comparative public administration.[30] The ideal-type authority systems of Max Weber

---

[28]Karl Deutsch, in defense of functionalism, stresses that, as applied to social science rather than the biological or medical fields, functionalism has "remained open to the much greater richness of combinatorial possibilities inherent in social systems . . . . In some ways, this structural functional approach permits greater freedom than do the 'ideal types' of Max Weber. [It] obviously allows for *functional equivalence*: the same social function may be fulfilled by different combinations of different structural units." Deutsch, *The Nerves of Government, op. cit.*, pp. 48-49.

[29]One of the most often cited criticisms of structure-functional analysis is Carl G. Hempel, "The Logic of Functional Analysis," in Llewellyn Gross, ed., *Symposium on Sociological Theory* (New York: Harper, 1959), pp. 271-307. A recent attempt to appraise the utility and limitations of the functional approach is a symposium edited by the sociologist Martindale. See D. Martindale, ed., "Functionalism in the Social Sciences," Monograph 5, *Annals of the American Academy of Social and Political Science* (Philadelphia, February, 1965). Almond has sought to provide his response to some of the criticisms in his recent article, "A Developmental Approach to Political Systems," *op. cit.*

[30]See Fred Riggs, *Administration in Developing Countries: The Theory of Prismatic Society* (Boston: Houghton Mifflin, 1964), p. 95. The prolific scholarly output of Riggs is strongly influenced by the writings of Talcott Parsons, whose basic scheme of societal organization readily lends itself to formulations of stringent developmental interdependence. See Talcott Parsons, Robert F. Bales, and Edward A. Shils, *Working Papers in the Theory of Action* (Glencoe, Ill.: The Free Press, 1953); Talcott Parsons, *The Social System* (Glencoe, Ill.: The Free Press, 1951). For an interesting application of the Parsons scheme to the role of bureaucracy in economic development, see Bert F. Hoselitz, "Levels of Economic Performance and Bureaucratic Structures," in LaPalombara, *Bureaucracy and Political Development, op. cit.*, pp. 168-98.

have their counterparts in administrative sectors. These are carefully spelled out by Alfred Diamant in what is one of the best short
discussions of Weber's administrative theory available to us in
English.[31] Thus, in a traditional authority system, we would find
administrators recruited to their roles because of personal, traditional, or kinship ties to the ruler. Such administrative systems are
extremely diffuse in the sense that spheres of authority and responsibility are not clearly laid out; canons of rational administrative
organization of training for specialized administrative office, or of
appointment on the basis of skill are usually lacking. In such
systems we find that certain administrative positions are sold or
owned and therefore inheritable.

In a charismatic situation, of course, administrators are appointed
by the leader and follow and obey him because of his perceived
superhuman qualities. As I noted previously, in its extreme form
everything in such a system turns on the overriding sense of
identification with and loyalty to a single person. This person — the
leader — can demand enormous sacrifices; the idea of working for a
salary and seeking mobility in a rational administration hierarchy is
simply alien to such a situation. Loyalty to the leader is the overriding criterion of selection to and retention in administrative posts;
criteria of competence and the careful delineation of spheres of
authority and responsibility have little if any importance.

It is in a legal-rational authority system that one expects to find
that particular pattern of administrative organization and behavior
that Weber defined as a *bureaucracy*. A bureaucratic system mani-
fests characteristics of hierarchy, authority, obedience, rationality,
and specialized administrative roles. Bureaucrats do not own their
positions and cannot sell or pass them on by inheritance. They are
not "tax-farmers," or any other kind of official who takes a percentage of what he extracts, but are salaried. They are not recruited or
promoted for reasons of family or friendship, but, rather, on the
basis of universal criteria, such as competitive examinations. They
are professionals who view their work as a career and who are in a
relationship of command and obedience to others because of laws
and other written regulations.

Just as there are specifically intended administrative counterparts for Weber's ideal-type authority systems, some writers at-

---

[31]For a very useful schematic portrayal of administrative characteristics under each
of Weber's ideal-type authority systems, see Diamant, *op. cit.*, pp. 88-90. For
Weber's own discussion of the characteristics of bureaucratic organization, see his
The Theory of Social and Economic Organization, op. cit., pp. 329-40.

tempt to construct ideal-type administrative systems from the pattern variables of Talcott Parsons. The most ambitious effort of this kind is represented by Fred Riggs's "Agraria and Industria." In this article, Riggs attempts to describe the important administrative patterns that one would find in an "Agrarian" and in an "Industrian" society. In the former, as he depicts it, administration would be remote from the people, little able to assure the geographic integrity of the social system. Governmental and administrative functions would be limited to law and order, defense and transportation. A high degree of diffuseness, particularism, ascription, and arbitrariness would govern administrative recruitment and decision-making. Agraria would be closely tied to what I have called above the primitive side of the pattern variable dichotomies.

In Industria, on the other hand, public administration would be influenced by the other choices in the Parsonian dichotomies. There would exist considerable differentiation of roles; achievement and universalistic standards applied to administrative recruitment and decisions; hierarchial, rational, and differentiated administrative structures; and considerable intervention of the public sector in the affairs of society. In short, this early typology by Riggs tends to identify the administrative systems of premodern societies with the traditional ideal-type of Max Weber and certain of the patterns described by Parsons. For the modern systems, the criteria of legal-rational bureaucracies and the differentiation-achievement-universalistic-disciplined side of the pattern variables are the defining characteristics.[32]

As in the case of political development, then, those who are particularly interested in bureaucratic development as an integral part of the broader process have sought to construct models or typologies that are closer approximations of the mixes or dualities existing in the real world. The Comparative Administration Group of the American Society for Public Administration, chaired by Riggs, is prominent in the field.[33] Following the publication of his

---

[32]Fred Riggs, "Agraria and Industria: Toward a Typology of Comparative Administration," in W. J. Siffin, ed., *Toward the Comparative Study of Public Administration* (Bloomington: Indiana Univ. Press, 1957), pp. 23-116. My summary is very brief and perhaps does not do justice to an article that contains much wisdom about such matters or the impact of social organization and values on administrative behavior. It should also be noted that, taking his lead from Wittfogel, Riggs attempts to differentiate the administrative patterns of "hydraulic" as opposed to "rainfall" systems. See Wittfogel, *Oriental Despotism, op. cit.*

[33]The Comparative Administration Group is primarily responsible for heightened scholarly activity in this field. It has organized special seminars and conferences dealing with both the empirical and theoretical problems of administrative development and change. Of great interest to the reader would be the "Occasional Papers,"

"Agraria and Industria," Riggs displays some uneasiness with the creation of ideal-type administrative systems based on the dichotomous pattern variables of Parsons. His response to this problem is primarily that of spelling out in considerable detail the character of administrative organization and behavior one finds in mixed—or what he denominates "prismatic"—societies.[34] "Prismatic" is a concept designed to identify behavior that falls somewhere between polar extremes which are identified as "fused" (read "functionally diffuse" in the Parsonian sense) as opposed to "diffracted" (read "functionally specific," or specialized, or differentiated). Fused and diffracted social systems—and therefore the structures and behavior that go with them—are meant to be ideal-type constructs that have no pure equivalents in reality. Riggs specifies the characteristics of each polar type and then proceeds to indicate that since most systems are prismatic (i.e., mixed), major attention must be paid to the manner in which fused and diffracted characteristics are juxtaposed and combined in prismatic societies. Riggs does not intend, however, to equate prismatic with transitional societies, noting that the latter term implies movement while a prismatic society may either remain essentially unchanged or move toward or away from development.[35] He professes to view administrative systems in an input-output context involving a dynamic relationship between input of "goals, resources, and demands," on the one hand and output of "related goods, services and regulative acts," on the other. How such a machine actually operates, he argues, will be

---

circulated by the CAG in mimeographed form. Because they constitute working drafts, these papers cannot be made the objects of quotation in the present essay. Nevertheless, the reader would be well rewarded to solicit from CAG copies of important occasional papers by Fred Riggs (e.g., "The Ecology of Development," "Administrative Development"); Jesse Unger (e.g., "The Military Role in Nation Building and Economic Development"); Nicolaas Luykx (e.g., "The Role of Rural Government in Agricultural Development"); S. N. Eisenstadt (e.g., "Continuity of Modernization and Development of Administration,"); and Alfred Diamant (e.g., "Political Development: Approaches to Theory and Strategy," and "Bureaucracy in Developmental Movement Regimes: A Bureaucratic Model for Developing Societies"). The last mentioned paper by Diamant is a splendid piece—in my view the best demonstration of the possibility of relating ideal-type constructs to several dynamic factors of political and bureaucratic development.

[34]Riggs's work has appeared in a number of learned journals over the years. However, most of the articles pertaining to his theoretical concerns are included (in somewhat modified form) in his *Administration in Developing Countries: The Theory of Prismatic Society, op. cit.* The term prismatic derives from optics. Riggs evidently has a compulsion to introduce unusual and novel terminology in the field, some of which is felicitous, but much of which is unnecessarily confusing. Nevertheless, much of what he has to say is worth the burden of having to endure the jargon.

[35]*Ibid.*, Chs. 1, 13.

in great measure determined by the prismatic mix of diffuse and diffracted structures.

A number of other writers argue quite persuasively that the Weberian legal-rational ideal-type is far from adequate in helping us understand patterns of public administration in the developing countries or in leading us to workable insights regarding what sorts of administrative changes might be required to assist in the achievement of developmental aims. Robert Presthus, in an interesting analysis of Turkish administrative organization, warns that what I have elsewhere called the democratic *norms* grafted onto Weber's concept of the bureaucracy may simply not be workable or needed in the Middle Eastern context.[36] His analysis clearly suggests several of the limitations inherent in the fact that Weber's conceptions of the bureaucracy not only emerged in the West but also reflected demands on public administration that are very different from the kinds of problems that developing-area bureaucracies must confront today. In such a situation, therefore, what Presthus denominates a "welfare bureaucracy," with characteristic patterns of its own, may be required and may constitute a much more useful model of developing bureaucratic systems.[37]

Other scholars have also concluded that the Weberian model of rational bureaucracy may often be inappropriate for developing societies. Inoki notes that development in Japan was aided—indeed required—by a bureaucracy involving both premodern and legal-rational patterns of public administration.[38] In similar fashion, Carl Beck, in a study of development in Eastern Europe, cautions against the notion that political or bureaucratic structures grow automatically out of other social and economic transformations or that economic and social change everywhere leads to the kind of rationality in administrative organizations and decisions that is identified with the theories of Weber.[39]

Perhaps the most extensive empirical example of the difficulties involved in attempting to use a Weberian concept or model of the bureaucracy to understand non-Western administrative systems is found in Berger's study of the Egyptian bureaucracy.[40] What he finds is that, despite formal administrative organization that might

---

[36]See LaPalombara, *Bureaucracy and Political Development, op. cit.*, pp. 50-55.
[37]Robert V. Presthus, "Weberism Versus Welfare Bureaucracy in Traditional Society," *Administrative Science Quarterly*, VI (June, 1961), 1-24.
[38]See Masamichi Inoki, "The Civil Bureaucracy: Japan," in Ward and Rustow, *op. cit.*, pp. 294 ff.
[39]Beck, *op. cit.*, p. 298.
[40]Berger, *Bureaucracy and Society in Modern Egypt, op. cit.*

suggest a close approximation to a modern or legal-rational bureau-cratic system, much of what one actually sees in Egyptian admin-istration remains premodern and traditional. Berger's field work would tend to show that not much has occurred to modify this situation and that, indeed, the patterns of Egyptian administration are so deeply rooted as to have succeeded in overcoming often quite earnest attempts by previous British colonial adminstrators to bring about change or reform.

Alfred Diamant makes a valiant effort to defend and "resurrect" Weber from the telling criticisms of scholars like Presthus, Beck and Berger. Weber, he notes, was not so naive as to believe that his ideal-typical constructs had unqualified correspondence in the empirical world. A complete reading of Weber, he tells us, would show that he anticipated mixed situations and that, therefore, a frequent shortcoming in research is to neglect asking probing questions about the nature of the authority system in any society about which one seeks to explicate public administration. Since authority systems may very well contain patterns of legitimacy that reflect traditional, charismatic, and legal-rational considerations, it is obvious that failure to execute this first step in analysis may lead to the kinds of "surprises" that Berger writes about, as well as to entirely premature and unjustified rejections of the utility of Weber.[41]

Evaluation

I have suggested that Riggs is the major American scholar who has tried to apply the concepts and theories of Weber and Parsons to public administration. While his work is too vast and important to be fully critiqued here, the following observations may serve to highlight the range of concerns that typify it and the problems it raises.

1. In a theoretical sense, Riggs has not freed himself from the serious limitations implicit in the use of ideal-types or the pattern variables. Although he recognizes that his diffuse and diffracted systems are as empirically unreal as the polar types of Max Weber,

---

[41]These points are scattered throughout Diamant's article, *op. cit.* However, they are summarized on pp. 82-86. My central reservation about this piece is that Diamant feels compelled to read into Max Weber a degree of insight into empirical variations or "mixed systems" that is exaggerated. It seems to me that it is Diamant, not Weber, who is expounding an entirely sophisticated understanding about the complexities inherent in comparative analysis of bureaucratic organization and development in the contemporary world.

in much of his writing the prismatic patterns are analyzed as if the polar types were empirically possible and, indeed, as if movement occurs toward one or the other of the poles. Thus, in his discussion of the prismatic model, he indicates that "the viewpoint adopted in this book is that a significant tendency exists for action in traditional societies to be predominantly ascriptive, particularistic and diffuse; whereas choices in modern societies are more likely to be achievement-oriented, universalistic and specific." Although Riggs insists that the central tendencies are "hypothetical" rather than a matter of "definition," it is difficult to see how this escape hatch can be held ajar given his own admission that the ideal-types do not correspond to any empirical system (and therefore the inference that all empirical systems are necessarily prismatic).[42] What we have here is Parsonian nectar in Riggsian bottles; its appeal to one's intellectual palate remains as problematical as before.

2. We are greatly in Riggs's debt, however, for the many striking descriptions he provides of the process and patterns of public administration in prismatic (really transitional, developing) societies. His broad approach to this problem rests on his insistence that we must know more about the "ecology" of administration before we can either reach a full understanding of administrative patterns or provide realistic prescriptions about effecting administrative change. Thus, while he continues to cast such descriptions within a framework he calls models, what he has to say alerts us to the great variety of administrative arrangements that one is likely to find in prismatic or mixed societies. His attempts to test some of his concepts against the empirical experiences of several Southeast Asian countries provide us with an opportunity to probe his meaning of such notions as "formalism" and "heterogeniety" in societies undergoing change.[43]

3. As Riggs notes, the ecological approach to public administration is designed to show how such factors of the broader environment as politics, economic conditions and patterns, religion, and social organization and mobility relate to the kind of public administrative organization that emerges in a given society. Many of us feel that this emphasis on ecological or environmental factors can, if overdone, take politics out of political science — that is, it tends to make the kind of political (and therefore public-administrative)

---

[42]Riggs, *Administration in Developing Countries: The Theory of Prismatic Society, op. cit.*, pp. 22 ff.
[43]The full flavor and impact of his contribution here can be gleaned from a complete and careful reading of the above volume. However, his concern with "administration ecology" is treated primarily in *ibid.*, Part Two, pp. 99-237.

configuration one finds in a society a largely or wholly dependent factor without any discreet or independent development capability or potential of its own. There are those who argue that efforts to cast administration within a conceptual framework as comprehensive as that of Parsons leads to exactly this pitfall. Riggs, however, does not think so. He notes that, in underlining the need for looking to environmental factors, one must do more than enumerate them and must also try to show exactly how these factors impinge on an administrative organization and behavior. He then says:

> But an ecological approach is not deterministic. It does not suggest that environmental conditions shape administrative behavior to such an extent that no choice is possible, that whatever appears is inevitable, hence unchangeable. Rather, ecological forces set boundaries, they give the ranges within which choice is possible. What is really frustrating to the program — and policy — oriented man is the attempt to do the impossible. The operator is most successful when fully aware of the constraints within which he must work. . . . Valid administrative ecology will demonstrate what is possible within the framework of reality, what the probable consequences of various possible courses of action are. Thus it will reveal unsuspected dimensions of choice, of autonomy, by illuminating new alternatives that have not hitherto been considered.[44]

Where, then, does all of this intellectual concern with political and administrative development leave us? What we seem to have are a number of formulations that do in some measure rest on assumptions about the nature — at least the central tendencies — of traditional, transitional and modern societies. These characteristics are assumed to set the broad parameters, the limits, within which administrative change or development can occur. How narrow or broad the range of development choice may be will presumably vary with the nature of environmental or ecological factors, although it is not clear from most of the writing on the subject exactly how deterministic such notions of administrative change may be. It is clear, however, that relatively little attention has been accorded political and administrative development or change as independent phenomena that can to some extent function apart from other sectors of society. Indeed, the very concepts of transitional, prismatic, or mixed systems (where traditional and modern organizations and behaviors exist side by side) should imply that such independent development is possible. To "explain" such mixtures by returning to the economic, social, or environmental conditions that make them possible is to be tautological and to display exactly the kind of determinism about political development that is one of the less felicitous outcomes of recent interdisciplinary research.

An Alternative Approach: The Challenge of Crisis and Capacity

The functional approach to development has led to much greater emphasis on the "output" or "capability" side of political system organization and behavior. That is, we are now led to ask not merely what factors seem to influence the kind of political organization that emerges in society, but also what the political system *does* — and how what it does influences its own transformation as well as changes in the broader society. The political system, then, is no longer viewed largely as a dependent phenomenon, but, rather, as something whose current configuration, as well as its potential for transformation, is at least in part independent of social, economic, and psychological factors in society.

It seems clear that a number of Western scholars have been moving independently in the direction of this kind of formulation. However, since many of these scholars have been in one way or another associated with the work of the Committee on Comparative Politics of the Social Science Research Council, I shall summarize their various contributions within the context of that Committee's work.[45]

An early conference on the role of public administration in the political development process spotlighted the enormous difference in developmental potential that the structure of public administration could make.[46] Papers prepared for this conference emphasized such generalizations as: (1) Weberian notions of bureaucratic characteristics associated with legal-rational authority systems are not essential to economic modernity; (2) a lack of balance in the evolution of political structures may actually impede democratic political development; (3) economic development may require certain kinds

---

[44]*Ibid.*, pp. 428-29.

[45]As I noted previously, the Comparative Administrative Groups has played an equally salient role in the field of comparative bureaucracy. Moreover, scholars like Riggs, Braibanti, Eisenstadt, Dorsey, Beck, LaPalombara, and others have had relationships to both groups.

[46]See LaPalombara, ed., *Bureaucracy and Political Development, op. cit.* Many of the central generalizations and hypotheses proposed by various authors are summarized in my introduction to this volume, pp. 3-33.

of *political* capacity before it can proceed; (4) the nature of the higher reaches of the public administrative hierarchy will deeply influence what kind of polity emerges; and (5) the ability of the bureaucracy to manage variations in demands placed on the political system is a vital dimension for measuring political development.[47]

S. N. Eisenstadt, the author of the last observation, has been a major figure in pointing our direction to the capability aspect of political system performance. Eisenstadt views political systems as being under constant demands from the society at large. The measure of a system's flexibility over time is its ability to respond to these demands in terms of new policies and organizations. Although Eisenstadt, too, seems to fall into the trap of assuming that a developed political system is one which grants political power to ever-widening segments of society, his writing has been of primary importance in alerting us both to the utility of gauging political development in terms of governmental output and of noting, therefore, how the political sector itself can be a critical factor in effecting change.[48]

In a volume on political development in Turkey and Japan, Ward and Rustow define a modern polity as one characterized by (1) differentiated and functionally specific governmental or political units, (2) high integration among governmental structures, (3) rational and secular procedures in political decision-making, (4) high volume, great scope or magnitude, and considerable effectiveness of political decisions, (5) wide positive identification with the history, territory, and identity of the state, (6) widespread political participation, (7) allocation of political roles on the basis of achievement rather than ascriptive standards, and (8) rule of a secular impersonal system of law and courts.[49] In the concluding chapter, of this work much attention is paid to the capacity of these systems to cope over time with a series of salient historical problems or "crises."

---

[47]Beck, "Bureaucracy and Political Development in Eastern Europe," in *ibid.*, pp. 268-300; Riggs, "Bureaucrats and Political Development: A Paradoxical View," *ibid.*, pp. 120-67; Spengler, "Bureaucracy and Economic Development," pp. 199-232; Fritz Morstein Marx, "The Higher Civil Service as an Action Group in Western Political Development," *ibid.*, pp. 62-95; Braibanti, "Public Bureaucracy and Judiciary in Pakistan," *ibid.*, pp. 360-440; Eisenstadt, "Bureaucracy and Political Development," *ibid.*, pp. 96-119.

[48]*Ibid.* For a striking application of his own formula to the bureaucratic systems of over twenty historical empires, see Eisenstadt, *The Political Systems of Empires, op. cit.* See, especially, Ch. 2, as well as the references to his own work listed by Eisenstadt in his chapter in LaPalombara, *op. cit.*

[49]Ward and Rustow, *op. cit.*, p. 7.

Ward and Rustow, following Eisenstadt, make the important point that, in viewing political development over time, it is necessary to identify and to distinguish two kinds of problems that the system must face, namely, "(1) those which are set or predetermined in such a manner as to be wholly or largely beyond the controls of the leaders of the modernizing societies and (2) those which are amenable to some significant degree of influence or control by these leaders."[50] They suggest that such things as geographical problems, the timing or sequencing of stimuli or demands, and the nature of a system's traditional heritage fall into the first category and constitute the "givens" of problems of political development. In the second category, however, fall the problems or crises mentioned above. For Ward and Rustow these include the following: (1) the extent to which traditional patterns can be exploited for modernizing goals, (2) the crises of identity, (3) the crisis of security, (4) the problems of leadership and followership, (5) the crisis of economic development, (6) the crises of integration, penetration, and participation, and (7) the crisis of distribution.[51]

Thus, in this formulation of development, the emphasis on output performance is central. In similar fashion, others have articulated the problem of governmental capability. Almond, for example, speaks more recently of development as involving the ability of a political system to deal with four sets of problems that he defines as integrative capability, international accommodative capability, participation capability, and distributive capability.[52] Others have evolved a somewhat more comprehensive formulation of development which rests on a "syndrome" of the historical impulses toward differentiation, equality, and capacity. The functional performance of any political system is to be judged in terms of how it manages to react to the kinds of "loads" (or demands, or challenges) it experiences as historical crises, such as those already described, are encountered.[53]

What we seem to have, then, are characterizations of political

---

[50]*Ibid.*, p. 465.

[51]*Ibid.*, p. 466.

[52]Almond, "Political Systems and Political Change," *op. cit.* See his refinement of this analytical scheme in his "A Developmental Approach to Political Systems," *op. cit.*

[53]An initial statement of this approach is sketched by Coleman, ed., *op. cit.*, pp. 13-18. An illustration of the importance of crises "loads" on the emergence and subsequent impact of party systems on development is contained in LaPalombara and Weiner, *op. cit.* A full treatment of this formulation will be found in Leonard Binder, James Coleman, Joseph LaPalombara, Myron Weiner and Lucian Pye, *Crises of Political Development* (forthcoming).

systems which continue to draw in some measure on the kinds of structural and behavioral descriptions that relate to Weber's ideal-types and Parsons' pattern variables. To put this differently, there is still much attention paid to the need for identifying what might be called the dominant patterns or the central organizational tendencies that one can associate with traditional, transitional, and modern social and political systems. Beyond this, however, there is the further conviction that the functional performance of a political system is of vital importance to a fuller understanding of development and that, in looking at this performance, one will want to pay particular attention to the varying ability of political systems to handle demands or crises.

Thus, some of us have found it convenient to view political (and bureaucratic) evolution within a context of challenge-and-response, or as a process over time whereby political systems respond to changes in the kinds of demands they encounter. Evolution or change is not considered "natural" or "inevitable." A given configuration (equilibrium, in one restricted sense) may exist over a long period of time. Moreover, while development may well include an increased capacity to adapt to increases in demand, no particular pattern of adaptation is yet considered optimal. To put this succinctly, no assumption is made that *a* specific way, say that of the United States, of responding to challenge represents the optimal way. Finally, I should stress that development, as I am using it here, is not to be equated with *increased* capacity. Indeed, a system's capacity to handle demand may actually diminish, and it is assumed that out of such failures will emerge other sets or types of developmental consequences for the system. I recognize that the notion of retrograde steps or political "backsliding" makes the use of a term like "development" infelicitous and that it would be better to follow the sociologists who prefer the term "change."[54] However, I am using these terms interchangeably, stressing that, in speaking of capacity, I intend to suggest that for any political system there may be more or less of this quality demonstrated over time and that we really do not yet know what combination of capacity is essential for certain kinds of development or change in society.

---

[54]In *Bureaucracy and Political Development, op. cit.*, p. 35, I noted that so much confusion surrounds a term like "development" that we should suspend its use. One reviewer of that work indulged himself in the gross misinterpretation that I simply want to terminate research and discussion about political development. I would still opt for a moratorium on the term's use, but bow to a developmental trend which is clearly and overwhelmingly in the direction of greater usage — and, I fear, greater confusion.

In thinking about political evolution, then, we are interested in challenge and the political system's response to it. In a much wider sense, of course, a whole society responds, but we are interested primarily in that sector of society that exercises physical compulsion or that handles what Easton calls the "authoritative allocation of values." Inference from history suggests that there are particularly salient demands that directly challenge the capacity of political systems. These challenges — or crises — can occur for most kinds of polities (e.g., empires, villages, tribes, nations), but we shall discuss them as they have emerged in and affected the nation-state.

For purposes of pinpointing the matter of the capacity of a political system, it is useful to think about six salient historical crises, namely, those of legitimacy, integration, identity, penetration, participation, and distribution.[55] We may define these briefly as follows:

Legitimacy. This concept refers to the basis upon which the exercise of political authority is established. A legitimate political system is one whose decisions are generally and widely accepted as just and proper by those who are ruled. As we noted earlier, legitimacy can be based on such things as tradition, charisma, or a set of legal-rational rules. A system that must rely heavily on physical force to extract obedience has less legitimacy than one that does not. Maximum legitimacy would exist where there was complete consensus regarding the "right" of those who govern to do so.

Integration. There are two important dimensions to this concept. One involves geography and refers to the ability of the political system to maintain the physical integrity of the nation-state. A nation whose borders are ill-defined or which are subject to incursion from outside or to secession from within is badly integrated in this sense. Integration also involves a process dimension and raises the question of whether the internal procedures that characterize politics are well understood and conducive to harmonious and stable interactions between subjects and rulers, among subjects, and among the various kinds of political-administrative subdivisions that the nation-state may include.

Identity. This crisis pertains to the individual subject and whether he has a clear conception of the nation-state and of his own

---

[55]One student with considerable direct experience with technical assistance programs urges that we focus on the relationship between prominent ends and necessary administrative means rather than engage in abstract theorizing and model-building about administration and development. He then offers an interesting typology of administrative systems that corresponds to the central goals and values of the societies. Edward W. Weidner, "Development Administration: A New Focus for Research," in Heady and Stokes, *op. cit.*, pp. 97-115.

place in it. It also refers to a somewhat reified notion of the "total nation" which has a sense of its own identity and role within the context of the broader world environment. Clearly, the interdependency of integration, legitimacy, and identity is very strong.

Penetration. This crisis refers to the ability of the central government to make its presence and authority felt in all of the outlying reaches of the nation. One form of penetration is military and is closely associated with the crisis of national geographic integration. It raises questions about centralization and decentralization and about the extractive capacities of the central governmental apparatus.

Participation. This crisis occurs whenever segments of the population not previously involved in some aspect of political decision-making demand such involvement. Its most common manifestation in recent decades is seen in campaigns for extended suffrage, but it is not limited to that. For example, the demand for legislative representation at the center by colonial areas is also a participation crisis. The same is true of demands for statehood emanating from previous territories of the United States.

Distribution. This crisis involves demands for major changes in the way in which goods and services are allocated in society as well as for the creation of new goods and services. Although it generally centers on obviously economic considerations, it also involves such things as education, public health, and the like.

All political systems will at some time confront all of these crises, and each of them will severely test the system's managerial and creative capacities. Although it is obvious that many factors we have called environmental will have important bearing on both the occurrence of these crises and the political system's response to them, it would appear that the most important questions to raise concerning crises are: (1) the sequence in which they occur, (2) how many crises occur over what period of time, (3) how long particular crises remain essentially unresolved, and (4) the relationship between these crises and the goals, values and resources of the society involved.

Contrasts between the histories of Western and non-Western nations provide examples that illustrate the central importance of the just-mentioned considerations. In Great Britain, the nation successfully dealt with the problems of legitimacy, identity, integration, and penetration (pretty much in that order) before the more recent crises of participation and distribution became major challenges to the polity. In sharp contrast, in Italy and Germany there occurred a piling up of crises at the time of national unification in the nineteenth century, and some crises (e.g., penetration) occurred out of sequence, so to speak, so that one could think of centralized and geographically integrated nation-states long before these nations had begun to cope with crises of identity, legitimacy, and process integration. The French and Russian revolutions reveal, for example, that neither prerevolutionary system was able to deal adequately with the ideologically based crises of participation and distribution that preceded these upheavals.[56] Continuing instabilities in French politics suggest that the Russian revolutionaries have been much more successful than the French in the management of salient crises. That the Russians have had recourse to devices that are ideologically unacceptable to many of us in the West should not obscure what I would call superior Russian capacity.

It is obvious that the study of Western history will not reveal *the* formula associated with a particular kind of crisis management and ensuing development. If the West could provide suggestive answers, the incredible clustering of crises and the overwhelming "load" on the political systems confronting most of the states of Asia and Africa would seriously hinder the applicability of Western solutions to local problems. Most of the countries in Latin America have resolved the crises of geographic integration and national identity during more than a century of independence. Yet they are still plagued by very heavy crises loads. The difficulties of legitimacy and penetration were never adequately managed; to these lingering crises have now been added those of participation and distribution.

The dilemma facing the political systems in transition is that the multiplicity of demands they confront requires unprecedented intervention by government and bureaucracy. Today's transitional societies must telescope into years the crisis management which was accomplished over generations in older nations. Not only must frontiers be protected, soldiers recruited, taxes collected, and internal law maintained, but simultaneously the kind of administrative machinery that will facilitate or manage economic or industrial growth, revolutionize agricultural productivity, and increase the availability of such welfare values as education, sanitation, health, and recreation must be provided. Picture the United States at the

---

[56]The Soviet decision to rely for bureaucratic management on both foreign administrators and technicians identified with the Tsarist system is well known. Not as widely understood, however, is the long history of Russian failures to effect administrative reforms, or the difficult and essentially long-range steps taken by Soviet leaders to fill the administrative gap. See Merle Fainsod, "Bureaucracy and Modernization: The Russian and Soviet Case," in Joseph LaPalombara, ed., *Bureaucracy and Political Development* (Princeton: Princeton Univ. Press, 1963), pp. 233-67.

time of the election of 1800, which raised grave issues of legitimacy and identity, also having to face such problems as Southern secession, the drive for universal suffrage and mass education, the rise of the trade union movement, the problems of rapid industrialization and urbanization, and the contemporary demands for the extension of civil rights and more and more "welfare capitalism" administered by government. Add to this picture widespread illiteracy, a scarcity of administrative and political leadership, extremely limited physical resources, and a population growth rate of explosive proportions. Finally, visualize this nation living in a world which included a number of much more materially affluent nations and in which communications technology made the material gap a matter of widespread knowledge. Only when we conceive of such a situation can we come close to understanding the nature of the problems that challenge the political leadership of many of the developing nations today.

In attempting to assess, then, what kind of administrative organization and behavior a country must have, we must know something about the tasks at hand and the priorities which the system assigns to various goals. Is the overriding commitment to be that of coping with the distribution crisis? If so, the political system will have to produce experts in economic planning, agricultural production, industrial management, and the like. Some sort of institutionalized administrative substitute for the entrepreneur will be essential. Bureaucrats and administrative procedures designed to assure the implementation of economic developmental plans will have to appear. Or must the energies of the political system be directed primarily toward integration? For many countries in Africa the crisis of geographic integration overshadows all others. Bureaucratic means of holding the real estate together must be devised. Or is the central crisis perceived as that of participation? And so on.

It is only after one has understood the relative priority assigned to the goals of the system that discussions about what kinds of administrators and administrative organization are best attuned to reaching them in a given situation make much sense. It will not do to say that all goals or crises are of equal importance, for this is rarely true in practice and, in any case, would certainly lead to contradictory strategies, perhaps even chaos, if a political system reacted on that basis. And it will not suffice to look at one of the developed countries for a pat administrative formula because, as we have noted, rarely will such a country's history represent the kind of clustering of crises that is true of the transitional societies of today; rarely will the role of the polity in the solution of such crises be as prominent as is likely in countries ideologically committed to vast public-sector intervention. Nor will it be sufficient to search out the ways and means of breaking down traditional cultural characteristics, both because tradition has remarkable staying power and because tradition may actually be an aid rather than a bar to certain kinds of development.

The developing countries present a wide variety of crises configurations and of administrative resources that might be made to deal with them. The Indian civil service, often called the very best in the world, proved effective in managing the crises of integration, participation, and penetration. But these law-and-order bureaucratic generalists are not well-attuned to resolving the crisis of distribution, particularly where it is assumed that the bureaucrats will fill planning, entrepreneurial and innovative roles.[57] How to balance the instrumental policy of economic development with the goal of encouraging democratic development is crucial since the very patterns of administrative organization that are positively attuned to rapid economic growth may very well be detrimental, perhaps fatal, to democratic development. Obviously, the latter outcome does not automatically flow from economic affluence but must also be made the object of careful political and bureaucratic planning.[58] Many Asian and African countries reveal systems of public administration unable to cope with many of the crises we have mentioned. In others, centrifugal drives may take the form of repressive, one-party arrangements.

Nor is effective response of administrators assured by the existence of a highly trained law-and-order bureaucracy. Many Western countries clearly demonstrate that, as government becomes increasingly involved in social and economic spheres that are alien to a law-and-order tradition, new kinds of administrators and administrative structures must be created. The public corporation, central planning agencies, new development agencies, as well as the complex range of administrative structures produced by the Soviet Union reflect in part our understanding that formal administrative organization that hews closely to established norms of rationality

---

[57]Ralph Braibanti has written extensively about the value to a developing country of a well-trained, intellectually alert, and law-and-order-oriented bureaucracy. See his "Reflections on Bureaucratic Reform in India," *op. cit.*, and his "The Relevance of Political Science to the Study of Underdeveloped Areas," in Ralph Braibanti and Joseph J. Spangler, eds., *Tradition, Values and Socio-Economic Development* (Durham: Duke Univ. Press, 1961), pp. 139-211.

[58]See my comments on this problem in LaPalombara, *Bureaucracy and Political Development, op. cit.*, pp. 48-61. Cf. the important chapter by Riggs, "Bureaucrats and Political Development: A Paradoxical View," *op. cit.*, pp. 120-67.

may actually reduce a system's capacity for managing changes in demands. It is Eisenstadt's insight, fortified by extensive historical research, that the most viable administrative system is one that can produce new behavior and organization in response to changes in demands. Nothing yet suggests that such response must be "modern" in the sense of being free from such influences as tradition, corruption, particularism, and other characteristics said to be incompatible with "modernization."

Conclusion

There are a number of concluding observations implicit in what I have said thus far. They will not add up to a neatly packaged formula regarding what kinds of administrators or administrative arrangements are optimally conducive to coping with the historical crises that beset nation-states. They may help us better to understand what kinds of questions must be asked and answered before any of us can prescribe regarding what the relationship between public administration and development is or can be in various places.

1. Existing abstract models of administrative and political systems are not very useful in helping us to understand the relationship between public administration and economic, social and political development. These models are far removed from reality, they tend to reflect the often erroneous perception the theorist has about the administrative system or systems he knows best, and they tend to obscure, or in any case are not sufficiently discriminating about, the conditions and characteristics of mixed (that is, all) systems.

2. Abstract models lead to quite unjustified generalizations about so-called traditional, transitional, and modern systems. What confronts us empirically is the great variety of values, organization, and behavior that one encounters in the traditional sectors of specific societies. This point has been forcefully made concerning the disparities of village life in a vast subcontinent like India, but it is also valid to some degree for any society, including those that are presumably modern. To assume that the idealized traditional society is unequivocally incompatible with such national goals as economic or political development is to ignore potential sources of support and/or to needlessly complicate the problems of crisis management.

3. Before one can make any decision about administrative organization and behavior, it is necessary to ask: (1) What kinds of crises confront the system? (2) Which of these crises have the highest priority for attempted solution? and (3) To what extent can existing structures, including those of public administration, be utilized in the business of crisis management? A strong tradition of hierarchical authority and obedience, for example, might be utilized for the disciplined management of industrial development, even if the tradition is based on particularistic and ascriptive considerations such as family or kinship. Japan offers a striking example of this kind of exploitation of tradition. Similarly deeply rooted patterns of administrative leadership and control exercised by an intellectual bureaucratic elite may be quite functional for the solution of certain developmental crises. Such patterns growing out of mandarinate and colonial histories in Asia are very strong and do not necessarily constitute impediments to economic and social development, although they may present grave problems for democratization.

4. How much efficiency, rationality, and professionalism the public administrative sector requires cannot be arbitrarily established. Corruption by modern standards may be something less immoral in other parts of the world. The history of the West itself suggests that corruption may be a spur to risk-taking and entrepreneurial dynamism in the bureaucracy. The availability of "spoils" may actually constitute an important, perhaps vital, means of encouraging such countervailing power centers to the bureaucracy as political parties and trade unions. Insistence on efficiency and rationality may, in the short-run, involve too radical a departure from tradition and therefore set up avoidable impediments to long-run change.

5. It is vital in every system that the administrator develop empathy regarding those persons in society whose cooperation is necessary if many of the historical crises are to be adequately managed. Ideas of what is organizationally or behaviorally possible derived from exposure to Western education and culture (or an abject dependence on Western formulae) are almost certain to cause more tension and instability than would be the case if attention were empirically and pragmatically directed to the indigenous situation. Programs of village development, of assuring process and geographic integration, of encouraging national identity require that administrators know something about the village. This is true not only of field administrators, who must leave their offices and actually go out and look at rice fields and the

village power structure, but also of administrative planners who prescribe broad developmental goals.

6. The matter of administrative organization and articulation both at the center and in the provinces is of vital importance. Ideological commitment to the unitary state may intensify local, communal, or linguistic hostilities to the central power. Reliance on patterns of field administration inherited from colonialism may aid the law-and-order function but be detrimental to the felicitous solution of distribution and participation crises. Similarly, central administrative organization dominated by lawyers and reflecting overriding attention to problems of defense, internal order and extractive activities like military recruitment and taxation will not be conducive to the successful execution of developmental programs that require technical specialists and that catapult the government into a wide range of social, economic and welfare programs.

7. What the improved capacity of bureaucracies to deal with change in demands clearly seems to require everywhere is some new institutions, a commitment to empiricism, and training or educational programs that are consonant with the tasks at hand. To what extent established administrators can be retrained to emphasize empirical approaches to problems and to be experimental in the use of organizational devices is everywhere problematical and, if historical experience is any teacher, almost everywhere discouraging. Those nations fortunate enough to have a strong ideology of social, political, and economic change are better situated in this regard than some others. Charismatic leaders might also be useful in this regard, but only if they, themselves, succeed in recruiting a group of skilled guardian bureaucrats who are single-mindedly commited to change. The problems encountered by leaders such as Castro, Nasser, Sukarno, Diem, and Nkrumah suggest that they can be impeded both by their own limitations and by the frightening scarcity of human resources available.

While it may sound terribly banal or bromidic, the solution to this problem is essentially long-term and lies primarily in education. Lenin recognized that the creation of the kind of bureaucratic managers fully compatible with the ideological aims of the Bolsheviks would require at least a generation. The agonizing and persistent problems growing out of the tense relations between party and bureaucratic and industrial elites in the Soviet Union suggest that a half-century is too short a time in which to create a happy balance between the demands emerging from society and the ability of the bureaucratic apparatus to meet them. This experience is clearly not encouraging for developing nations less endowed with material resources than the Soviet Union and far less prepared than the latter was in 1917 to produce the human skills essential to crisis management.

8. Finally, I should note that for those who are interested in a particular kind or direction of political development, namely pluralistic democracy, the problems we have been exploring here are enormously complicated. The overwhelming need to maintain the nation-state intact does not conduce power-holders to encourage or tolerate opposition, civil liberties, or countervailing centers of power. Long-range goals of economic growth may quickly lead to measures designed to repress demands for greater consumption or more equitable distribution of economic and welfare values. The use of traditional bureaucratic elites to effect important law-and-order and economic development functions cuts against the idea of broader recruitment to the bureaucracy or a more democratic relationship between bureaucrat and citizen. Thus, to cite the case of Mexico, the impressive material transformation of that society under the essentially dictatorial leadership of PRI, has not been matched by the growth of democratic pluralism or by a new pattern of relationship between bureaucratic rulers and subject citizens. [59] Whether, as some hope, democracy may later emerge out of the one-party patterns that now characterize many of the developing states is certainly open to question. We can be fairly certain that administrative patterns and educational experiences leading to bureaucratic roles that do not consciously pose democracy as an end in view will not aid in the realization of such a mission.

---

[59]See the materials on Mexico in Almond and Verba, *The Civic Culture, op. cit.* Cf. Robert Scott, "Mexico: The Established Revolution," in Pye and Verba, *Political Culture and Political Development, op. cit.*, pp. 330-95.

III Empathic Accuracy and Innovation

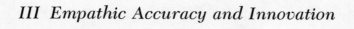

Chapter 5
Empathy

Henry Clay Smith

Department of Psychology
Michigan State University

The question of the level of empathy has been of basic philosophic and psychological concern.[1] Hume and other philosophers in the tradition of "epistemological loneliness" have viewed man as being essentially alone. They see him as capable of understanding the behavior of other men but incapable of really understanding their experiences. Following this tradition, behaviorists have attempted to understand men through a study of their behavior alone.

By contrast, most clinicians assume that man can understand others by assuming that their experiences are similar to his own. It should be apparent from this that when we say that we are all pretty much alike it does not mean that we must all be psychotic, or that we must all have children, or that we must all have had the experience of our parents dying. In fact we need not have had these experiences. Rather, in the way in which all yearning is the same, all pain is the same, and all fantasy is the same, we can have these experiences. The method whereby we may become aware of the relationship between experience and behavior is through the use of systematic self-observation. Thus at the extreme, the behaviorist sees empathy as the source of all error; the clinician, the source of all truth.

Empathy, as we define it, is the tendency of a perceiver to assume that another person's feelings, thoughts, and behavior are similar to his own. Blackman defines empathy and distinguishes it from the related terms *projection, identification,* and *sympathy* in the following way:

---

[1] D. Bakan, "Clinical Psychology and Logic," *American Psychologist,* XI (1956), 655-62.

Empathy is the ability to step into another person's shoes and to step back just as easily into one's own shoes again. It is not projection, which implies that the wearer's shoes pinch him and that he wishes someone else in them; it is not identification, which involves stepping into another person's shoes and then being unable or unwilling to get out of them; and it is not sympathy, in which a person stands in his own shoes while observing another person's behavior, and while reacting to him in terms of what he tells you about his shoes—if they pinch, one commiserates with him, if they are comfortable, one enjoys his comfort with him.[2]

This definition implies that when we think we have stepped into another person's shoes we actually have; our definition implies that we can only be sure that we are being empathic and not being projective by comparing the similarities we assume between ourselves and another person with the actual similarities between ourselves and him.

Freudians, non-Freudians, sociologists, and psychologists stress that similarity to others forms the foundation for understanding them.[3] What they do not stress is that assumed similarities can be wrong as well as right, can lead to mistaken as well as correct judgments. The focus in this chapter is, therefore, not on empathy alone, but, rather, it is on empathic *accuracy,* the ability of an individual to perceive correctly the ways in which he is like another person and the ways in which he is different.

In this chapter we shall discuss four topics: (1) the relationship between empathy and empathic accuracy and how each is measured, (2) the social-psychological processes which are correlated with the process of empathy, (3) the personality of the empathizer, and (4) the implications for the administrator and administration.

The Measurement of Empathy and Empathic Accuracy

Although everyone assumes some similarity between himself and others, some are more empathic than others. There are three

[2]N. Blackman, K. Smith, R. Brokman, and J. Stern, "The Development of Empathy in Male Schizophrenics," *Psychiatric Quarterly,* XXXII (1958), 546-53.

[3]Cf. O. Fenichel, *The Psychoanalytic Theory of Neurosis* (New York: Norton, 1945); H. S. Sullivan, *Conceptions of Modern Psychiatry* (New York: Norton, 1956); G. H. Mead, *Mind, Self and Society* (Chicago: Univ. of Chicago Press, 1934); and C. R. Rogers, "Relationship between Real Similarity and Assumed Similarity with Favorability Controlled," *Journal of Abnormal and Social Psychology,* LIX (1959), 431-33.

related measures which will aid us in dealing with empathy and empathic accuracy: (1) the empathy score, (2) the actual similarity score, and (3) the empathic accuracy score. The empathy score is a measure of *assumed* similarity. The common way of measuring empathy is to have people answer questions as they themselves would answer them and then answer the same questions as they think someone else would answer them. The number of questions that a man answers for others in the same way he answers them for himself is his empathy score. Table 1 illustrates this method of measuring empathy.[4]

The actual similarity score is obtained by comparing the response of an individual about his own feelings, thoughts, or behavior with the responses of another individual. The actual similarity score is the number of times in which two people have *independently* made the same response about themselves. We can, therefore, measure the actual similarity between them without either being aware of the other. We cannot, however, measure assumed similarity (empathy) without having a perceiver make a conscious attempt to predict the responses of another person. The empathic accuracy score is measured by dividing the assumed similarity score (empathy score) by the actual similarity score (see Figure I).

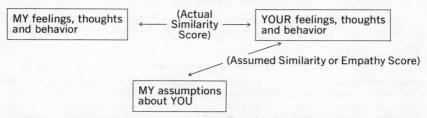

FIGURE I.   Measures related to the Empathic Accuracy Score. The **actual similarity score** is the number of similarities between myself and you regardless of whether I know about them or not. The **assumed similarity score** (empathy) is the number of similarities I assume between myself and you regardless of whether they are based on correct observations or mistaken projections of my own attitudes on to you. The **empathic accuracy score** is the assumed similarity score divided by the actual similarity score. If the ratio is less than one, I have assumed less similarity between myself and you than actually exists; if more than one, I have assumed more similarity than actually exists.

---

[4]D. Livensparger, "Empathy Inventory," unpublished manuscript, 1965. The content of empathy measures have varied widely. Livensparger used items from the Strong Vocational Interest Blank; in June Chance and W. Meaders, "Needs and Interpersonal Perception," *Journal of Personality*, XXVIII (1960), 200-10, items from the Edwards Inventory were used; Rogers, *op. cit.*, employed the Gough Adjective Check List; Rosalind F. Dymond, "A Scale for Measurement of Empathic Ability," *Journal of Consulting Psychology*, VIII (1954), 164-71, used the MMPI. F. K. Strayer, "Empathy and Social Perception," *Dissertation Abstracts*, XXI (1960), 244.

One might think that a perceiver who had a perfectly accurate *level* of empathy with a person would also have perfect empathic accuracy. That this is not necessarily correct is illustrated by Table 2, a hypothetical response to the first four items in the test in Table 1.

In this example, the perceiver assumes he is similar to the person on two items (musical comedy and auctioneer) and is actually similar on two items (manufacturer and auto salesman), but he is wrong in all of his specific assumptions about similarity and dissimilarity. The reason for introducing this example is that it is fairly true of what happens in many life situations. For example, Bronfen-

---

TABLE 1.   EMPATHY INVENTORY

This inventory measures three things: (1) your knowledge of the interests of the majority of men; (2) your knowledge of the interests of the majority of women; and (3) your own interests. Follow the separate directions for each part.

(1) Knowledge of Men

A large and representative group of educated men checked whether they liked or disliked the various occupations, activities and school subjects below. Mark one (1) if you think the **majority of men** checked that they **"liked"** the interest. Mark two (2) if you think the **majority** checked that they **"disliked"** the interest. Note that the numbering skips lines on the answer sheet (1,2,3,4, ... 9,10,11,12, ... 17, etc.) **Mark your answers in agreement with the numbers.**

1. Manufacturer   2. Musical comedy   3. Auctioneer   4. Auto salesman
9. Art galleries   10. Symphony concerts   11. Auto racer   12. Auto repairman
Etc.

(2) Knowledge of Women

A large and representative group of women checked whether they liked or disliked the various occupations, activities and school subjects below. Mark one (1) if you think the majority of women checked they **liked** the interest. Mark two (2) if you think the majority checked that they **disliked** the interest. Note that the numbering skips lines as in part (1).

65. Costume   66. Proof reader   67. Companion to   68. Accountant
    designer   elderly person
73. Bank teller   74. Magazine writer 75. Telephone   76. Buyer of
                                           operator   merchandise
Etc.

(3) Personal Interests

The following is a list of occupations, activities and school subjects, etc. You are to indicate whether you like or dislike each of the items. If you like the item, mark one (1) on the answer sheet. If you dislike it, mark two (2). Note that the items are numbered so that you now return to the top of· the answer sheets and use the numbers left blank.

5. Manufacturer   6. Musical comedy   7. Auctioneer   8. Auto salesman
Etc.

S. D. Livensparger, "Empathy Inventory," unpublished manuscript, 1965.

brenner, who found a correlation of .86 between empathy (assumed similarity) and actual similarity, found only a correlation of .21 between empathy and the degree of empathic accuracy.[5] That is, individuals were much more accurate in predicting their general level of similarity or dissimilarity to another person than in predicting the specific items on which they would make the same or a different response.

Individuals tend to underestimate their similarity to others. For example, Livensparger, using the test shown in Table 1, determined the three measures described above for fifty-seven college men and women. He multiplied the empathic accuracy score by 100. When the result was 100, it indicated that the student's empathy and actual similarity scores were identical. He found that the average student assumed too little similarity (94). The individual variations, however, were very wide, some students having scores of less than 50 and some having scores of more than 150.[6]

The problem of empathic accuracy seems to be most acute at the extremes: Individuals tend to overestimate their similarities to

TABLE 2. HYPOTHETICAL RESPONSES

	Manufacturer	Musical Comedy	Auctioneer	Auto Salesman
Responses of the Perceiver	"dislike"	"dislike"	"like"	"like"
Responses that the perceiver assumes for the person	"like"	"dislike"	"like"	"dislike"
Response of the Person	"dislike"	"like"	"dislike"	"like"

those that are most like themselves and to overestimate their dissimilarities to those that are least like themselves. Clinical psychologists as well as laymen suffer from this difficulty. Giedt had 48 clinicians judge a series of patients of varying ages and backgrounds and with different problems. He concluded:

> Raters seemed particularly likely to misjudge patients whose socioeconomic and cultural status was either quite close to their own or quite distant from their own. . . . The patient whose socioeconomic and cultural position was most distant from that of the raters — a rather nomadic

---

[5]U. Bronfenbrenner, J. Harding, and Mary Gallway, "The Measurement of Skill in Social Perception," in D. C. McClelland, ed., *Talent and Society* (New York: Van Nostrand, 1958).
[6]Livensparger, *op. cit.*

fellow who shared few of the high aspirations probably characteristic of most of the raters—seemed to be least well understood, and his behavior was often interpreted on the basis of an improper frame of reference. Thus reading pulp magazines and having been involved in fights as a boy—behavior which probably differed from that of the raters—was incorrectly related to impulsivity and lack of control. The patient who had a fairly high-level, managerial status had an outlook on life perhaps so close to that of the raters that they could hardly accept the possibility of serious psychopathology in him. This patient was rated far too high in adherence to reality, apparently on the assumption that no high-level person such as this could be very unrealistic.[7]

The clinician has the greatest difficulty in judging those who are most or least like himself. He seems to have a similar difficulty in dealing with these extreme groups in a therapy situation. Carson and Heine had sixty clinical trainees give therapy once a week for sixteen weeks to sixty patients. Before therapy, clinicians and patients completed the *Minnesota Multiphasic Personality Inventory*. Patients were assigned to clinicians on the basis of their similarity or dissimilarity to them. The sixty clinician-patient pairs were divided into five groups, the first group being composed of those with the most similar profiles and the fifth group being composed of those with the least similar profiles. After the sixteen weeks, the success of therapy for each pair was independently determined. Patients in the groups that were most and least like their therapists were least benefited by the therapy; patients who were moderately like their therapists (the three middle groups) were most benefited by therapy.[8]

Processes Leading to Empathy

Four interrelated social-psychological processes frequently associated with empathy are identification, attraction, generalization and familiarity.

Identification is the process by which a person acts like another person without being encouraged or taught to do so. Children identify with their parents: A daughter feeds and cares for her doll

[7]F. H. Giedt, "Comparison of Visual Content and Auditory Cues in Interviewing," *Journal of Consulting Psychology*, XIX (1955), 407-16.
[8]R. C. Carson and R. W. Heine, "Similarity and Success in Therapeutic Dyads," *Journal of Consulting Psychology*, XXVI (1962), 38-43.

as her mother feeds and cares for her; a son walks, talks, and thinks like his father. In a similar manner, spectators at a sport identify with the athletes, and students identify with other students. The process is reciprocal: We feel, think, and act as we think others are feeling, thinking, and acting; we assume that others are feeling, thinking, and acting as we are. We empathize with those with whom we identify.

Attraction is related to empathy. The more we like a person, the more we assume that he is like us. But liking someone, while related to assumed similarity (empathy), need not rest on actual similarity. Convincing evidence comes from a study of seventeen students at the University of Michigan. They were all transfer students, all strangers to each other, and all residents of the same cooperative house. In return for spending five hours a week being interviewed and filling out questionnaires, they were given free room and board for the semester. The men were given no voice in the selection of roommates, but (within the limits of the university regulations) they were given complete freedom to conduct the house, including the cooking and eating arrangements, as they chose. Before their arrival, each of the seventeen men filled out a questionnaire covering attitudes toward a wide range of issues: classical music, immortality, sexual morality, house rules, university regulations about driving, etc. During the semester, the men completed a variety of personality inventories and rated themselves and each other on numerous rating scales. They also reported whom they liked and disliked. From these data, an index of each man's liking for each of the other men was calculated and also an index of his assumed similarity (empathy) to each of them. Result: the greater the attraction, the greater the empathy ($r = .69$).[9]

It is not surprising that students assumed that those they liked were like them. It *is* surprising that there was no relationship between attraction and actual similarity. A quite different study reached the same conclusion. Silkiner correlated the favorableness of foreign student attitudes toward the United States and the degree of assumed similarity (empathy) between their interests and those of the typical American man. Result: the more favorable their attitude, the greater their empathy. He then correlated favorableness of attitude with actual similarity. Result: no relationship.[10]

---

[9] T. M. Newcomb, "The Prediction of Interpersonal Attraction," *American Psychologist*, XI (1956), 575-86.
[10] D. S. Silkiner, "A Cross-cultural Study of the Measurement, Determinants and Effects of Stereotype Accuracy," unpublished master's thesis, Michigan State Univ., East Lansing, 1962.

Generalization is a key process in empathy: "When a person finds that he has some characteristics in common with another person, he tends to perceive himself as having other characteristics like that person."[11] If we are aware of a few dissimilarities, we assume many more.

Generalization works both ways: We ascribe our traits to the person we perceive as similar; we also ascribe *his* traits to ourselves. Burnstein and his associates brought more than a hundred junior high school boys together in the school gymnasium and asked them to complete a "describe yourself questionnaire." One part of the questionnaire asked them to rate their excellence in swimming, ability to hold breath under water, etc. Two weeks later, the boys were separated into groups of a dozen each and then addressed by a "deep-sea diver" who described his career and stressed his excellence in swimming, ability to hold his breath under water, etc. In some groups, the diver (a confederate) stressed that he was similar to the boys: He was born and raised in their rural neighborhood, went to the same school, had a father who worked in the same factory that employed most of the fathers of the boys, etc. In other groups, the diver stressed that he was *dissimilar:* He was born and raised in a big city, went to a large city school, had a father who was a fisherman, etc. At the end of each group meeting, the diver asked the boys to again rate themselves on their excellence in swimming, etc. The boys who had heard the "low similarity" speech rated themselves about as they had two weeks before; the boys who heard the "high similarity" speech changed their ratings of themselves so that their characteristics were more like those that the diver described himself as possessing.[12]

Familiarity is correlated with empathy. The longer we know a person, the more we tend to assume we are like him. Students were brought into a room two at a time and seated at different desks so that they could not see each other. Each then took a test which pictured twenty-four situations with three different kinds of responses. Each chose the response that he would make in each situation. The pair was then very briefly introduced to each other and asked, even though they did not know each other very well, to fill out the test as they thought their partner had filled it out. Assumed similarity was measured by determining the number of situations in which a student picked the same response for his partner as he had picked for himself. The pairs of students were

---

[11]E. Burnstein, E. Stotland, and A. Zander, "Similarity to a Model and Self-Evaluation," *Journal of Abnormal and Social Psychology*, LXII (1962), 257-64.
[12]*Ibid.*

then given two topics to discuss for twenty minutes. Afterward, each member of the pair was to answer the test as he thought his partner had. Higher assumed similarity after interaction was found.[13]

The relationship between empathy and accuracy also increases with the length of acquaintanceship. In the conclusion to his intensive study of the members of a cooperative house, Newcomb states:

> Early acquaintance is characterized by a continuing process of reciprocal scanning: What kinds of things does this person view as important? Whatever they are, how does he feel about them, and also about the things I regard as important (including myself)? If the discrepancies seem not too glaring, explorative communication continues, and with it comes the possibility of changes in the scale of importance, and in attitudes toward things of varying degrees of importance. In the long run (four months, in my own investigation), attraction and association came to be relatively concentrated upon those who are perceived, usually with a considerable accuracy as having notions similar to one's own of what is important and as having attitudes similar to one's own toward important things.[14]

Interrelations among variables. The process of identification, attraction, generalization, and familiarity are intimately interwoven: We identify with those we like, we like those with whom we identify, etc. The relationship, for example, between familiarity and attraction has been formulated as the Law of Propinquity: "As the frequency of interaction between two persons increases, the degree of their liking for one another increases." The law is pervasive.

Beier and Stumpf reached the same conclusion. They started out to determine the influence of various kinds of cues on judgments of intelligence, sociability, and other personality characteristics. To do so, they presented four persons one at a time to over two hundred students under different conditions: (1) The students heard only the voices of the subjects from behind a screen; (2) the students then heard the subjects and saw them making gestures but did not see their faces; (3) the students heard their voices and saw their faces and observed them making gestures; and (4) the students had all of these cues and also heard the subject discuss a topic for

---

[13]J. Bieri, "Changes in Interpersonal Perception Following Social Interactions," *Journal of Abnormal and Social Psychology*, XLVIII (1953), 61-66.
[14]Newcomb, *op. cit.*

three minutes. The students rated the subjects after each presentation. The more familiar students became with a subject, the more favorable their ratings became.[15]

The ratios of empathy to actual similarity scores vary with the saliency of the processes of identification, attraction, generalization, and familiarity. People identify more with their own than the opposite sex. Consistently, Livensparger found erroneously high levels of empathy with the same sex (108) erroneously low levels with the opposite sex (81).[16] American students have more obvious similarities to and familiarity with American than foreign students. Silkiner, using a test roughly similar to that shown in Table 1 (see p. 114), measured the levels of empathy of American and foreign male and female students to American men. He reported the empathy scores as follows: for the American male students, 78; for the foreign male students, 60; for the American women, 70; and for the foreign women, 51. All groups were in reality more similar than they assumed. Foreign women, however, underestimated their similarity to American men by the greatest amount.[17]

The Personality of the Empathizer

Chance and Meaders measured differences in personality between those people who assumed little and those who assumed a great deal of similarity to two individuals that they heard on tape recordings.

The authors concluded that those who assumed high similarity (empathy) had a "highly developed need for social interaction although strongly tinged with dependence upon and conformity to the constraints that others impose." Those who assumed low similarity were "nonconforming, impatient with custom and authority, disinclined to plan and to accept schedules, wanting to be in the limelight, not strongly motivated toward seeking contacts with others, seeking new experiences, and preferring aggressive modes of behavior."[18] Table 3 summarizes these findings.

A similar result emerged from a study using a different approach. Leaders were first asked to describe themselves by rating their agreement with statements such as "I like good food" and by

[15]E. G. Beier and J. Stumpf, "Cues Influencing Judgments of Personality Characteristics," Journal of Consulting Psychology, XXIII (1959), 218-25.
[16]Livensparger, op. cit.
[17]Silkiner, op. cit.
[18]Chance and Meaders, op. cit.

choosing from pairs of adjectives such as "calm-exciting." Each leader was then asked to use the same alternatives in describing the man he thought was his best and the man he thought was his poorest subordinate. The number of statements on which a leader assumed that the best and poorest subordinates were like himself were counted. Finally, the difference in assumed similarities to the best and to the poorest workers were determined. Those leaders who

TABLE 3. PERSONALITY CHARACTERISTICS OF HIGH AND LOW EMPATHIZERS

Low Empathizers	High Empathizers
Expressive	Inhibited
Dominating	Submissive
Independent	Dependent
Aloof	Gregarious
Cool	Warm
Aggressive	Unaggressive

Source: Chance and Meaders, "Needs and Interpersonal Perception," Journal of Personality, XXVIII (1960), 200-210.

assumed about the same amount of similarity to these opposites were found to be more dependent on others, more concerned about the attitude of others toward them, and more unwilling to reject unsatisfactory workers. Those leaders who assumed much more similarity to the best worker than to the poorest worker were more independent, more indifferent to the attitudes of others, and readier to reject people they judged to be unsatisfactory. They were distant from people.[19]

The aloofness of the nonempathizers may be related to childhood experiences. Stotland and Dunn measured the degree of identification of students who were watching another student in an anxious situation. They compared the anxiety levels of firstborn children with students who had at least one older brother or sister. Students with older siblings were more anxious. "The first and only born . . . react as if they only use the other person's performance level as a guide to self-evaluation and do not really 'feel with' him."

Stotland and Dunn also compared the empathic anxiety of students with low and high self-esteem. Those of high self-esteem

---

[19]F. E. Fiedler, "Leadership and Leadership Effectiveness Traits: A Reconceptualization of the Leadership Trait Problem," in L. Petrullo and B. M. Bass, eds., *Leadership and Interpersonal Behavior* (New York: Holt, 1961).

identified more with the student in trouble. "These results are reminiscent of the clinician's belief that only those who really love themselves can love others."[20]

Sources of Empathic Errors

While some people are more accurate in judging others, all make errors. Here we shall briefly consider six of the most common and influential of these errors: (1) the rigidity of levels, (2) the prevalence of simple thinking, (3) the dangers of psychological-mindedness, (4) the error of least effort, (5) faulty stereotypes, and (6) the cancerous hypothesis.

Even after the briefest exposure, we can gain a clear picture of what a person is like. Our pictures, however, vary widely from the darkest gray to the rosiest pink. Some people think that most people are "no damn good" while others think the best of everyone. The general level at which a perceiver operates reflects a stable and central personality quality. It also has a pervasive influence on all of his judgments of himself and others. The problem is not so much the level that a perceiver has as the rigidity and inflexibility of his level. More or less regardless of his own qualities, who he is judging, or what he is judging, a perceiver tends to stick to a constant level. Those who have the highest empathic accuracy are those who have learned to realistically adapt their level to changing persons and situations.

We perceive a person as a unified and simple whole. So strong is the tendency to think in simple terms that it is hard to avoid describing everyone as either "bad" or "good," "right" or "wrong," "strong" or "weak." One common way of achieving a simple picture of a person is to fail to observe or to forget facts that do not fit. The same result can be achieved in the opposite way. We can accumulate an excessive number of facts, many of which are ambiguous and some of which seem to conflict. Then it is possible to unconsciously pick facts that fit the picture we had before we began accumulating them.

The use of "psychology" and psychology-mindedness is a potent source of error, for preoccupation with the psychological underground leads one to overlook significant facts that lie on the surface. The preoccupation may also lead to the view that we are all moved by primitive and blind impulses when, in fact, we are largely

---

[20]E. Stotland and R. E. Dunn, "Empathy, Self-Esteem and Birth Order," *Journal of Abnormal and Social Psychology*, LXVI (1963), 532-40.

reasonable players of social roles. Also, it is hard to see in the underground and thus easy to mistake our own projected feelings for the reality. Perhaps most relevant of all, the most enthusiastic proponents of psychological-mindedness are not those with deep involvement with others but those with a desire to protect and enhance their own self-esteem. Mastery of the "psychological point of view" may be comforting, but it may also be deceptive.

It is possible to surface after a brief dip in the literature of empathy with the idea that we are generally preoccupied with assessing the fundamental nature of the people we meet. In fact, we are usually interacting with others in well-defined situations and are playing rather specific roles. The question before us is not: What is he like? It is: What do I do next? In such a situation, we naturally strive to *reduce* the information we need to sustain the interaction process. We seek to know the least amount about another person that is consistent with playing an immediate social role effectively. While this principle of least effort is helpful in playing our social role, it is not helpful in increasing our empathic accuracy.

A stereotype is our picture of the social role that the members of a particular group play; stereotype accuracy is the adequacy of our knowledge of these roles; and stereotyping is the process of applying our knowledge of these roles to making predictions about how individuals playing them will behave. Stereotyping is inevitable; it is, also, on the whole, very helpful. Still, stereotypes can be mistaken and misused. Stereotype accuracy depends, in part, upon the number of persons in the group we have known. Not infrequently, the number is one. We meet one Australian, form an impression of his personality, and use that impression in making predictions about all Australians. Even more serious, the number may be zero. Children and adults learn stereotypes from those about them without any firsthand experience with the groups: Koreans, Negroes, Jews, Texans, Catholics, etc. One of the most certain ways of reducing empathic errors is through training in stereotype accuracy.

One sort of error is so typical of judgments of personality, so persistent, and seemingly so unavoidable that it should be constantly borne in mind. It is the result of a hypothesis that, like cancer, grows in a wild and uncontrollable way. A Texas company, for example, needed a new head for their research and development section. The autocratic president announced his choice. The members of the section unanimously objected to his appointment saying that he was "unimpressive." His dwarf-like physique played a large part in the informal discussions of his unimpressiveness, strongly suggesting that the group was generalizing from this single physical quality to many psychological ones. Nonetheless, the man was appointed, was highly successful, and was eventually promoted to a higher position. The country was combed for his replacement. There was general agreement on the best available man although it was incidentally remarked by those who recommended him that "he tends to talk a great deal when he is nervous." He came, was interviewed, and was rejected because he seemed "arrogant, egotistical, and opinionated." Again, it seemed clear, there was a wild generalization from one obvious behavioral trait to many subtle ones.

The Improvement of Empathic Accuracy

To be effective, training designed to improve empathic accuracy should focus upon the unified person, should make it easy for the trainee to change his theories about people, and should provide realistic feedback. Like all principles, these are easier to state than to apply successfully. Sensitivity training laboratories, analyses of clinical interactions, and role-playing are three widely used efforts to apply them.

Sensitivity Training Laboratories

The procedures of sensitivity training involve a "laboratory" composed of 30 to 150 people, meeting in a conference setting for two or three weeks. A training group meets for thirty to forty hours, carrying on a study of its own processes. Most laboratories also involve a wide range of other activities: lectures and demonstrations reviewing material from the social sciences, consultation on back-home problems, and planned exercises. The exercises may range from replications of classic experiments in social psychology to full-scale organizational simulation designs that continue for a day or two.

To determine whether training achieves all or any of its goals is extraordinarily difficult. The persons appearing for human relations training are highly self-selected, and it is excessively difficult to get comparable pools of subjects to serve as members of control groups. Ordinarily the number of participants in any particular training laboratory is relatively small. Where training laboratories are composed of persons from widely spread geographical areas, getting accurate follow-up measures is difficult; where laboratories are held with members of an ongoing organization, it is almost impossible to separate the presumed outcomes of the laboratory. In an effort to solve these problems, Miles used thirty-four elementary school principals attending a two-week training laboratory at Bethel, Maine, in 1958. Each principal was matched with another principal who did not attend the conference. In addition, each participating principal gave names of six to eight associates on the job who could describe his job behavior.

Miles determined that there was no change in either the experimental or control group in a leadership behavior scale given before and after training. There was a change in both the experimental and control groups in their participation habits as measured by a group participation scale. There were significant changes in the experimental but not in the control group in the way they perceived themselves: "listens more," "communicates better," "shares decisions more," "gives help to teachers," etc. However, there was no relation between the amount of this change and the initial expressed desire for improvement. "If anything the relationship was inverse . . . a high wish to change in this sample was a kind of defensive protestation."[21]

A feedback technique is often utilized in Sensitivity Training. A rule is sometimes made by the trainees that before anyone can speak of his ideas he must first repeat what was said and felt by the person who had spoken before him. Comments after using the technique are, commonly, "For the first time in my life I find that I am really listening to what others say." The pattern has some obvious advantages over the client-to-therapist or supervisor-to-trainee type of feedback: (1) The relationships involved are not those of superior-inferior type; (2) the perceiver obtains feedback from the rest of the group as well as from the person perceived; and (3) each trainee has a chance to be the perceiver, the person being perceived, and the observer of perceiver-person interactions.

Analyses of Clinical Interactions

The training of clinicians is consciously directed at the goal of empathic accuracy: Does the therapist, for example, feel a "slight depression and mild anxiety" because he is realistically identifying

---

[21]M. B. Miles, "Human Relations Training: Processes and Outcomes," *Journal of Counseling Psychology*, VII (1960), 301-6.

with the client or because he is projecting some of his own irrelevant feelings into the situation? One way of answering the question is for the therapist to communicate back to the client what he assumes the client is feeling. The client can then correct or amplify the therapist's impressions. Another way is to have the expert supervisor listen to the taped interview and to correct what he judges to be empathic errors. While such knowledge of results is more adequate than in a formal course, it may not be adequate enough to increase accuracy. It may have its most significant effect in the tendency of the clinician to identify with his supervisor rather than his client, i.e., to attend to the inner feelings of the client in the way that he thinks his supervisor does.

Having trainees discuss responses they would make in specific situations may be helpful in developing some therapeutic skills. Such discussions, however, do not give the trainee any knowledge of how well he understands a particular person. If the format were changed it might. Suppose, for example, that trainees were first presented with an actual interaction sequence between therapist and client and were then given five alternative responses of the client to the last remark of the therapist, one of which the client actually made. If the trainee makes the correct choice in a series of such sequences, he would be given some objective knowledge of his understanding of the person. The first selection of such sequences and alternatives might result in all the trainees failing to choose the correct response. However, this problem would be readily solved by trying out the sequences and eliminating or revising those that were inadequate.

A more serious problem is that both trainer and trainee may resist the win-lose nature of such situations. Such resistance might be reduced by selecting and testing the interaction samples so that trainees could be exposed to them according to their difficulty. Trainees are often anxious and defensive in realistic social interactions. To meet this difficulty, the initial cases could be tape recorded and only the final ones would be actual interactions.

Role-Playing Session

Practice in playing the role of a person might be of considerable help in improving empathic accuracy. In role-playing the player pretends he is the person and acts out situations as he thinks the person would behave in them. Bronfenbrenner and Newcomb have given a helpful analysis of some of the aspects of the person which the role-player should be aware of and attempt to incorporate into his portrayal of the person:

Verbal content: slips of the tongue, omissions and blocks, sudden shift in train of thought, frequent repetitions, etc.

Voice characteristics: speed, rhythm, pitch, intensity, dropping or raising of voice, change in speed, etc.

Bodily movements and postural adjustments: relaxed, jerky, abortive, controlled, immobilized, etc.[22]

The comments of both the trainer and other trainees may be of help in developing the accuracy of the role-player's performance.

Role-playing has been used for many purposes. The critical differences between role-playing for developing empathic accuracy and for other purposes are: (1) The participants play the roles of actual persons with known responses instead of fictional persons with unknown responses; (2) the stress is upon the exact imitation of another person rather than upon a free interpretation that encourages the role-player to project his own personality into the situation; and (3) an exclusive concern with understanding the other person rather than with relating to the person in an affective way. The utility of role-playing for increasing empathic accuracy for a particular person could be determined by comparing the accuracy of predictions for the person before and after his role was played.

Implications for the Administrator

Can an administrator make mistakes by having too much empathy, i.e., by assuming too much similarity between himself and others? He can and does, for he often jumps to the conclusion that, because a person is like him in obvious ways, he will be like him in less obvious ways. He is, therefore, very likely to assume too easily that other administrators will think and act like himself. He is also likely to err by assuming too little similarity between himself and his subordinates, by assuming that his subordinates will think about a problem less like he does than they actually do.

Can an administrator have too much empathic accuracy, i.e., understand people too well for his own good or the good of the organization? The commonsense answer would be "no," for it is a

---

[22]U. Bronfenbrenner and T. Newcomb, "Improvisations—An Application of Psychodrama in Personality Diagnosis," *Sociatry,* I (1948), 367-82.

centuries old principle that "The good leader knows his men." The best empirical check of the principle was made in a military setting. In this study, infantry trainees in the process of completing their six-month tour of duty were asked for the following facts about themselves: (1) first name, (2) last name, (3) whether or not during the past week they had been on KP, (4) whether or not during the past week they had been on passes or leave, (5) their rifle qualification score, (6) the amount of schooling they had completed, (7) their main job or activity before entering the Army, (8) their principal hobby or interest, (9) their ambition for a future civilian career. Then the squad leaders were given the last names of the trainees under them and asked to provide the same information about each trainee (first name, rifle scores, etc.). A squad leader's answers were corrected against the answers given by the trainees themselves. Each correct answer was awarded one point. The average number of correct answers for his men was the squad leader's *interpersonal knowledge score.*

Was interpersonal knowledge related to leadership effectiveness? As a measure of effectiveness, each squad leader was separately rated by his sergeant, trainee guide, and platoon leader on a scale from 1 ("the very best type of squad leader") to 7 ("the worst kind of squad leader"). In addition, each squad leader took a battery of leader-reaction tests that required him to perform as a leader in three tactical situations, to take part in leadership group discussions, and to lead a squad through dismounted drill. When interpersonal knowledge scores were related to each of these measures of effectiveness, *all* the measures correlated significantly with interpersonal knowledge.[23] Common sense is vindicated: People who know people are more successful in dealing with them.

What are the qualities of the administrator with high empathic accuracy? Motivation is the first essential: Men learn what they want to learn. The people of high empathic accuracy are those who find their greatest satisfactions in human relations, who are considerate and responsible in dealing with others, who want to give to others rather than to get something from them, but who are not dependent on them. Openness to new experiences is another essential. Those who are most understanding of others are sympathetic to new ideas about people and capable of looking at old facts in new ways. They are curious, plastic, nondefensive, skeptical, tolerant, liberal, and ready for change. Learning about people also

---

[23]M. Showel, "Interpersonal Knowledge and Voted Leader Potential," *Journal of Abnormal and Social Psychology,* LXI (1960), 87-92.

requires boldness—a willingness to approach people, to ask questions, and to express feelings and get responses to them. Studies consistently indicate that those of high empathic accuracy are active and forceful people to the point that they are sometimes described (and describe themselves) as egotistical and conceited. Finally, they are intelligent. They are capable of considering and making sense out of the fragments of facts they gather about people by the use of complex concepts.

Chapter 6
Empathy and Managerial Communication

David K. Berlo

Department of Communication
Michigan State University

In discussing the function of empathic communication within a formal organization, we first need to look at what we mean by communication. People use the word when they mean better reading and writing, telegraphy, or many other activities. For our purposes, we shall define communication as a social process involving the transmission of messages which are intended to elicit desired meanings. Human communication is a social transaction in which both parties presumably receive sufficient satisfaction to warrant continued interaction.

Within a formal social system, communication is the process which binds the organization. The boxes on an organizational chart denote the roles which exist in the system. The lines which connect those boxes, the "channels" of the organization, refer to the flow of formal or officially recognized communication within the system. In an organization, communication is the process most used to give and receive instructions, to gain compliance with policy, to influence and be influenced. Communication is basic to the accomplishment of work objectives, as well as to the kind of interpersonal support which is necessary to loyalty and satisfaction among the members of the organization.

Effective communication is important at all levels within an organization; however, it becomes crucial when supervision and management are involved. The worker on the line primarily manipulates things rather than symbols. He works with objects, with the tools of the trade. His work usually is somewhat dependent on the work of others; however, in large part his primary relationships are with physical objects. The manager, on the other hand, in large part manipulates symbols. He will work with physical objects;

however, most of his success or failure is attributed to his competence in working with people as well as with things. He is totally dependent on others, and his primary relationships are communicative.

Given communication as the binding process within the organization, it seems apparent that an understanding of the process can contribute to effective managerial behavior. Unfortunately, many of us lack this understanding. We analyze the technical processes of production in great detail; however, we all too often simply take communication for granted as something we do, as something that comes naturally. This lack of concern explains in part the frequent breakdowns within an organization that can be traced to a failure in the communication complex.

The Communication Process

An understanding of communication rests on the acceptance of a philosophic point of view that suggests that reality, particularly social reality, is something we build rather than something we discover. Until early in this century, the prevailing philosophic framework suggested that reality is a discoverable, that it "exists" in the world around us, and that the perceptive individual trains himself to observe things as they are. Since that time, a different frame has been revived, namely, that reality is a construct. What is real to an individual rests on the way in which he builds his world rather than in his discovery of what the world is.

This is a particularly viable idea when it comes to our judgments about people. It may be difficult for some to accept the idea that the word mile refers to a certain physical phenomena only when people agree that it will; however, it should not be as difficult to accept the idea that a word like competent does not have its basic referent in the physical world. Rather, a man is competent if and only if his peers, subordinates, and superiors *say* he is.

Perhaps the point can be made more easily in the game of baseball. One who argues that reality is discoverable would define a ball or a strike in terms of a physical location of the ball, the plate, the batter's height, and similar variables. The "construct" point of view suggests that a ball is a ball if and only if the umpire says it is — regardless of its physical location at the time.

Obviously, if we are to play the game of baseball, we need to follow some rules to relate what we call something and where it is; however, in the final analysis, a term is used "when we call it" rather than "when it is." By the same token, the game of social organization must have its own rules which must be followed if we are to play together. But, again, the decisions as to what *really* is a good product, a competent supervisor, an ethical firm are social decisions. Good, competent, ethical, and the like are terms we use to build a reality for ourselves, not terms we use to refer to what we have discovered.

Given the idea that reality is a construct, we can derive our first communication principle: Meanings are in people, not in physical events. By this we mean that the meanings for the symbols we use to communicate are found in the people who use the symbols, not in the symbols themselves. Words, gestures, memos, corporate policy, and the like are meaningless in and of themselves. Their utility rests in toto on the interpretations, the meanings, that people assign to them. It follows also that meanings cannot be placed in receptacles and shipped from place to place. Meanings are not transmitted, only physical events are transmitted. If we choose our events carefully, they will elicit the meanings we intend. The criterion, then, for choice of the "right" word or event rests on its meaningfulness to the receiver, not on any arbitrary criterion of its real meaning, or its correct meaning.

The primary communication question is not "What messages should I use to convey the correct meaning for what I intend?" Rather, it is "What messages can I construct which have the best chance of eliciting the meanings I want from the intended receiver of those messages?"

An analysis of the communication process and its effectiveness within any organization must start with an analysis of the people who are communicating, with their meanings, and with their beliefs and knowledge. The meanings that we have for the symbols we use are learned. They come from our own backgrounds and experiences. Since no two people have exactly the same experiences, it follows that no two people have *exactly* the same meanings for anything.

This gives rise to a second communication principle: Perfect communication between individuals is inherently impossible. There is some error in all human communication transactions. This means that the effective manager does not ask whether his communication will be distorted in reception. He assumes that it will be distorted and builds corrective mechanisms into the system from the start.

When we communicate about specific things, and with people whose professional backgrounds and experience are pretty much like our own, these distortions can be minimal. However, as the topic of communication becomes less denotative, more abstract, and when the experiences of the other communicator begin to differ significantly from our own, the probability of communication breakdown rises rapidly. In that situation, the effective manager needs to have a thorough understanding of the way in which communication occurs and be sensitive to the problems that evolve from differences in meaning and interpretation of the same symbolic event.

One more basic communication principle needs mention: All, or nearly all, communication is purposeful. We communicate to have an effect on others. We want people to believe as we believe, to look at the world as we do, to know things we want them to know. We also communicate to affect ourselves. We want to structure our own life to give it the meaning or significance we desire. We communicate to make contact with our environment, to develop our own self-concept, to affect people in ways consistent with our self-perceived best interests.

Many of these communication objectives involve an intent to influence the behavior of others, to persuade them to our point of view. In fact, all communication is in part persuasive. Some people like to believe that they can avoid persuasion, that they simply provide people with information without influencing them. This is not possible. We may influence others intentionally, and we may influence others unintentionally. We cannot avoid influencing them.

In summary, then, we have suggested that communication is a social process involving transactions between two or more people in which messages are sent and received to elicit the desired meanings. Communication is the matrix for management of any formal organization. It is crucial to the attainment of organizational objectives. Furthermore: (1) the meanings in communication transactions are found in the people who communicate rather than in the symbols they use; (2) people's meanings come from experience. Given that experiences differ, meanings inevitably differ; (3) effective communication is difficult—complete fidelity of human communication is impossible; (4) communication is purposeful, and many of our communication objectives involve an attempt to influence the behavior of others; (5) effective communication requires successful predictions about how others will respond.

This analysis suggests that the first step in using communication effectively is a thorough analysis of the intended receiver, of the person for whom the message is intended. In designing our own communication behavior, we need to be able to predict the meanings which others have for various symbols, to predict the responses which they will make to message alternatives, to develop, in effect, a theory of how the other person will behave in a given circumstance. We need to have at our disposal a set of "if . . . then" propositions that we can use, e.g., "if I suggest such-and-such, then he will respond so-and-so." The ability to operate in this kind of scientific way is the basis for skilled use of interpersonal communication.

Predicting Communication Behavior

When we communicate, we have two alternatives in constructing our message. First, we can assume that things mean what they say. If we do this, we can simply ignore the receiver and just "put out messages" for whom it may concern. Given our earlier discussion, this alternative obviously is undesirable, and we can dismiss it as inadequate.

The second alternative is to attempt to predict the probable response to our messages. In part, we can do this without having any personal interaction with a particular receiver. By this we mean that we do not predict response on the basis of personal experience with the receiver, but we predict on the basis of things we know or believe *about* him, e.g., the groups he belongs to; his age, sex, race, religious or political affiliations; the roles he plays such as bookkeeper, salesman, farmer, husband, Scout leader; and the like — the categories in which we place him.

All of us carry meanings for each of these roles or categories, and we have beliefs or pictures in our minds as to how people in these categories will behave. We have a name for these beliefs. We call them stereotypes (if we do not like them) or expectations (if we do). Whatever we call them, we use them as a basis for predicting probable responses to messages. When we learn that an individual possesses some attribute or belongs to some category of people, we take what we know or believe about that attribute or category and predict that this individual will behave accordingly.

Predicting individual response from our knowledge of the responses of similar people is energy-saving and useful. At the same time, however, the use of role or attribute as a sole basis for predicting behavior has two dangers: (1) The particular individual's behavior may deviate from the behavior of most of his group; (2) our belief as to how most members of a group would behave may itself be in error.

For example, all of us have certain expectations about a man's behavior in certain circumstances when we learn that he is an accountant; however, Mr. X may not behave as most accountants would, and also most accountants might not behave as we believe they would. So, though knowledge of role is a legitimate basis for predicting response, we need to go beyond it in order to take into account individual variations in behavior and erroneous expectations on our part.

Going beyond categorical predicting we can predict meanings and response on the basis of our personal knowledge of the individual concerned. We use the knowledge we personally have of him. We try to put ourself in his place, to simulate his beliefs and temperament, to take his role, to look at the world as he looks at it.

Our knowledge of both the categories to which a person can be assigned and the individualistic behaviors of which we are aware contribute to our theory of how Mr. X will respond. There is a name we use for the development and use of this kind of a theory. We call it empathy. Empathy can be defined as the set of predictions we make as to the probable responses of another person. It is based in part on our expectations as to how people in this person's role will respond and in part on our hypotheses as to how this particular individual will respond. When our predictions are accurate (high empathy), effective communication is facilitated. But, as we shall note in a moment, not all predictions are accurate. In this case, inaccurate empathizing can be a significant source of communication error, as can no predictions at all.

Bases for Empathic Predictions

Given the importance of predicting the receiver's responsiveness to communication, what characteristics contribute to the predictions we make? There are two clusters of characteristics that we use. The first cluster does not involve knowledge about the intended receiver, and the second one does involve such knowledge.

First, all of us have our own view of the world, our general beliefs about how human beings behave. We carry this generalized worldview around with us and use it as a basis for predicting all events in which we are engaged. The more sophisticated this view is, the more likely we are to be successful empathizers. Sophistication comes from increased knowledge of the nature of human behavior, from training in the social sciences, and from sensitivity to behavior observed on the job and elsewhere. This implies, and rightly so, that the wider the breadth of experience an individual has, the more types of situations in which he will be able to have an accurate view of the world. However, whether our view is accurate or not, each of us certainly has his own view — and we project it to others as one basis for prediction.

Our predictions are also affected by our own tolerance along several dimensions. Individuals vary in their tolerance for ambiguity, in their tolerance for complexity, and in their tolerance for conflict. A primitive view of the world is to see it in black or white terms, that is, as "everyone is pretty much like me," or "everyone else is very different from me and my group." These assumptions are an insufficient (and often quite erroneous) basis for prediction; however, they are a beginning. Other people are like us in some ways, but different from us in other ways. Moreover, in many situations, our data are insufficient to predict, and our analysis must remain ambiguous, at least temporarily. In these situations, the notion of tolerance becomes important. If the manager cannot handle both similarities and differences (low tolerance for complexity), if he must "fill in the blanks" so that he has certainty as to his predictions (low tolerance for ambiguity), or if he tends to distort what he sees to fit his own view of the world (low tolerance for conflict), his predictive capacity is seriously diminished.

In summary, then, a good empathizer has the ability to carry with him a sophisticated view of human behavior which allows for complexity as well as differences between his and others' behavior and which can tolerate uncertainty of prediction along dimensions on which he has inadequate data. Empathic predictions also assume a quantity of data about the roles the receiver plays and about individualistic characteristics of the receiver himself. These predictions are useful to communication. Also, these predictions are in large part received through communication.

How do we get the information we need to predict response? First, we need to observe and catalogue everything we can learn about the individual. Fortunately, this information is easy to obtain if we are sensitive to it. Everything a man says, everything he does, tells us something about him — even though he ostensibly is talking about something else. The subject of most sentences is, in part, "I." The good empathizer is sensitive to these kinds of data. He systematically collects information, both about the roles or attributes which a man has and the idiosyncratic behaviors which he performs. These data form a general base for predicting response.

We also gather information as we communicate with others. All communication has some effect, i.e., some response is made to everything we say to one another. If we pay careful attention to the responses we elicit, these responses give us some idea of the effects we are having. The responses elicited are the result of our communication. By careful observation, we can gain knowledge of these results. In communication theory, we call this knowledge of results "communication feedback." By this we mean that the consequences of our messages should be observed and fed back into our own system so that we can evaluate how well we are doing—and take corrective steps where necessary. The efficient use of feedback helps any communicator attain his immediate objective. It also provides information which can be filed away for future predictive use.

Given the view of the world which we have, our knowledge of the roles which the receiver occupies, our basic data on his knowledge and beliefs which we have gained through observation and feedback, we can begin to anticipate what will happen when communication occurs. Instead of simply sending a message and observing the response (an action-reaction sequence using feedback), we can hypothesize that *if* we were to send such-and-such a message, *then* the receiver probably would behave so-and-so. This anticipatory feedback is available because of man's capacity to hypothesize, to symbolize events before they occur. Anticipatory feedback is a term which can be interchanged with empathy.

The Varying Need for Empathy

Hopefully, we have provided enough information on what the communication scientist means by empathy, and we have discussed its role and function in effective communication. Undoubtedly, in any communication situation, empathy will increase communication effectiveness. However, the process we have described is highly energy-consuming and equally time-consuming. Furthermore, the manager is not a professional social psychologist, or can he devote all of his energy to "people-reading." The question is pertinent, then, as to how much energy is "enough," how much is "too much," and so on.

We can best answer this by isolating the factors in an organizational situation which determine the amount of empathy which is necessary to effective management. In particular, we can look at four such factors: (1) the complexity of the work-task; (2) the clarity and distinctiveness of roles and functions; (3) the relative importance of task productivity and group maintenance as management objectives; (4) the number of people with whom the manager must communicate interpersonally.

Each of these factors affects the amount of energy which can or should be devoted to developing empathic predictions. First, let us consider the complexity of the task. The more complex the work situation is, the more we need interaction and empathy. In a simple, repetitive, highly denotative task situation, minimal communication is needed; therefore, we have little need to take differences in meaning and response into account. As the task increases in complexity, or as it becomes abstract rather than denotative, the need for frequent and subtle interpersonal communication goes up. There is a corresponding increase in the need for empathy.

Similarly, the need for empathic communication is minimal when each role within the organization is very clearly defined, when each function is clearly differentiated from all other functions within the system. In other words, when each person has a prescription for exactly what he is supposed to do, and there is no overlap in function among people, communication is reduced and the chances of communication breakdown are also reduced. Empathy is also easier to achieve in this situation because excellent predictions can be made from role without the necessity for much personal knowledge of the occupant of that role.

The differentiation of role is particularly relevant with respect to the responsibility for decision-making. In a highly centralized decision-making structure, questions as to what to expect from another or what he expects from you are minimal; therefore prediction is easy, and empathic communication is less important. When decision-making is shared among occupants of many roles, when individual judgment and initiative are encouraged, empathy becomes more important for the day-to-day decision-making of each person in the group.

A third factor affecting the need for empathy is related to the objectives of the organization. The goals of any organization can be described in a number of ways. For our purposes, we will isolate two major objectives: task productivity and maintenance of the group. Task productivity refers to those work objectives which are the basis for existence of professional and product-producing organizations, as contrasted with simple leisure or other nontask groups. All groups, however, have the objective of continued existence, of maintenance of the group over time. This goal sometimes contributes to task-oriented objectives; however, at times, energy must be diverted from productivity and directed to maintenance.

Group maintenance involves such things as satisfaction with membership in the group, group morale, feelings of identity, or meaningfulness as a group member. Accurate empathic predictions are one of the best bases for building member satisfactions. The empathic communicator builds rapport and loyalty among those with whom he communicates by anticipating their needs and responses and behaving in accord with them. Given that loyalty, all of the energy of the group can be directed toward task productivity. There is minimal dissatisfaction with membership and minimal danger that the group will break apart; therefore, empathic communication is less needed. Paradoxically, of course, if empathic communication has not been the typical pattern of managerial interaction, one seldom finds high loyalty and satisfaction. This suggests that the time you need empathy most is when you do not have it and vice versa.

Finally, the possibility of empathy is determined by the number of people with whom one must communicate. In a narrow span of managerial responsibility, with a relatively small set of colleagues and subordinates, considerable data can be gathered on which to base communication predictions. Given a situation in which many people report to one individual, or a situation in which frequent interaction is required with sizable groups, little attention can be placed on particular and specific predictions of individualistic responses. In short, then, the more people one must communicate with, the more expensive it is to empathize and the less emphasis we give to empathic predictions.

These four factors affect the extent to which empathy can and should be utilized in effective managerial communication. Within this context, the question of "how much empathy" is easier to answer. Undoubtedly, accurate empathic predictions are always desirable. The question of "how much" is one of practicality, i.e., how much effort and resources can I devote to acquiring accurate information. As the group size increases, more effort is needed per unit of information gain. In a highly centralized decision structure, with maximum clarity and distinctiveness of roles, a simple repetitive task of a denotative nature, and low needs for group maintenance, energy invested in empathy has less importance and less payoff.

Of course, such a situation may be undesirable in terms of other managerial objectives. If so, and if changes are introduced on any of these factors, corresponding changes must be introduced to allow for better and more frequent interpersonal communication; therefore, accurate empathic predictions become more crucial to success. Considerable attention to empathy is crucial in a group in which power and decision-making is shared, in which roles overlap and interact, in which the problems faced are abstract and connotative in nature. If a relatively small number of people are connected in this group, maximal empathy is also possible.

Implications of Empathic Communication

We have dwelled on the nature of empathy and its role in increasing one's communicative influence. Undoubtedly, the use of empathic predictions in communication does have this effect; however, there are at least two other implications of the use of empathy as well. The first has to do with the effect of empathy on the empathizer himself, i.e., what happens to the individual who makes use of empathy in his relationships toward others. The second has to do with the desire that most managers have for empathy *from* their subordinates and colleagues. We have talked about how the manager empathizes with others, but how does the manager aid others to empathize with him, and what implications does this aid have for his own role in the organization?

When we make use of empathic predictions, we create a set of hypotheses about how another person will look at a situation. We attempt to analyze things as he would, to simulate his beliefs and goals. In so doing, we in effect are creating a set of messages about the situation, messages which the other person might be expected to create. These messages have an audience — ourselves. By empathizing, we expose ourselves to an array of data and arguments that may or may not be compatible with our original view as to strategy, or even as to our basic objectives themselves.

We know that all communication has some effect; therefore, it is reasonable to argue that these messages we create have an effect on us. In short, as we try to view the world from another's point of view, and create messages representing his point of view, we change to some extent and begin to look at the world ourselves somewhat more like he does. This has value in that his viewpoint may provide us with new insights and information and may alter our prior decision on the best way to attack a problem or implement a decision.

It may go farther than that. We actually may change our communication objectives as a result of empathy, as well as simply change the strategy and tactics through which we achieve those objectives. To put it differently, we may not only change how we will attempt to get what we want—we may also change what we want. This kind of communication in which we are consciously willing to alter objectives as well as strategy is the extreme of open human communication. It permits maximum interaction between human beings and is a prerequisite for intimacy of personal awareness and experience.

But it has its limitations, too. For one thing, the objectives may be fixed and unchangeable; therefore, empathy may produce reduced commitment on the manager's part to the attainment of the given objective and a corresponding reduction in his effectiveness. Secondly, if we go to the extreme of role-taking and manage to gain a fairly complete understanding of what motivated a person to do something, what factors caused his behavior, what values and needs he had, we approach "being" the other person. We reduce our empathic predictions and increase our sympathetic relationships with the receiver. At this point, it is difficult if not impossible to correct behavior which is antagonistic to the organization's objectives. We become ineffectual. When we are sympathetic rather than empathic, it is difficult to take punitive action, to apply reprimands, to issue orders which will not be satisfying to the recipient.

In short, then, we are suggesting that empathy has an instrumental value. It helps us predict the responses of others and helps us accommodate our messages to those predictions in ways which will heighten the desired effects. But empathy also can have other consequences, some good and some bad. These include the possibilities that (1) the predictions we make serve as messages to ourselves, and alter our strategy for accomplishing change, the objectives we had in mind, or both; (2) through sympathy, we will incapacitate ourselves to take action that the other person might not see as in his best interest.

A second implication of the empathy concept relates to the manager's desire to have others empathize with him. Most managers will testify that they desire and expect their subordinates to predict what the manager wants and how he will react in given situations. Such predictions are of value in improving the effectiveness of an organization; however, the manager often is unaware of what is necessary on his part if such predictions are to be possible, and he overlooks the implications which such predictions have.

As for what is necessary, it is clear that the subordinate must study the manager just as we have suggested the manager studies others. The subordinate who is going to predict his boss needs to gather basic data on the roles the manager occupies, the attributes he has, and the personal characteristics he exhibits. The manager must help others gain this information about him. In his communication with others, he needs to reveal himself, to expose his own thoughts and feelings. He also needs to provide feedback to others on how well they are doing with him, on what kinds of acts on their part satisfy him and what ones displease him, on what messages he understands or agrees with, and on what messages he does not understand or disagrees with.

Some managers consciously take this responsibility to provide information to others. Many pay no attention to it, or fail to see its relevance to their own function. Some consciously or unconsciously resist giving information about themselves to others. Why is this?

The consequence of prediction in social relations is control. When others give us information about them which enables us to predict their responses, we gain some control over their behavior. By the same reasoning, when we allow others to get information about us which enables them to predict our responses, we give up some control over our own behavior and transfer that control to them. If we want others to predict us so that they can anticipate and satisfy our desires and needs, we have to be willing to let them influence us as well. We have, in effect, to share the managerial role with them. Our unwillingness to do this often precludes the possibility of free and reciprocal interchange of influence and communication.

Everyone would agree that one purpose of communication is the sharing of information; however, we often fail to understand that another purpose of communication is the hiding of information. We often talk with the conscious or unconscious intent of inhibiting others in their attempts to learn about us. We communicate to hide. We communicate to raise barriers around us for self-protection.

In all the preceding discussion, several managerial stances have been implied. As summary, it may be helpful to review and relate them by looking at some typologies of managerial philosophy with respect to communication, empathy, and interpersonal relationships.

First, there is the managerial type who believes that meanings are in words and events rather than in people. This kind of stance implies that things will be said once — and only once. Effort will be expended in selecting the "correct" words and behaviors to express managerial objectives; however, little or no energy will be spent in predicting responses to messages, or in trying to anticipate the feelings of others and tailoring messages to fit. Little or no attention will be devoted to gathering information about others, to getting feedback on the effectiveness of communication, or to empathizing at all. Under this view, managerial communication consists primarily of telling people what they are supposed to do and assuming that they will do what they are told — if they are competent and motivated. When communication fails, an analysis is made as to which other person is responsible — and blame is assigned.

The second managerial type recognizes that meanings are in people and does analyze those with whom he works. But this analysis is strictly for instrumental purposes. The sole objective of the analysis is the gathering of data which will allow for better predictions of others, more effective influence of them, tighter control of them through communication. This manager carefully refrains from attempting to look at the world through another man's belief system except as a technical exercise. He might be typified by a statement of the order "I'm not interested in people as people, I'm just interested in people as statistics." This second type also refrains from giving any information about himself which might allow others to exert influence over him. He believes that management is a function and is to be performed solely by that subset of employees who are designated as managers.

A third managerial type recognizes that meanings are in people and empathizes constantly. He gains information about others and gives information about himself freely and with abandon. He can look at any given problem from everybody's point of view and can defend a large set of alternatives with equal rigor and vigor. He is interested in people as people and can empathize to the point where he begins to assume the personality of any individual with whom he is interacting, that is he sympathizes; consequently, he finds it difficult to take any action whatsoever when he is in a situation of ambiguity or tension. He begins to look on management as a human experience in which the goals and needs of all must be guaranteed at all times.

Our fourth and final type of manager has a communication orientation. He recognizes the inherent subjectivity of all interpersonal interaction. He recognizes that perfect communication is not possible and that some distortion of messages and breakdown of communication is inevitable. He carefully gathers all the data about others that is appropriate to the kind of situation in which he works. He empathizes but does not "become" the other person by sympathetic identification. He acknowledges the fact that empathy will change his outlook on the world and welcomes this experience, although he realizes that he must guard against it at times. He recognizes that others need information about him and provides it. He believes that management is a process in which all are engaged regardless of rank within the organization. He recognizes that influence is inherent in communication and encourages it up the chain of command as well as down. He does not attach blame to communication breakdowns, because he realizes they are inevitable. He also knows that when you pin responsibility for communication errors on people the chances of breakdown go up. He knows this himself, and he trains his staff to understand this, too.

One could argue that none of these types exists in its pure form within a given manager, although we may believe that some of the descriptions given apply fairly completely to managers we know. The communication bias clearly favors the fourth type. It is a useful exercise for the manager to ask himself three questions with respect to these typologies:

1. Which one best describes my present managerial behaviors?
2. Which one would most of my colleagues place me in?
3. How can I get my present behavior and others' perceptions of me closer to what they should be?

References

1. Asch, Solomon, *Social Psychology* (New York: Prentice-Hall, 1952).
2. Berlo, David K., *The Process of Communication* (New York: Holt, 1960).
3. Gompertz, Kenneth, "The Relation of Empathy to Effective Communication," *Journalism Quarterly*, XXXVII (1960), 533-46.
4. Halpern, H. M., "Predictive Empathy and the Study of Values," *Journal of Consulting Psychology*, XIX (1955), 449-52.
5. Jarrard, L. E., "Empathy: The Concept and Industrial Applications," *Personnel Psychology*, IX (1956), 157-67.
6. Lerner, Daniel, *The Passing of Traditional Society* (Glencoe: The Free Press, 1958).

7. MacLeish, Archibald, "The Poet and the Press," *Atlantic Monthly*, CCIII (1959), 40-46.
8. Mead, G. H., "A Behavioristic Account of the Significant Symbol," *Journal of Philosophy*, XIX (1922), 157-63.
9. Mead, G. H., *Mind, Self and Society* (Chicago: Univ. of Chicago Press, 1934).
10. Speroff, B. J., "Empathy and Role Reversal as Factors in Communication," *Journal of Social Psychology*, XLI (1955), 163-65.
11. Sullivan, H. S., *Conceptions of Modern Psychiatry* (Washington: W. A. White Psychiatric Foundation, 1947).

Chapter 7

Game Theory and
Administrative Decision-Making

William A. Gamson

Department of Sociology
University of Michigan

Game theory deals, most generally, with the study of decision-making in situations in which each individual must consider the actions of other individuals in making his own choices. Typically, it has focused on those situations in which there is some degree of conflict of interest between the parties involved. Perhaps the "theory of games" is an unfortunate title for a theory which covers situations that may involve our most vital interests and values. The word "game" connotes a certain frivolity and casual involvement that frequently seems inappropriate or even offensive. Schelling has suggested the "theory of interdependent decision,"[1] and this seems more suitable if considerably less catchy. At any rate, "game theory" remains the current usage, requiring the reminder that it covers a general theory of decision-making in conflict situations.

This paper is in no way an overall review or evaluation of game theory. It makes no attempt to examine such important questions as, for example, the current status of the theory of n-person games.[2] Here, the concern is with the effect on individuals of exposure to the style of thinking and concepts of game theory. Any theory focuses our attention on certain features and chooses to ignore others. To what new insights or clarifications of thought does game theory lead us? What confusions does it help us to avoid? And, finally, in what ways may its characteristic focus blind us to certain aspects of conflict situations?

[1]Thomas C. Schelling, *The Strategy of Conflict* (Cambridge: Harvard Univ. Press, 1960).
[2]For an excellent nontechnical review, see Martin Shubik, "Game Theory and the Study of Social Behavior: An Introductory Exposition," in Martin Shubik, ed., *Game Theory and Related Approaches to Social Behavior* (New York: Wiley, 1964).

Imagine an individual who is neither mathematician nor behavioral scientist. He is interested in neither the mathematical development of game theory nor the application of game theoretical models to behavioral science problems. However, in the normal course of his life, he is confronted with a great many decisions in which he must consider the possible choices of others when he makes his own choices. What might he learn from exposure to game theory?

The Live, Reacting Opponent

Consider the difference between a game of chance and one which involves a live, reacting opponent. The first kind, a *game against nature*, has many interesting features. A player may be faced with difficult choices of strategy in risky situations—for example, should he pursue a course with a small chance of a great payoff or, alternatively, one with a rather good chance of a very modest payoff? An essential feature of this decision is the fact that the choice he makes will not itself alter the probability that the strategy will lead to the desired outcome. Whether he chooses to bet on red or black in an honest game of roulette will not alter the probability of either of these colors coming up. The roulette wheel will not thwart or help him. Lady Luck may seem capricious at times, but her impersonality and indifference to efforts to charm her has been repeatedly demonstrated.

The situation changes fundamentally when the game involves a live, reacting opponent. Our strategy choices must now be based on the assumption that what our opponent does will depend in part on what he thinks or knows we will do. Of course, if our opponent is unaware of us or indifferent to our actions, then this situation is no different from a game against nature. But he may become aware and no longer indifferent if our actions begin to affect him. When our opponent is aware of us, a new dimension has entered—we must consider our own actions partly as communicative acts. To do so involves a kind of mental role-playing. We ask ourselves, if I were he and saw myself making such moves, what would I make of them and how would I respond?

The introduction of a live, reacting opponent gives game theory a certain amorality. The logic of the analysis creates a tendency to view opponents' strategic problems in the same spirit we view our own. The abstract, pure players in game theory are not "good guys" and "bad guys." One can as easily and naturally consider player A's strategic problems as player B's. By its built-in tendency to view the world from an opponent's vantage point in considering strategic problems, game theory contains a check on fanaticism, self-righteous crusading, and dogmatic ideology.

The style of analysis involved in game theory is a problem-solving mode that may be used by people with diametrically opposite goals. It does not tell us what we ought to want, but it does suggest how we ought to act, *given* that we have certain goals. For a person committed to a particular set of values, such open-mindedness may seem overly cool and detached. But zeal appeals only when the cause is one's own. When it is not, then the freedom from dogma in game theory represents the voice of reason and emancipation.

The distinction between a game against nature and one with an opponent seems simple enough, perhaps even obvious. Yet, note how the distinction can alter the validity of arguments on civil defense in the following example. If a nuclear war comes, the civil defense advocate often argues, it is certainly better to have fewer rather than more people killed. If the number of possible dead can be reduced at some reasonable cost, then surely it is desirable to do so. And even if the financial cost is high, surely we should not be deterred when human lives are at stake. Under this line of reasoning, the arguments of civil defense opponents appear open to ridicule, as in the following letter to the editor of the Harvard Crimson:

> It has been brought to our attention that certain elements among the passengers and crew favor the installation of "lifeboats" on this ship. These elements have advanced the excuse that such action would save lives in the event of a maritime disaster such as the ship striking an iceberg. Although we share their concern, we remain unalterably opposed to any considerations of their course of action for the following reasons:
>
> 1. This program would lull you into a false sense of security.
> 2. It would cause undue alarm and destroy your desire to continue your voyage on this ship.
> 3. It demonstrates a lack of faith in our Captain.
> 4. The apparent security which "lifeboats" offer will make our navigators reckless.
> 5. These proposals will distract our attention from more important things, i.e., building unsinkable ships. They may even lead our builders to false economies and the building of ships that are actually unsafe.

6. In the event of being struck by an iceberg (we will never strike first!) the "lifeboats" would certainly sink along with the ship.
7. If they do not sink, you will only be saved for a worse fate, inevitable death on the open sea.
8. If you should be washed ashore on a desert island, you will be unaccustomed to the hostile environment and will surely die of exposure.
9. If you should be rescued by a passing vessel, you would spend a life of remorse mourning over your lost loved ones.
10. The panic engendered by a collision with an iceberg would destroy all vestiges of civilized human behavior. We shudder at the vision of one man shooting another for the possession of a "lifeboat."
11. Such a catastrophe is too horrible to contemplate. Anyone who does contemplate it obviously advocates it.[3]

The analogy to a natural, maritime disaster may seem plausible enough until we remind ourselves that an iceberg is not a live, reacting opponent. The iceberg does not monitor the actions of the passengers and crew of the ship for information on their intentions. It does not make its own ship-striking behavior contingent to some extent on the actions of the passengers. The detached and indifferent (and, we might add, cool) iceberg will not alter its course because of the presence or absence of lifeboats; the probability of a maritime disaster is unaffected by the precautions taken on the ship in this game against nature.

This is not so, of course, if the game involves a live, reacting opponent. The game has been changed in a profound way which makes the satire of the lifeboat letter quite pointless. It is possible that a civil defense program will be monitored by an opponent for information on the intentions of the originator. If we put ourselves in the position of the iceberg, it is quite conceivable that we should find the initiation of a program for the evacuation of Soviet cities and the construction of massive fall-out shelters quite threatening. We might, for example, believe that it undermines the deterrent power of our nuclear weapons and leaves us open to nuclear blackmail. How we might react under such circumstances is a matter of conjecture, but at least the conjecture recognizes the contingent nature of the interaction between Soviet actions and our own.

---

[3]Herman Kahn, *Thinking About the Unthinkable* (New York: Horizon Press, 1962), pp. 88-89. Kahn introduces it as "Perhaps the best, if somewhat satirical, summary of the arguments against civil defense. . . ."

A Taxonomy of Games

In classifying conflict situations, game theory suggests what features are essential for understanding decision-making under conditions of conflict. The term zero-sum game has become part of the patois of many intellectuals with no specialized knowledge of game theory. Its use is often more related to the pretensions of the user than to the point he is making, but this should not blind us to the importance of the taxonomy of which the zero-sum category is a part. The fundamental distinction focuses on the relationship among the rewards or payoffs to the different players. A game is called "zero-sum" if the gains and losses of the players add up to zero regardless of the outcome. Thus, in a two-person zero-sum game, whatever one player wins the other necessarily loses.

The zero-sum game is a *pure conflict* game. There is no area of common interest among the players, and strategy is designed accordingly. Outside of the parlor, there are few such games. Most conflict is mixed with elements of common interest and interdependence. War, for example, is clearly not a zero-sum game since under some outcomes *both* parties may suffer severe losses. Strikes, house-buying, political maneuvering in a bureaucracy, and racial conflict are all nonzero-sum situations with important elements of mutual dependence as well as conflict. "These are the 'games,'" to quote Schelling, "in which, though the element of conflict provides the dramatic interest, mutual dependence is part of the logical structure and demands some kind of collaboration or mutual accommodation—tacit if not explicit—even if only in the avoidance of mutual disaster."[4]

Schelling has suggested that the zero-sum game serves as one limiting case in a theory of interdependent decision—the case of pure conflict. At the other end, we have the *pure collaboration* game in which players win or lose together since they have identical interests with respect to all outcomes. Such pure coordination games are essentially trivial under conditions of full communication—the players need simply coordinate their actions in their mutual interest. However, there are many situations in which the coordination problems are complicated by communication problems. Under such circumstances, these games have a good deal of intrinsic interest which Schelling has exploited brilliantly. To illustrate, imagine a man who loses his wife in a department store without any prior agreement on where they are to meet. What

---

[4]Schelling, *op. cit.*, p. 83.

strategy should he use for finding her? The problem involves the coordination of predictions about the other's behavior, "to identify the one course of action that their expectations of each other can converge on."[5]

One can gain insights by examining the way people handle a series of such problems in tacit coordination. Typical examples from Schelling include, "You are to meet somebody in New York City. You have not been instructed where to meet; you have no prior understanding with the person on where to meet; and you cannot communicate with each other. You are simply told that you will have to guess where to meet and that he is being told the same thing and that you will just have to try to make your guesses coincide," or, even simpler, "Name heads or tails. If you and your partner name the same, you both win a prize."

These may be regarded as problems whose solution embodies certain strategic principles. The "solution" may depend more on imagination than logic; any solution is arbitrary in the sense that, if an alternative also occurs to the other party as a solution, then it is a good one no matter how silly it may seem. The major characteristic of solutions to tacit coordination problems is the prominence of the alternative. A husband and wife who vigorously argued about the merits of a particular painting might well find it the most suitable meeting spot because it is still very much on their minds when they accidentally become separated in an art museum. Besides conspicuousness, uniqueness is an important and related principle. If the husband and wife in the art museum had disagreed on several paintings but agreed on only one, the latter would be a less ambiguous alternative despite the fact that they had less dramatic discussion about it. In sum, pure coordination games like pure conflict games isolate a recognizable class of situations with basically similar strategic problems.

Between the limiting cases of pure conflict and pure coordination games is a rich and varied assortment of situations involving *both* conflict and common interests. The prototype and most interesting of these *mixed motive* situations is the *prisoner's dilemma*. The name derives from an anecdote used to illustrate it.

> Two prisoners charged with the same crime are held incommunicado. If both confess, both can be convicted. If neither confesses, neither can be convicted. But if one confesses but the other holds out, the first not only goes scot free but gets a reward to boot, while the second gets a more severe punishment than he would have got if both

[5]*Ibid.*, p. 54.

confessed. Should a rational prisoner confess or hold out under these circumstances?[6]

The dilemma is a real one with no easy solution. If each pursues the reward, both suffer. If each is trustworthy, both gain. But the solution is unstable because a temptation exists for both parties. If one is *certain* that the other will be trustworthy, then it pays him to inform and gain the reward. If, on the other hand, he is certain the other will *not* be trustworthy, then it *still* pays him to inform because if he alone is trustworthy, then his penalty will be more severe. By such logic, both prisoners, unable to communicate, may be led to a solution in which both do worse than they would by remaining trustworthy.

The prisoner's dilemma has stimulated an increasing volume of research. It offers possibilities to study, in a controlled and systematic way, a conflict situation which contains many of the basic elements of everyday conflict situations. Rapoport has given precise meaning, in the prisoner's dilemma context, to such terms as trustworthiness, perfidy, forgiveness, vengefulness, greed, repentance, trust, and distrust.[7] One may examine a wide variety of situational and personality characteristics which are related to these behaviors. Such experimental conflict situations are likely to be a valuable source of insight for the participant as well as for the experimental observer.

Like the idea of a live, reacting opponent, the idea of a mixed-motive game seems a simple one. Yet, quite frequently, situations of this type are misconstrued as pure conflict or pure coordination games. To illustrate *both* tendencies, let us examine that complicated conflict or series of conflicts called the Cold War. The Soviet Union and the United States, the major protagonists in this conflict, have clear areas of common interest ranging from the avoidance of nuclear war as an absolute minimum to a large number of outcomes which both desire. Both may realize their own goals better, for example, through trade relations which bolster both economies; both might find their own goal realization aided by the containment of Chinese influence in Southeast Asia. On the other hand, there are conflicts of interest as well—each country wishes to maintain or extend its influence in some areas at the expense of the other.

This mixed-motive situation is sometimes treated as a pure con-

---

[6]Anatol Rapoport, *Strategy and Conscience* (New York: Harper and Row, 1964), p. 290.
[7]*Ibid.*, pp. 142-59.

flict situation. Consider the following arguments: "The Soviet Union desires a leveling off of the arms race so it can divert resources to non-military programs. It also desires increased trade with the Western nations as a way of bolstering its economy. Since the Soviet Union is our opponent, we should not aid it in these objectives," and "The Soviet Union would like to see Candidate X elected President of the United States. Therefore, we should all vote for Candidate Y." The validity of both of these arguments depends on the pure conflict assumption — only then does it follow that benefit to an adversary is injurious to one's own cause. If we are locked in a mortal struggle, then the actions which bolster the Soviet economy necessarily injure us. But once we admit the existence of common interests, then simply knowing how an action affects our opponent does not tell us how it affects us. Will a wheat deal with the Soviet Union help the United States economy and remove the cost of storing surplus grain? Will Candidate X, whom the Soviet Union prefers, help keep us out of war while protecting our vital interests? If so, then the fact that such outcomes happen to please the Soviet Union as well is adventitious. Only in a pure conflict situation can one infer the payoffs to one adversary from knowledge of the payoffs to the other.

United States-Soviet relations are also treated sometimes as a pure coordination game. People who see the avoidance of nuclear war as the overriding interest of both countries frequently view the actions of both major powers as a form of madness. In this view, the placement of missiles in Cuba, the American blockade of these missile shipments, the buzzing of American planes in the Berlin air corridor, the U-2 overflights of the Soviet Union are all manifestations of the failure of both countries to keep in mind their overriding common interest — the avoidance of nuclear war. The operative word in this argument is "overriding" for, as Wohlstetter points out, "to call this interest overriding boils down to saying that all other interests are unimportant, that they can and should be neglected."[8] This argument, then, amounts to an assumption that a pure coordination game is the most suitable model for United States-Soviet relations.

The existence of important elements of conflict does not make a situation one of pure conflict; where important elements of common interest exist, the situation is not simply one of pure coordination. The taxonomy of interdependent decision suggested by

---

[8]Albert Wohlstetter, "Sin and Games in America," in Shubik, *op. cit.*, p. 224.

Schelling is a conceptual tool which is useful in avoiding such mistakes.

Coalition Formation

The just-discussed taxonomy of games can be applied to situations involving more than two participants, i.e., the n-person game. Here, however, the zero-sum situation is no longer an adequate model of pure conflict since it is frequently possible for a sub-group of players to combine and gain at the expense of those who are excluded from the coalition. It seems useful in n-person games to define the limiting case of pure conflict as one in which coalitions are excluded. They may be excluded for two reasons: (1) There is no incentive for them since a coalition cannot increase the payoff that its members would get acting individually, that is, coalitions are unnecessary, or (2) the rules of the game prohibit coalitions — for example, by making communication and negotiation among the various players impossible.

Pure coordination games in the n-person case are characterized by the fact that there exists some solution which maximizes the reward for all players. In such situations, there is no reason to exclude any participant, since in pursuing his own interests he is aiding others to achieve their own. The problem the participants face is one of coordination and mobilization of all available resources for the most efficient achievement of the group's collective goal.

The mixed-motive, n-person game is one in which there are both elements of conflict and coordination. The central problem is the problem of coalition formation — who will join with whom under what kind of arrangement? There is an element of conflict guaranteed by the fact that all do not prefer the same outcome. There is an element of coordination guaranteed by the fact that there exists, for at least two of the players, the possibility that they can do better by coordinating their resources than by acting alone.

Some of the principles suggested by the theoretical and experimental work on coalition formation are not obvious — or, at least, not obvious until they have been stated explicitly. Two of these will serve for illustration. We may call them the Strength-Is-Weakness principle and the Playing-To-Win-Is-Playing-To-Lose principle.[9]

---

[9]The points made in the following sections are developed more fully in William A. Gamson, "Experimental Studies of Coalition Formation," in Leonard Berkowitz, ed., *Advances in Experimental Social Psychology* (New York: Academic Press, 1964), I.

1. Strength-Is-Weakness

It turns out, paradoxically, that in some clearly specifiable situations, the player who starts in the initially strongest situation is in the strategically weakest position. Because of his strength, he is likely to be excluded from any coalition which may occur. To illustrate this, imagine a political nominating convention with three leading candidates, each with absolute control over the votes of his followers. Candidate A, at the start of the convention, controls 48 per cent of the votes, Candidate B controls 30 per cent, and Candidate C controls 22 per cent, with a simple majority needed for nomination.

Now assume that the participants share an expectation that one ought to get from any agreement an amount proportional to what he brings into it. It follows from this "parity" principle that a coalition will form in which the total resources of the coalition are as small as possible while still being sufficient.[10] In the example given, this means that the coalition between B and C with 52 per cent of the vote will be preferred to A and B with 78 per cent or A and C with 70 per cent. Candidate A will find his initial position of strength to be a weakness for it will lead to his exclusion from the winning coalition.

It is not true, by any means, that initial strength is *always* weakness. Work on coalition formation suggests when this is true and when it is not. It makes explicit the conditions under which being the front-runner invites a coalition of opponents, but it also suggests conditions under which one ought to strive to be the front runner. In a more general way, it gives some sense of the dynamics of shifting alliances in multi-person conflict situations and makes the "strange bedfellows" of politics seem less mystifying.

2. Playing-To-Win-Is-Playing-To-Lose

This principle is quite similar to the Strength-Is-Weakness principle, but it refers to the style of play rather than to the initial strength in resources. In conflict situations in which coalitions are possible, a ruthless pursuit of one's interest may frequently backfire. If one is known to be a particularly hard and skillful bargainer,

---

[10]The argument is presented more fully in William A. Gamson, "A Theory of Coalition Formation," *American Sociological Review*, XXVI (June, 1961), 373-82. William Riker, *The Theory of Political Coalitions* (New Haven: Yale Univ. Press, 1962), arrives at an essentially similar point by a slightly different line of argument.

one who will exact whatever he can from any situation, he is likely to be a less attractive coalition partner than one who seems more tractable. It is one of the ironies of coalition situations that those players who make the least effort sometimes do best. Again, the significance of this principle is not simply to suggest strategies for devising winning coalitions, but to give greater insight into, for example, how some people manage to be their own "worst enemy."

Some Blindspots of Game Theory

The concepts employed in game theory alert us to certain significant aspects of decision-making in conflict situations. They suggest essential distinctions such as those between a game against nature and a game against an opponent and among pure conflict, pure coordination, and mixed-motive games. The prisoner's dilemma and the work on coalition formation are attempts to gain insight into extremely complex and omnipresent phenomena. Still, it is always possible that the style of thought and conceptualization of particular problems may act as blinders: By directing the focus in a particular way, important aspects of decision-making are blocked off.

Before examining such blindspots, it is worth pointing out an important advantage of game theory even when the content is imperfect. The advantage derives from the *explicitness* of assumptions in game theory in contrast to the elusive, implicit assumptions contained in more informal and less systematic discourses. The claim which Shubik makes for mathematical models in general is applicable here,

> If for no other reason, the application of mathematical methods to the study of human behavior has great value in that bad simple mathematical models can be spotted in far less time than bad verbal models. The same poor assumptions and conclusions clothed in four hundred pages of words require much more time to locate the basic structure and with it the errors, fallacies, and omissions.[11]

In short, if the "essentials" which are selected by game theory are misleading or too narrow, at least they are so clear and precise that one may specify with precision what they omit or distort. Clarity simplifies the critic's task and aids those who would do better.

---

[11]Shubik, *op. cit.*, p. 5.

Early Stages in the Decision Process

The world does not present us with a well-defined set of alternatives to which we can then attach a measure of value. Instead, we are presented with situations. Which aspects of these situations are defined as problematic and which are not is a matter of great consequence, for the problematic aspects will be acted on.

Game theory deals with the final stages of the decision process. It assumes a definition of the problem. It does not take the creation of a well-defined set of alternatives as something to be explained. Nor does it accept constraints from the existing social structure as problematic; such constraints are taken into account as part of the "rules of the game," but understanding their source and nature is not a matter of concern to the theory of games.

What important aspects of decision-making might we miss by such a late entry in the process? First, we might forget the fact that defining a problem in a particular way has many consequences for later choices. The statement of a set of alternatives is an implicit definition of a problem which itself acts as a major constraint. In many cases, it may be the critical part of the decision process. Once having defined the problem in a particular way, certain alternatives may appear so compelling that the problem of choice is then trivial.

It is not clear from game theory, for example, that the preparation of an agenda for a meeting is an important source of influence. An agenda is a rule for discussion and such rules are rarely completely neutral. By controlling the inclusion and exclusion of certain topics and their order of discussion, a particular orientation toward a problematic situation may be encouraged or discouraged. Similarly, the inclusion or exclusion of certain individuals with particular definitions of a problem is not important simply because of the preferences they might have on different alternatives; it affects the range and kinds of alternatives considered. Much of the influence of committee reports comes not from the persuasiveness of the arguments they muster to support their preferences but from the definition of the problem they impose. In sum, the process of arriving at a particular set of alternatives for consideration is no trivial stage in the total decision-making process.

Game theory also envisions players who know what they want. Their preferences for particular alternatives may change as they acquire more information about how these alternatives affect their goals, but the goals themselves are assumed to be stable. Game-theory man is not ambivalent; he is not simultaneously attracted and repelled by the same goal states.

Nor does game theory help us to understand the sudden shifts in intensity of commitment and involvement which seem to characterize many social movements. Individuals suddenly become willing to put aside their daily work and to risk personal injury or death by going to Selma, Alabama, to participate in a demonstration for Negro voting rights. Game theory can handle such actions after the fact by, for example, invoking such goals as self-esteem, which may be hurt by failure to participate in the Selma demonstrations. But the kind of radical shifts in the priority of goals which are involved in the social movement and the attendant mobilization of energy and resources which may significantly alter the outcome of a decision is not something to which game theory directs our attention.

Synoptic Decision-Making

Very much in the spirit of game theory and individual decision theory is a strategy of problem-solving which Braybrooke and Lindblom call "synoptic." The essence of the synoptic model is the "call for a systematic canvassing of possible alternative policies, for a similarly systematic analysis of the consequences of each possible alternative possibility, and for policy choices to serve goals or objectives somehow separately established."[12]

Braybrooke and Lindblom attack this advice strongly. The concession that a comprehensive search for alternatives is, after all, an ideal that can never be achieved in practice is no defense against the main thrust of their attack. They argue that it should not even be used as an abstract goal in making policy choices. Their argument centers on the failure of the synoptic model to incorporate simplifying strategies. "To insist on comprehensiveness," they point out, "is to rule out at the start many techniques for simplification, since omission is a chief principle of simplification." The synoptic model assumes the existence of a set of alternative policies but "the search for alternatives is an especially demanding and costly part of the problem-solving process."[13]

Against the synoptic model, Braybrooke and Lindblom match their strategy of "disjointed incrementalism." Boulding suggests, only half facetiously, that this strategy can be reduced to two propositions: (1) "Never do anything unless you have to; (2) If you

[12]David Braybrooke and Charles E. Lindblom, A *Strategy of Decision* (New York: The Free Press of Glencoe, 1963), p. 38.
[13]*Ibid.*, pp. 50, 51.

have to do anything, do as little as possible."[14] If the phrase "disjointed incrementalism" seems recondite, then it may bring joy to policy-makers when they discover that they have been speaking disjointed incrementalism all their lives. The strategy shuns comprehensiveness and limits investigation of alternatives to those whose known or expected consequences differ incrementally from the status quo. Thus it offers a solution for the basic problem of simplification which every decision-maker must face. The authors claim for their strategy the merit of reflecting and justifying what successful policy-makers actually do.

Policy Innovation

It may not be quite fair to tax game theory with the synoptic strategy of policy-making for they are connected in spirit rather than through any logical route. There are other reasons, however, for doubting the helpfulness of game theory with respect to policy innovations. A creative innovation frequently comes from a redefinition of a problem. Starting from certain premises, certain alternatives seem available and, yet, neither the one presently being pursued nor any of its competitors seems very adequate. The administrator in such situations is forced to pursue what appears to be the best of a bad lot.

However, his assumptions about the nature of the problem create a particular set which may make certain alternatives invisible or extremely difficult to conceive. To find a more satisfactory solution, the administrator must reorganize the problematic situation in such a way that new alternatives become visible. If we ask, for example, how we should respond to Communist aggression in Southeast Asia, we may find our choices highly restricted and unattractive. If we ask ourselves how we should deal with nationalist and anti-colonial forces in Southeast Asia when an opponent is attempting to exploit these forces for its own benefit, the list of alternatives will look quite different.

Game theory, in taking the players' goals and strategy alternatives as a starting point, does not seem to raise the sort of question that leads to reorganization. If the definition of the problem is taken as given, then all problems may be treated as technical ones.

---

[14]Kenneth Boulding in a review in the *American Sociological Review*, XXIX (December, 1964), 930-31.

Perhaps it is this tendency that leads some writers to feel that those who think in the game theory mode see events in a manner devoid of any sense of their human significance. By excessive focus on the rationality of means, the goals of action are left unquestioned. Rapoport suggests a grim, hypothetical case which carries such a tendency to its ultimate extreme:

> I tried to imagine what would happen if a scientist carried out and reported investigations that led to the arguments once presented by Jonathan Swift in his morbid essay [A Modest Proposal.] Suppose, I thought, a scientist felt concerned about the food problem in the post-nuclear-attack period and carried out calculations on how many adult lives could be saved by judicious utilization of babies' flesh. Being of a humanitarian disposition, the scientist would also be understandably concerned with the moral problem, but being a scientist, he would try to "solve" this problem also. At first he would convince himself that as far as the babies were concerned, there would be no suffering to speak of. The slaughtering could be carried out without the infliction of pain, and, of course, the babies would not be subjected to any mental anguish either, being unaware of what was happening. The real problem would be seen to lie in the attitudes of the adults, particularly of the parents of babies. Clearly then, our scientist would conclude, research should be directed along lines aimed at discovering means, possibly conditioning procedures, possibly narcotics, to remove the psychological obstacles to a rational solution of the food problem. If, say, a drug could be found that would do the trick (make parents less resistant to the scheme), the solution would be almost within grasp. Of course, the problem would still remain of how to induce adults to take the drug. But this problem could also be treated as a technological problem (as every problem can be made to appear) and its solution could be referred to appropriate specialists.[15]

One does not have to accept any given definition of a problem to use game theory. It is even possible to suggest that one has misconceived a particular situation, for example, as a pure conflict situation when it is a mixed-motive game. Still, the focus of the theory is on the appropriateness of alternative means. It lies beyond the province of the game theorist to ask if the players really want or need what they think they want.

---

[15]Rapoport, *op. cit.*, p. xxi.

Conclusion

Game theory is the source of many useful insights into decision-making under conditions of conflict. The distinctions between a game against nature and one against an opponent and among a pure conflict, a pure coordination, and a mixed-motive game are valuable pieces of intellectual baggage. So is the model of the prisoner's dilemma game; to understand that a conflict situation in which one is personally engaged fits this model might well be a major step in helping an administrator and some adversary avoid a mutually destructive set of actions. In conflict situations involving more than two parties, it is extremely helpful to understand when apparent strength may be weakness and vice-versa.

Game theory is less helpful in understanding certain other aspects of interdependent decision-making. In particular, by its focus on the late stages of the decision process, it does not help us to understand the kind of constraints which stem from the definition of the problem. Nor does it seem very helpful in understanding sharp changes in involvement and commitment of the sort that accompany social movements. It does not raise general questions about what goals players ought to be pursuing nor does it, in other ways, contain pressures to reexamine basic premises. Such limitations should not be taken as criticisms of game theory. It addresses itself to certain problems, as any theory does, and not to others. To point out limitations in this case is simply to warn against expecting the theory to be helpful on these questions which it does not address.

Chapter 8
Learning About Group Processes in Decision Making

Alvin Zander

Research Center for Group Dynamics
University of Michigan

Can a public administrator develop a broader perspective of the processes involved in group problem-solving and decision-making? The answer is certainly, Yes. There are facts, concepts, beliefs, and expectations for him to learn as well as patterns of interaction among these, and there is no great problem in comprehending what is currently known. But an understanding of group processes which will be useful in the day-by-day activities of a professional career requires more than a body of information. It requires an ability to use knowledge in identifying the nature of events, their origins, and their consequences. It demands, further, that the learner develop insight into himself, his style as an administrator, and the effects of his style. These noncognitive learnings are not easy to acquire and, thus, are likely to be fully grasped only when appropriate conditions for learning are present.

Can a public administrator who has attained a broader perspective be taught to use this information wisely on his job? The answer once more is, Yes, of course. But appropriate conditions must again be present if he is to make the best application of his knowledge and if he is to help his colleagues benefit from his learnings.

Under what conditions will a public administrator develop a better understanding of group processes and a better use of these learnings in his career? Under what conditions will he fail to do these things? Our purpose is to consider answers to these queries. In doing so we draw in part upon concepts and results of research in group dynamics. The study of group dynamics attempts to identify the laws of behavior in groups, to learn why groups behave as they do, and to explain why they have particular effects upon their members. We also borrow from the writings of persons who have a special interest in teaching leaders and members how to be skilled performers in their social units.

Understandings of Group Processes

There are several approaches one may adopt in studying phenomena in groups. What a person actually learns depends upon which of these approaches guides his efforts. Each tends to make salient separate features of the interaction among members.

One approach is immediately familiar. It requires that a person attend to the issues and arguments involved in a conference, evaluate the soundness of the evidence presented by participants, weigh the validity of the logic employed, and consider the rewards and costs inherent in the alternative solutions offered. The student, in brief, is primarily interested in the content and value of the ideas put forth in the discussion. This is a familiar approach since it concerns what is most easily seen when observing a conference — the process of decision-making.

There can be no doubt that a good administrator, whether he be chairman, consultant, or member, must be skilled in discussing the substantive topics of his profession. His training and experience equips him to do these well. But there is more to group decision-making than this. Indeed, the capable social engineer is one who can perceive at levels of awareness beyond the substantive discussion, who can see a variety of phenomena which are significant in determining the nature of the group's decision. Cyert and March contend that many decisions in business firms are not at all the product of rational problem-solving.[1] Bales has developed an observation check list to be used in exhaustively categorizing all of the behaviors displayed by members in a problem-solving meeting. Half of his twelve categories are concerned with the task of the group, asking questions and seeking answers. But the other half are concerned with what he calls social-emotional behaviors, positive and negative reactions to ideas and styles of behavior offered in the meeting.[2] His research demonstrates that in many problems these social-emotional behaviors are not noise in the system but are as

---

[1]R. Cyert and J. March, *A Behavioral Theory of the Firm* (Englewood Cliffs, N. J.: Prentice-Hall, 1963).
[2]Robert F. Bales, *Interaction Process Analysis: A Method for the Study of Small*

pertinent to the quality of the group's solution as the members' task-oriented behaviors. This first approach, then, is important but narrow.

In a second approach, the learner seeks to understand basic theories developed by social scientists. He learns what properties in a group generate particular consequences in the behaviors or products of the members and why. There is more to be mentioned here than it is useful to describe. A recent volume by Barry Collins and Harold Guetzkow, provides a valuable review of these group properties. Material in this book and others demonstrates that an adequate psychology of putting heads together is developing.[3] Consider the following examples of pertinent findings.

Sets of individuals go about problem-solving in ways that are quite different from the methods used by persons working independently of one another. When groups are at work, moreover, interpersonal relations among members often become obstacles to effective performance. The ability of one member to influence others decides the quality of the group's decision, and his power to influence can arise from various sources. The differences in social power among a number of people affects their behavior toward one another, their expectations, their frequency of communication, and the content of their messages as well as their readiness to accept certain solutions. The style of communication among those around a conference table is determined by a set of variables such as the importance of the topic, participants' expertness on the topic, the value of the group for the member, and the persons who are taking unpopular positions in the group. Interpersonal conflicts arise in a group if members have similar goals and if resources are scarce, or if the goals among members are too different. Interpersonal trust and a willingness to engage in rational thinking, rather than to affect laden defenses of own views, are necessary for resolution of conflicts. Members who understand how others feel about a given situation or who understand themselves well, two different aspects of what is commonly called social empathy, are better able to perceive what is going on in a group.

There is a body of evidence, then, indicating what leads to what in face-to-face conferring. Ideally, with the aid of such information, a manager who desires situation X to exist in his organization need only create that condition (Y) which is known to generate X.

---

[3]B. Collins and H. Guetzkow, *A Social Psychology of Group Processes for Decision Making* (New York: Wiley, 1964). Also see D. Cartwright and A. Zander, eds., *Group Dynamics: Research and Theory* (Evanston: Row, Peterson, 1960); and G. Homans, *Social Behavior: Its Elementary Forms* (New York: Harcourt, 1961).

Because theories of group behavior reveal how certain consequences can be generated by particular conditions, it is usually true, although paradoxical on the face of it, that men of affairs find more value and ease of application in abstract and explanatory material than they do in descriptive accounts of phenomena, even though these accounts may be more closely related to the administrators' work experiences.

A third approach to the study of groups examines the abilities necessary for a person to participate effectively in group problem-solving or decision-making. Three types of skills have been described by Matthew Miles.[4] They are phrased in terms of training problems or needs.

Sensitivity. How confident am I of the things I notice in the interaction among members? Do I have blind spots—are there things members do that I never seem to notice? Or do I notice certain things especially well—such as going off on a tangent—because they bother me personally in some way or have special significance for me?

Diagnostic ability. Do I understand why person X seems to be getting off on tangents? Is it a case of the group's goal not being clear? Or is it that person X would like to be the center of things? Or is it that the group does not care to work on this particular topic and would rather be doing something else? Am I or someone else failing to do whatever is needed in order to move the group along?

Action skill. Can I speak up and help the group by doing whatever is necessary? Can I do it in a way that will be useful? What will be the consequences? Can I take care of those consequences?

A fourth approach is suggested by the previous ones. It emphasizes that there are several domains of concepts, theories, and skills in understanding events in groups. These domains are cognitive, affective, and behavioral. To comprehend fully the complications of group decision-making, certain cognitions must be attained by the administrator in training (cognitive domain). He must also generate an understanding of his own expectations and methods of defense (affective domain) and must practice ways of behaving in accord with his intentions (behavioral domain). An administrator is a man of action. He must know laws of social behavior, but he must be able to use these understandings in his work with others. He requires, then, a rare combination of social engineering skill and knowledge. Teaching and understanding of group processes by

---

[4]M. Miles, *Learning to Work in Groups* (New York: Teacher's College, Columbia Univ., 1959).

appropriate coverage of each of these domains has been discussed by Watson and Lippitt, Miles, and Bradford, Gibb and Benne.[5] Adequate treatment of this fourth approach would probably cover most of the other approaches as well.

Conditions for Effective Learning

There is quantitative evidence that persons can improve their comprehension of cognitive, affective, and behavioral conditions of groups and of themselves as members. Dorothy Stock has summarized the results from many empirical investigations into the results of training for group membership. Briefly, she reports that all of the following have been affected by opportunities for learning about group processes: perceptions of the self, own affective behavior, perceptions of congruity between self-percept and how one would prefer himself to be, sensitivity to the feelings or behavior of others, role flexibility, awareness of procedures in reaching group decisions, ability to diagnose difficulties in a group, behavioral skills, and self-confidence.[6]

Not all people make these changes as a result of an opportunity for learning, just as some persons never learn to be administrators. For most individuals these changes occur only if the conditions are appropriate. Some of these conditions have been identified: What a person is like when he enters training seems to have a great deal to do with the learning he takes away with him. He must have a readiness to learn, aroused by an awareness of an inadequacy in his performance.[7] But he must not be anxious about his needs since these persons appear to learn less in such a setting.[8] He must not have a strong need to protect his perception of himself if he is adequately to enter into consideration of changing his managerial methods.[9]

---

[5]Jeanne Watson and R. Lippitt, *Learning across Cultures* (Ann Arbor: Institute for Social Research, Univ. of Michigan, 1955); Miles, *op. cit.*; L. Bradford, J. Gibb, and K. Benne, eds., *T-Group Theory and Laboratory Method* (New York: Wiley, 1964).

[6]D. Stock, "A Survey of Research on T-Groups," in Bradford, Gibb, and Benne, *op. cit.*

[7]Dorothy Stock, "Factors Associated with Change in Self-Percept," in D. Stock and H. Thelen, eds., *Emotional Dimensions of Group Culture* (New York: New York Univ. Press, 1958); S. Mathis "Development and Validation of a Trainability Index for Laboratory Training Groups," unpublished doctoral dissertation, Univ. of Chicago, 1952.

[8]Jeanne Watson, "Some Social-Psychological Correlates of Personality," unpublished doctoral dissertation, Univ. of Michigan, Ann Arbor, 1952.

[9]Mathis, *op. cit.*

Certain properties of the learning situation make it more likely that one will develop a better understanding of group events and one's own behavior. Students of training in group interaction emphasize that the following conditions are necessary:

(1) An opportunity for the trainee to learn basic concepts by reading, listening to lectures, and observing groups at work.

(2) Membership for the trainee in a discussion group which is given maximal freedom to develop its own goals and methods and a minimal amount of limitation or definition of a member's tasks—a group learning laboratory.

(3) Members are expected to participate actively, and to observe the nature of their own behavior and that of others.

(4) Topics of discussion which become, under the guidance of a professional teacher, descriptions of the events in the group itself, attempts to understand why those present perceive the same event differently, overt discussions of their reactions, and efforts to identify the origins and effects of these. Participants will learn, in short, what to perceive in interpersonal phenomena and how to explain among members cause and effect in the processes which elsewhere are seldom discussed, except in anger or dismay. These discussions are a form of feedback, new inputs of information into the system of learning and its parts.

(5) For the events in (4) to occur effectively, members must develop a climate in which they trust one another to be helpful rather than derogatory or degrading in their interactions.

(6) Given the foregoing, the learner must try out new forms of belief, feeling, or action while he is secure in the knowledge that the consequences will be suitable for learning and growth rather than potentially damaging to him.

(7) The trainee must be provided a chance to plan new behaviors which he will employ on his job and an opportunity to hear appraisal and evaluation of these plans.

(8) The trainee must be given follow-up advice, at a later time, based on appropriate evaluation and reinforcement in order that he might maintain the will and the skill to apply his learnings in his professional work.

Transfer of Training

We have said that there is much to learn about group behavior and that people can learn these many things, even when it requires changes in attitudes or interpersonal skills to do so. We have illustrated, in passing, types of learnings one may develop about group processes. We have stressed that appropriate conditions are necessary to foster such learning.

Easier learning and performance in situation *Q* because of previous learning about situation *P* occurs if there is transfer of training. To be maximally effective, an administrator must be able to transfer his training from classroom, study, laboratory, or previous professional experience to a new setting. It is useful to consider examples of evidence that this transfer can occur, scattered and incomplete though the evidence is. We will review (1) changes in a person's behavior on the job as a result of past training, (2) changes in the behavior of his immediate set of colleagues, and (3) changes in the larger system as a result of shifts in either (1) or (2).

1. Modifications in Professional Behavior

Miles examined the behavior of school administrators before and after a three-weeks training experience in managerial skills. His data were perceptions of the trainees by the person himself and by his colleagues. These protocols provided a measure of the amount of alteration in behavior over a ten-month period following the training program. The amount of change among trainees was compared with that among members of a matched control group who were not trained. The trained persons changed more than the untrained ones in the areas of increased sensitivity to others, equalitarian attitudes, and skills of communication and leadership. Trainees also modified certain personal traits, such as "more considerate, relaxed," and their ways of managing, such as "delegates more, aids group decision making."[10]

Bunker used the same type of pre and post measurements. He reports that after they had returned to their jobs from training participants were more clear in their communications, more willing to share responsibility with others, and more skilled in the analysis of interpersonal behavior.[11]

Lippitt describes changes in behavior among community-relations workers as a result of attending a workshop on problems related to their professional concerns. Six months after the training Lippitt reports that alterations included "a broadened view of the

[10]M. Miles, "Human Relations Training: Processes and Outcomes," *Journal of Counselling Psychology*, VII (1960), 301-6.
[11]D. Bunker, "Individual applications of Laboratory Training," *Journal of Applied Behavioral Science*, I (1965), 131-48.

problems of community relations, motivation to become more active in contributing to the solution of these problems, more effective use of specific skills in stimulating and leading others, more sophisticated planning of action strategy, new confidence in own potenialities and in available resources, and personal changes in prejudiced attitudes."[12]

Boyd and Elliss measured the effects of managerial training (called seminars) in a Canadian utility. They compared the consequences of laboratory training with the effects of a program consisting of case studies and lectures. As in the previously mentioned investigations, changes were assessed by obtaining information from colleagues of the trainees as well as from the participants themselves. Those who took part in the seminars changed to a significantly greater degree than those in the other program. The contents of the alterations are described by Boyd and Elliss as follows.

> One of the most frequently reported changes in behavior for the seminar groups was an increase in listening, which accounts for about 12 per cent of the reports. By listening is meant paying more attention to what other people are saying, being easier to communicate views to, and so forth. Equally frequent is better understanding and better contributions in group situations, such as in meetings. Third, but still accounting for 10 per cent of the comments was an increase in tolerance and flexibility. To a lesser extent the seminar participants were said to have more self-confidence and to express themselves more effectively.[13]

A consistent theme in the results of these investigations is that the participant develops greater sensitivity to his own effects upon others and to the motives and beliefs of others. We earlier called this social empathy. Margaret Luszki studied the effects of empathy in a careful laboratory experiment. She indentified persons who had developed different degrees of empathy as a result of their membership in small training groups. She observed that those who had greater empathy were more able to perceive, indentify, and accurately report events in a standardized group meeting acted out before them as part of the experiment than were those who had less empathy. Participants who had greater empathy, moreover, tended

---

[12]R. Lippitt, *Training in Community Relations* (New York: Harper, 1949).
[13]J. B. Boyd and J. D. Elliss, *Findings of Research into Senior Management Seminars* (Toronto: Personnel Research Department, The Hydro-Electric Power Commission of Ontario, 1962).

to be better adjusted personally and more mature.[14] Stotland reports that teams of persons were better able to persevere toward their own goals, rather than defer to an obstructing authority figure, the more they were confident that they knew what their teammates were thinking—a reasonable indicator of empathy.[15] It seems evident that empathy is a useful attribute of the effective administrator. It is likely, furthermore, that empathy can be best developed via a type of training that provides practice in this skill—book-learning is not enough.

2. Changes in Group Performance

An administrator who has changed his methods should be a source of change among his colleagues. Ideally, he should be a point of contagion for practices and procedures which improve the operations of any group in which he has a part. Although many of us have seen some one member be an effective influence for the improvement of a group's procedures, or a potent wrecker of a group for that matter, there is no empirical research into such problems.

Anecdotes abound describing situations in which a chairman or some insightful member leads the group into a discussion of its methods of work. Often, the member stimulates greater enthusiasm for his induction by providing data he has gathered in private about the frequency of participation among members, the number of times topics are left hanging, or some other innocuous piece of objective information which serves to get the conversation going. Such discussions, when well handled, can in principle generate important modifications in the methods of a working group. Indeed, the effort of managerial committees to improve their ways of work, with the aid of a counselor, is quite fashionable these days. We know of a managerial consultant who is fully occupied in advising top management committees how to improve their daily decisions.

We believe that it is possible for one member to attain the informal position of group consultant or teacher of group process, provided he is not rejected by others in the group for making an

---

[14]Margaret B. Luszki, "Empathic Ability and Social Perception,"unpublished doctoral dissertation, Univ. of Michigan, Ann Arbor, 1951.

[15]E. Stotland, "Peer Groups and Reactions to Power Figures," in D. Cartwright, ed., *Studies in Social Power* (Ann Arbor: Institute for Social Research, Univ. of Michigan, 1959).

attempt to do so. We base this belief, however, not upon studies which have followed up the effects of training but upon experiments in the modification of behavior. A number of investigations have demonstrated that attempts to influence a group have had consequences for the behavior of all members in ways relevant to our interests. It is useful to illustrate a few of these studies, especially those in which the agent of influence behaved in ways which were readily available to him and which were easy to perform.

Hastorf changed the participation rate of members and the approval accorded to these individuals by fellow members. In his experiment he first measured the frequency of participation of each member and the amount of regard accorded to each by groupmates. This was done by observing the discussion in the group on a standard topic. The member who was third from the top on these two criteria was then chosen as the *target person*. While the group discussed a second topic, the observers (said to be experts on group discussion) gave the members signs of approval or disapproval by means of red or green lights; each member was able to see the lights meant for him but could not see others' lights. A green light indicated that the statement just made (or the lack of participation in the last few exchanges) was a good one which was likely to be helpful to the group in the future. A red light indicated that a statement just made (or the lack of a statement) was bad and would hinder the group in the future. The target person was shown many more green lights than red ones in a prearranged program which had nothing to do with what he actually said. The other three members were given many more red lights than green ones. As a result the target person greatly increased his participation during the discussion of the second topic while the other members reduced their talking. At the end of the discussion, moreover, the target person rose in the esteem of the members and the others decreased in value. The reinforcement of the one member and the lack of reinforcement of the others had strong effects upon changing behavior.[16]

Obviously red and green lights need not be used in committee meetings. Wolff, for example, had fairly similar results from an experiment in which the chairman approved of certain remarks by members and disapproved of others. He found, in addition, that members who were approved more often were more attracted to the

---

[16]A. Hastorf, "The Reinforcement of Individual Actions in a Group Situation," in L. Krasner and L. Ullman, eds., *Research in Behavior Modification* (New York: Holt, 1965).

group than those who were disapproved more often.[17] Zander and Cohen observed that members provided more approval and acceptance to those in the group whom they had been led to believe were high in status and less approval and acceptance to those whom they believed were low in status. As a consequence, the individuals so treated (who were not aware that they had the status attributed to them by groupmates) were considerably more comfortable and outgoing in the former case than in the latter.[18] Because providing approval and disapproval is fairly easy for a chairman or a member to do and because it has clear consequences, it supports the belief that the behavior of a group as a unit can be modified by one who wishes to do so.

In an experiment closely related to the type we have just been considering, Emmy Pepitone increased the amount and quality of effort members exerted in a group by making them believe that their work was more important for the social unit. The participants in her experiment worked out of sight of one another. Half of these persons were told that their work was very important to the group and the other half that their output was a preliminary step for the group's performance. All members had, in fact, the same task to perform. Those who were told that they had the more important assignments produced more and better quality of output than those who were told that they had less important duties.[19] Burnstein and Zajonc have observed that persons who were promoted to higher status levels improved their quality of work while those who were demoted to lower status levels decreased their quality of work.[20] Thus, a member's evaluation of the role he is asked to occupy has noteworthy implications for the amount and usefulness of his effort.

The examples we have been citing may be conceived of as attempts to increase responsibility forces on a member, that is, forces acting on the member to behave in ways needed by others. Thomas has reported that members are more likely to feel responsibility toward the group, and thus to work harder in behalf of the group, the more they perceive that all members are in an interdependent relationship, a relationship in which each needs the work

[17]R. J. Wolff, "The Value of Member Contributions as a Determinant of Attraction to Group," unpublished doctoral dissertation, Univ. of Michigan, Ann Arbor, 1953.
[18]A. Zander and A. R. Cohen, "Attributed Social Power and Group Acceptance," *Journal of Abnormal and Social Psychology,* LI (1955), 490-95.
[19]Emmy Pepitone, "Responsibility to the Group and Its Effects on the Performance of Members," unpublished doctoral dissertation, Univ. of Michigan, Ann Arbor, 1952.
[20]E. Burnstein and R. Zajonc, "Individual Task Performance in a Changing Social Structure," *Sociometry,* XXVIII (1965), 16-29.

of others to do his own part.[21] We assume that greater interdependence is created in a group when it is to be rewarded or punished as a unit than when each member is to be rewarded or punished for his own individual effort. Zander and Wolfe examined this assumption in a study of managerial committees in a large utility. The committees were brought into a laboratory setting and were either told that they would be evaluated and rewarded on the basis of the group's total performance or that each separate member's output would be evaluated and individually rewarded. They were constrained to work on a task which resulted in better scores (for individuals and the group) the more that members collaborated with one another. The group reward condition generated better relations among members and more responsibility toward the group than did the individual reward condition.[22] Responsibility to the group has been created in experiments by Deutsch and by Raven and Euchus.[23] Here again, a relatively simple change in the views of members had important consequences for their behavior in the work of the group.

Confusion among members about the exact goal or path to the goal commonly creates discoordination among members. Raven and Rietsema varied the degree that members understood what they were doing and why they were doing it. Those who were more clear about their group's goal and the path to the goal produced more and had better interpersonal relations than those who were confused about the goal and the procedures on the task.[24]

A manager who would maximally improve his perspective on group processes, we have earlier asserted, must have feedback which helps him to revise and redirect his efforts. This point is no less true in attempts to improve the performance of a group. Zajonc for example, has demonstrated that the productivity of members is improved if they learn how well they are doing as individuals and as a group.[25]

---

[21]E. J. Thomas, "Effects of Facilitation and Interdependence on Group Functioning," *Human Relations*, X (1957), 347-66.

[22]A. Zander and D. Wolfe, "Administrative Rewards and Coordination among Committee Members," *Administrative Science Quarterly*, IX (1964), 50-69.

[23]M. Deutsch, "The Effects of Cooperation and Competition upon Group Process," *Human Relations*, II (1949), 129-52, 199-231; B. Raven and R. Euchus, "Cooperation and Competition in Means Interdependent Triads," *Journal of Abnormal and Social Psychology*, LVII (1963), 307-16.

[24]B. Raven and J. Rietsema, "The Effects of Varied Clarity of Group Goal and Group Path upon the Individual and His Relation to the Group," *Human Relations*, X (1957), 29-44.

[25]R. Zajonc, "The Effects of Feedback and Probability of Group Success on Individual and Group Performance," *Human Relations*, XV (1962), 149-61.

The use of data concerning aspects of the organization, so that these can be compared with evaluative criteria and so that decisions may be made about necessary changes in operations, is a familiar event in business firms, governmental agencies, political parties, and military units. These self-measurements are further examples of feedback about a group to a group. It has often happened, however, that the data gathered in a burst of enthusiasm for self-appraisal is later ignored and does not function as feedback at all. The problems involved in the effective use of feedback by organizations are themselves amenable to study and have become primary interests of the newly created Center for Research on the Utilization of Scientific Knowledge in the Institute for Social Research at The University of Michigan.

Self-study has been used not only by individuals and groups to examine their own processes but also by pairs of groups who have recognized that social conflicts exist between them and that remedies are needed. Blake and colleagues describe in stimulating detail the efforts of a group of managers and a group of labor representatives to understand one another by engaging in a two-day learning experience set up for that purpose. Since much of the effort by the members of the two groups required description and examination of their own group as well as the other group, their report also provides evidence that groups qua groups can help themselves to improve their own operations as well as, in this case, the relations between groups.[26]

What if all members in a group had a better understanding of group processes? Would better meetings result? Not necessarily. Training is no substitute for the desire to perform as well as one knows how to do. If all members have a better perspective on the problems inherent in collaborative effort, it seems reasonable to suppose that they are thereby equipped to improve the performance of the group if they desire to do so. Specifically, each member should be able to draw upon cognitions and behaviors which are helpful, to assist others to do their best, to understand more fully the needs of the organization, and, thereby, to make the social unit more effective in its joint efforts. The contention that groups might be improved in decision-making or problem-solving because their members are trained, in summary, rests on the assumption that a trained participant can help his group learn from past experience (as he has done) or that he can create properties in the group which have the consequences he and others value.

---

[26]R. Blake, Jane Mouton, R. Sloma, "The Union-Management Intergroup Laboratory: Strategy for Resolving Intergroup Conflict," *Journal of Applied Behavioral Science*, I (1965), 25-57.

3. Effects on the Larger System

Consideration of the effects in the larger organization resulting from the training of members and smaller groups, requires a generous use of speculation. We assume that the laws which govern behavior in smaller groups operate in larger groups even though the number of persons involved may introduce phenomena which strengthen or weaken adherence to these laws. There is support for this assumption in research on large organizations which has drawn upon theories originally tested in group experiments. Theories about societies or large associations have also been used in studies of behavior in small groups. Thus, there is no compelling reason to assume that we need separate theories for large and small groups.

Those who cannot comfortably accept this last assumption may remind themselves that large organizations are composed of smaller departments, bureaus, and the like. It is no doubt true that the most meaningful events for a member of a large organization occur within these smaller social units. Rensis Likert in *New Patterns of Management* devotes much of his discussion about effective administration to the activities of the manager in his staff meetings.[27]

Within each work group, moreover, each man has a limited number of persons who prescribe duties and expectations for him. Kahn and associates call these "role sets" and demonstrate that a manager's view of himself, his work, and his organization is largely determined by his set of satellite persons. He, in turn, can influence these satellites.[28]

If we accept that a person can be trained and that, as a result, he can help his own group, it follows that he can have as much effect upon the larger system as the smaller group has power within that system. Clearly, the more powerful the influencing agent, or the more powerful the group he influences, the more his efforts will have consequences for the larger organization. The largest consequences in any system, it would seem, occur when men at the top are changed and then seek to change others.

Conditions Fostering Transfer of Training

We have noted that learning his lesson well, having a strong faith in the value of training, and even committing himself to practical

---

[27]R. Likert, *New Patterns of Management* (New York: McGraw-Hill, 1959).
[28]R. Kahn, D. Wolfe, R. Quinn, D. Snoek, and R. Rosenthal, *Organizational Stress* (New York: Wiley, 1963).

use of such knowledge is not a guarantee that the trainee will be different on his job. It is fairly common, as an example, for a company to put foremen into a supervisory training program, to establish that the men learned and approved of the offerings, and yet to observe that many foremen do not apply their learnings when back at work. Why is this?

In a study of how much managerial trainees applied the teachings given them in a course on human relations sponsored by their company, Hariton observed that men whose superiors favored the content of the training given to the subordinates (usually because it agreed with the superiors' beliefs) were likely to behave in accord with the training; whereas those who had disapproving superiors behaved as though they had not taken the training course.[29] In another study (unpublished), training was found to be repressed by those who had received it because it made the student's practices too different from those followed by his colleagues. Thus, established customs may serve as restraints to the person who desires to change his style on his job. The remedy is apparent in the results. In order to prevent himself from objecting, the boss should be a learner before his subordinates are exposed. And in order for group standards to serve as supports rather than obstacles, the peers should be trained at the same time.

In his book, *Training in Community Relations*, Lippitt offers experimental evidence showing the value of social support in learning. Half of the participants attended a workshop as members of a team from their community. The other half came as solo trainees. Observations a number of months after the workshop revealed that those who were members of teams put more of their training into action than those who came alone.[30] Public agreements among managers to conform to certain practices in administration have been shown to generate more adherence to these agreements than individual and private pledges to follow the plan.[31]

The more an individual can link his learnings about group behavior to events in his everyday life, the more it is likely that his training will influence his assumptions and behavior in his work.

[29]T. Hariton, "Conditions Influencing the Effects of Training Foremen in New Human Relations Principles," unpublished doctoral dissertation, Univ. of Michigan, Ann Arbor, 1951.
[30]Lippitt, *op. cit.*
[31]L. Coch and J. R. P. French, Jr., "Overcoming Resistance to Change," *Human Relations*, I (1948), 512-32; J. Levine and J. Butler, "Lecture versus Group Discussion in Changing Behavior," *Journal of Applied Psychology*, XXXVI (1952), 29-33.

Miles tested this hypothesis, assuming that school administrators who had specific plans for change in their schools would more often apply what they had learned than officials who had vague plans unrelated to professional problems. His results did not validate the hypothesis, but it is so eminently sensible that it should have further study.[32]

Other untested hypotheses about the conditions which encourage transfer of training appear to be researchable. Administrators whose training increases their self-regard are more likely to act out their learnings. Those who are least afraid of uncertainty and ambiguity will more often attempt the changes that application of their knowledge implies. Participants who place high value on what they have learned and who believe that acting in accord with their knowledge can improve their social environments will more probably take the prescribed actions. Individuals who are members of an organization which values flexibility and creative problem-solving will be more favorable toward trying out new beliefs or behaviors. Persons who value promotions but perceive that there is little chance of getting ahead in their present place of employment will probably be most hesitant about trying unfamiliar forms of administrative behavior.

It would be helpful if we could confidently assure ourselves that the training of administrators had favorable effects upon their careers. Certainly most public and private organizations these days would assert that promotions are granted on the basis of ability rather than the race, color, or creed of the individual. Yet, it is possible that ability, and we may assume the improvements in ability created via training, may be more honored in the public relations handout than in the practices of those who decide promotions or other rewards. In a recent study of prejudice within a large firm which publicly denied that it allowed prejudice to determine promotions, Kahn and colleagues noted that criteria other than competence sneaked into decisions about the futures of men because the qualities required for many jobs were vague and thus unwittingy open to unsound judgments and because the fate-deciders incorrectly believed that others would disapprove of a nonprejudiced decision about a man in question who was a member of a minority group.[33] Would an administrator whose training makes him a deviant suffer the same fate?

---

[32]Miles, op. cit.
[33]R. Kahn, G. Gurin, R. Quinn, Ellen Baar, and A. Kraut, Discrimination without Prejudice (Ann Arbor: Institute for Social Research, Univ. of Michigan, 1964).

Summary

Men can be trained to improve their understanding and participation in group decision-making or problem-solving, or they can teach themselves to do so. They can also learn how to help others to learn. How well they adopt these learnings and how well they apply them, however, depends upon the presence of conditions which give support and practice in experimenting with new beliefs, attitudes, and behaviors.

IV Values, Ideology and Innovation

Chapter 9

Ideology and Administration:
A Case Study in Israel[1]

Alan Arian

Department of Political Science
Tel Aviv University

Ideology is inexorably involved in effective development and administration since societal values are generally formulated in ideological terms. The interactions between the public servant, his organization's ideology, and the societal ideology will be as important in determining his effectiveness as will his mastery over technical skills or human relations techniques.

It is obvious that the public servant will be affected by the accepted societal ideology just as he is by the pressures generated by more particularistic forces. While there are studies which deal with pressures from interest groups and political parties, the universalistic pressures—the societal ideology, the "public philosophy"—are generally overlooked.[2] In the public administration literature, little mention is made of the relevance of the societal ideology to the administrator.[3]

The existence of a societal ideology will have its effect upon the individual. Even an individual who is ideologically uncommitted will be affected by the general inclination toward given views. It is likely that this exposure will be even more pronounced in the case of a public servant who is highly exposed and contactable.

A preliminary attempt at studying the relations between the public servant and the societal ideology will be presented here. After developing a framework for the study based on role theory, it

[1] I wish to thank Professor Robert Scigliano for a careful reading of an earlier draft of this chapter.
[2] This is "macroscopic role consensus." See Neal Gross, Ward S. Mason, and Alexander McEachern, *Explorations in Role Analysis* (New York: Wiley, 1958), Ch. 7.
[3] See for example Herbert A. Simon, Donald W. Smithburg, and Victor A. Thompson, *Public Administration* (New York: Knopf, 1964), pp. 369-74.

will be applied to a case study dealing with legislators and senior civil servants in Israel.

I

It is my contention that decreased public acceptance of an ideology will cause stress, over time, in those members of a society who are expected to function in terms of that ideology. Change is generally accompanied by stress. Revolutions and elections both produce stress while facilitating change. Geographical movement, added education and adjustments in socioeconomic positions, produce stresses of varying degree.

An indicator of the decreasing acceptance of societal ideology, then, will be the extent of stress concerning the ideology evidenced by individuals who are in positions in which they are expected to act in accordance with the ideology. Changes in a society and its ideology are likely to occur long before they are reflected by the official actors of that system. The personnel of the society's institutions are likely to be caught in an ideological pincer until the systemic changes are integrated into the institutions of the system.

This consideration is not tautological. Individual stress is an indicator of an ongoing process in the system. It is not to be thought of (in this framework) as a contributing factor or a causal condition of ideological change within a system. Measuring ideological change in terms of stress is quite different from arguing that where there is change there is stress and where there is stress there is change.

The concepts of role theory will help to comprehend the effects of ideological change.[4] Role is defined as a generalized, societal set

4For applications of role theory, see Gross, Mason, and McEachern, *op. cit.*, John C. Wahlke, Heinz Eulau, William Buchanan, and LeRoy C. Ferguson, *The Legislative System* (New York: Wiley, 1962); Alvin Magid, "District Councillorship in an African Society: A Study in Role and Conflict Resolution," unpublished doctoral dissertation, Department of Political Science, Michigan State Univ., East Lansing, 1965. Cf. Lionel J. Neiman and J. W. Hughes, "The Problem of the Concept of Role — A Re-Survey of the Literature," *Social Forces*, XXX (December, 1951), 141-49; Stanfield Sargent, "Concepts of Role and Ego in Contemporary Psychology," in John H. Rohrer and Muzafer Sherif, eds., *Social Psychology at the Crossroads* (New York: Harper, 1951), pp. 355-70; Theordore R. Sarbin, "Role Theory," in Gardner Lindzey, ed., *Handbook of Social Psychology, Vol. I* (Cambridge: Addison-Wesley, 1954), I, 223-55; George Herbert Mead, *Mind, Self and Society* (Chicago: Univ. of Chicago Press, 1934); W. Coutu, "Role Playing vs. Role Taking: An Appeal for Clarification," *American Sociological Review*, XVI (April, 1951), 180-87; Michael Argyle, "The Concepts of Role and Status," *Sociological Review*, XLIV (1952), 39-50; T. M. Newcomb, "Role Behaviors in the Study of Individual Personality and of Groups," *Journal of Personality*, XVIII (1950), 273-89.

of expectations.[5] Here role will be defined as a systemic demand to conform to the accepted societal ideology. The expectation to conform to the ideology may be on the behavioral as well as the attitudinal level.

The perception that the actor held of the societal ideology was of concern to me. The actor who perceived the elements of the societal ideology as being constructive in the nation's development or as being accepted by most of the population was acknowledging the existence and significance for himself of the societal ideology. The actor who did not perceive these elements as being constructive or generally accepted was not cognizant of the role he was enacting.

A further aspect of the actor's orientation to the role he enacted was his view of the legitimacy of the ideology.[6] The notion of legitimacy is a useful concept in role theory. The question asked of the actor is usually, "Does the audience (society) have the right to expect 'x'?" Or the audience (society) might be asked, "Does the actor have the right to 'y'?" In this study, to approximate legitimacy in the usual sense of role theory, a question probed whether the respondent agreed with the elements which comprised the accepted ideology.

The problem in this conceptualization is that, although agreement with the elements of the ideology may have indicated perceived legitimacy of the societal ideology, disagreement with them could not be understood as perceiving the societal ideology to be illegitimate. The actor may have defended society's right to disagree with his opinion. The dimension which could be tapped by asking the question of whether the respondent agreed with the elements of the societal ideology was really the dimension of identification and not of legitimacy.

Indentification did for my model what legitimacy did for the Gross study. The juxtaposition of the two dimensions, perceived expectations of society and identification with the accepted ideology, may produce a conflict situation. It is this conflict situation which interests us both as an indicator of stress within the system and as an analytic tool which can aid us in operationalizing the concepts of role theory in a meaningful way.

The practical advantage of employing a conflict strategy in orienting the theoretical framework of role theory studies is important. The study by Wahlke and others, in which it is contended that role theory is used to study the role of the legislator, reduced itself to a

---

[5]Gross, Mason, and McEachern, *op. cit.*, p. 67.
[6]*Ibid.*, p. 58.

study of the position of legislator.[7] This was so because role is the dynamic aspect of position. Conversely, position is the static dimension of role. As the Wahlke study used role theory, the actors were basically motionless.[8] As Gross used a role conflict framework, the actors became alive and the term role, taken in conjunction with the notion of conflict, became meaningful.

Role is the societal set of expectations concerning the ideological position of an actor. He may agree or disagree with the elements which the research assumes to be the societal ideology. Should the actor, for example, perceive the demand made upon him, but disagree with its content, a potential stress situation would result. Stress, in operational terms, is possible when there is incongruency between an actor's perception of society's expectations for him and his own identification with the accepted ideology. Stress will be manifested in the respondent's reaction when confronted with a hypothetical action-oriented statement presented in terms of the stress-generating ideological element.

II

The "kibbutz ideology," it is generally agreed, was the societal ideology of Israel immediately prior to and following the founding of the State in 1948.[9] The kibbutz movement and its ideology represented more to the Israeli population during the trying years of the 1940's than an ideal structure to absorb immigrants or a strategic location during the War of Independence: The kibbutz ideology epitomized the pioneering spirit, the volunteerism and the self-sacrifice which contributed greatly to the success of nation-building. The kibbutz movement was a source of manpower for the political, economic and military struggles of Israel. The "leftist" orientation of the country during this period and the insecurity of

---

[7]Position, called location by Alvin Zander, Arthur R. Cohen, and Ezra Stotland, *Role Relations in the Mental Health Profession* (Ann Arbor: Research Center for Group Dynamics, Univ. of Michigan, 1957), p. 21, is defined as social location by Gross, Ch. 4. Sarbin's definition is presented in footnote 8.

[8]We may criticize Wahlke's formulation on the same grounds Gross criticizes Sarbin's definition of position as a set of expectations. Gross labels Sarbin's definition of position as predictive and questions Sarbin by imagining no expectations. If there would be no expectations, would there thus be no position?

[9]See Lester Seligman, *Leadership in a New Nation* (New York: Atherton Press, 1964), Ch. 2; and Shlomo Avineri, "Israel: Image and Reality," *The New Republic,* CLI (September 26, 1964), 9.

facing independence with an unstable economy and the possibility of war made the kibbutz and its ideology symbols which could be called upon to promote unity.

The kibbutz movement has never involved more than 10 per cent of the Israeli population. Nevertheless, the kibbutz movement has been more influential, ideologically, politically and economically than its numerical strength would indicate. When the research upon which this is based was being conducted in 1963-64, the importance of the kibbutz movement was still greater than its proportion of the population would suggest, but its ideology had declined in public acceptability.[10]

In spite of its loss of public acceptability, the kibbutz ideology seems to reflect most accurately the societal ideology of the pre-State period. This is because it has remained, over the years of independence, the most consistent and faithful ideology to the principles of the past. The kibbutz ideology is founded on a socialist base with strong Jewish nationalist (Zionist) overtones.[11] After reviewing the literature of the kibbutz movement for the past fifty years, I extracted ten elements as representative of fundamental principles of the ideology.[12] They are:

1. Complete mutual responsibility according to the principle "From each according to his ability, to each according to his needs." (cooperation)
2. The establishment of society without any differences in privileges or material possession. (equality)
3. The abolition of the private ownership of the means of production.
4. Society gives man his character, and society stands above the individual.
5. The image of the Jews must be that of a laboring nation.
6. The realization of the principles of the kibbutz ideology must take place within an agricultural framework.
7. The Jews of the world constitute a nation and not only a religion.

[10]See Alan Arian, *Ideological Change in Israel* (Cleveland: Western Reserve Press, forthcoming) and Avineri, *op. cit.*
serve Press, forthcoming) and Avineri, *op. cit.*
[11]The themes of socialism and nationalism are recurrent in the ideologies of many developing nations. See David E. Apter, ed., "Ideology and Discontent," *Ideology and Discontent* (New York: The Free Press of Glencoe, 1964).
[12]Cf. Melford E. Spiro, *Kibbutz: Venture in Utopia* (Cambridge: Harvard Univ. Press, 1956), Ch. 2.

8. General immigration of all Jews to Israel.
9. Those Jews in the diaspora who are at the summit of the economic pyramid must form its base in Israel.
10. Kibbutz values should be accepted as the values of all mankind.

The first five elements represent the socialist nature of the kibbutz ideology. Emphasizing cooperation, equality, the primacy of labor, society and public ownership, they may be found in the platforms of many socialist groups. The next four elements are more specifically nationalist and Jewish in character, although in numbers 5 and 9 Zionism takes on a socialist cast. The tenth element refers to the universality of the ideology's principles — especially the socialist elements.

It is not my intention to imply that the kibbutz ideology had or has exclusive title to all of the elements which comprise it. Other ideologies in Israel have adopted, more or less intensely, most of these elements, but the ideological positions in Israel today are still underscored by the pre-State formulations. Yet today, the kibbutz ideology is no longer dominant; many competing ideologies exist. Most challenged are the socialist planks of the kibbutz platform. It is obvious that the ideology which was an important factor in establishing the nation no longer reflects the needs or goals of the State adequately. Agriculture has given way to industry; physical labor is being replaced by machines. While the rhetoric of the past can still be heard, the society is no longer developing in the direction pointed to by the "accepted" ideology.

III

The data to be analyzed here were provided by interviewing one hundred Israeli "public servants." Sixteen of the respondents were Knesset (parliament) members; eighty-four were senior civil servants. Both groups were equally divided between those individuals who were either then or previously had been kibbutz members on the one hand and those individuals who were never affiliated with the kibbutz movement on the other.

The ten discrete ideological elements, representing the main components of the kibbutz ideology, were presented to each respondent in three different ways. First, he was asked to evaluate the public acceptance or utility of the ideological elements (subsequently referred to as the instrumental questions).[13] The respondent was asked to express his estimate of the proportion of the general population which might agree with the elements or with the contribution the ideological elements were making to Israel's development. Second, he was asked to evaluate the ideological elements (referred to as the ideological question) and say whether he agreed with them.[14] Third, the respondent was asked to reply to an action-oriented hypothetical situation based on the ideological elements (referred to as the personal practice statements).[15] For example, using the "inverting pyramid" element (number 9), each respondent was asked to what extent this principle was contributing to the development of Israel, to state whether he agreed with the principle and to empathize with a professional Jew abroad and report whether he would immigrate to Israel to aid in development.

The three ways in which the ideological elements were presented provide the basic components employed in this model: (1) an evaluation of the public acceptance or utility of the ideology — the instrumental questions: (2) an evaluation of the ideology in the present — ideological questions; and (3) a personal practice statement. The different combinations of these three categories will

---

[13]Elements 4, 7, 9, and 10 were presented in the public acceptance manner. Coding procedures used are explained in *Ideological Change in Israel*. Elements 1, 2, 3, 5, 6, and 8 were presented in the utility manner.

[14]These questions for each of the elements were worded in straightforward fashion, e.g., "Do you agree that all the Jews of the world should immigrate to Israel?"

[15]The personal practice statements were worded as follows (the numbers correspond to the listing in the text):

1. Given your present position, would you agree to receive the same salary for your work as does the physical laborer with a comparable family situation?
2. Are you willing to share your personal property in order to approach the goal of complete equality among men?
3. If you were a stockholder, would you agree to turn over your profits to the government?
4. If society were to dictate to you how to live and even how to decorate your home in a manner which clashed with your personal judgments, would you agree to follow the dictates of society?
5. Would you agree to having only workers' parties in Israel?
6. Would you agree to assist in the realization of the kibbutz ideology if the condition were that you become a farmer?
7. If you were an American Jew, would you agree to define yourself as being Jewish by virtue of religion and not by virtue of nationality?
8. Would you agree to nonselective immigration of all Jews to Israel within a short period of time?
9. If you were an experienced professional in the diaspora, would you be willing to immigrate to Israel even if it meant working at physical labor?
10. Would you be willing to actively aid in the establishing of the kibbutz's values as the values of mankind?

produce different theoretical types (see Table 1): (1) the "Ideologue" is one whose responses to the practice statements agree with the ideological questions but not with the instrumental questions; (2) the "Realist" is one whose responses to the practice statements agree with the instrumental questions but not with the ideological questions; (3) the "Consistent" is one who responds to all three statements in a similar manner; and (4) "Stress" results from incongruency between the three responses.

TABLE 1. RESPONSE PATTERNS DEFINED AND LABELLED

Instrumental	Ideological	Practice	Label
disagree	agree	agree	pro-kibbutz Ideologue
agree	disagree	disagree	anti-kibbutz Ideologue
agree	disagree	agree	pro-kibbutz Realist
disagree	agree	disagree	anti-kibbutz Realist
agree	agree	agree	pro-kibbutz Consistent
disagree	disagree	disagree	anti-kibbutz Consistent
disagree	disagree	agree	Stress
agree	agree	disagree	Stress

The levels of stress reported in Table 2 may be understood in one of two ways. Stress, according to the model, may indicate change which has not yet been integrated into the structure of societal values. Alternatively, stress may result from methodological error. Three examples will make this distinction clear. High levels of stress are observed for the "individual-society" element and the "laboring nation" elements. For the "agriculture" element, a relatively low level of stress is recorded. The stress manifested by the "individual-society" element is an example of change which has not yet been integrated into the value system of the society. The primacy of society over the individual, as demonstrated in the kibbutz ideology, is in contrast to the tendency within the society to develop individual initiative and private enterprise. Not only has the ethos of the country become increasingly individual-oriented, measures supported by the "socialist" parties in the government coalition aid individual-oriented values. The conflict between the statements defending a societal-orientation and the practice of supporting individual-oriented programs leads to this large degree of stress. This tendency can also be seen in the low percentages of

TABLE 2. RESPONSE PATTERNS FOR THE TEN ELEMENTS OF THE KIBBUTZ IDEOLOGY (IN PERCENTAGES) (N = 100)

Element	Ideologue		Realist		Consistent		Stress	Unknown[a]
	pro-	anti-	pro-	anti-	pro-	anti-		
1. "To each according..."	20	1	2	22	21	16	15	3
2. No difference in possession	22	2	1	9	14	39	9	4
3. Abolition of private ownership	13	1	0	16	5	40	20	5
4. Individual-Society	4	8	1	24	5	21	26	11
5. Laboring nation	6	2	0	12	32	6	39	3
6. Agriculture	11	6	12	22	14	18	13	4
7. Nation not only religion	1	1	5	1	61	0	24	7
8. Immigration	6	9	0	3	45	11	22	4
9. Inverting pyramid	15	1	6	3	14	17	34	10
10. Universal values	39	0	1	10	4	29	13	4

[a]Comprising those individuals who failed to answer any one of the three questions used in forming the response pattern.

pro-kibbutz responses (agreement with the kibbutz ideology) in the Ideologue, Realist, and Consistent categories.

The high level of stress which exists concerning the "individual-society" element may be contrasted with the relatively low level of stress for the "agriculture" element. The "agriculture" element of the kibbutz ideology has been publicly debated and thoroughly discussed in recent years. While ideological change has certainly taken place regarding this element during the past twenty years, the debate has been public and open. There is little inconsistency between the ideology of public statement and the practice of private interests. While there is no broad consensus concerning the element within the sample studied, there is not a high level of stress concerning the issue either.

The high level of stress recorded for the "laboring nation" element is a result, it seems, of a methodological error. This error was due to the personal practice statement for the "laboring nation" element (question 5). The question is probably more relevant as an index of democratic predisposition than as a probe concerning the respondent's readiness to accept in practice the principle of "the

Jews in Israel having an image of a laboring nation." To the extent that the question is not reliable, the model's label based on the unreliable question is not valid.

The ability of the model to discriminate meaningfully between levels of stress may be verified when selected sociological and political variables are cross-tabulated with the positions of the respondents on the ten ideological elements. For example, let us suppose that former kibbutz members have undergone a greater extent of ideological change regarding the kibbutz ideology than have individuals who are still kibbutz members or those who have never been kibbutz members. Then we would hypothesize that former kibbutz members will tend to be "Realists." Concomitantly, the present kibbutz members will tend to score highest as "Ideologues."

Another reasonable hypothesis is that as we move from political left to political right, pro-kibbutz responses will tend to decrease, stress will tend to increase. If there is a positive relation between leftist political tendency and positive evaluation of the kibbutz ideology, we shall find individuals identifying themselves with the "Marxist left" much more positive regarding the kibbutz ideology than the "Center" respondents are. Because the ideology is less acceptable to them, the "Center" respondents will tend to be much more sensitive to change in the public acceptability of the ideology and therefore will be much more likely to manifest stress than will the "Marxist left" individuals.

These two hypotheses are based on the assumption that one measure of ideological change is the observed stress in the ideological role being enacted by the respondent. The testing of these two hypotheses based on the model will provide an indication of the model's ability to interpret reality: (1) Among civil servants, former kibbutz members will tend to be "Realists," present kibbutz members will tend to be "Ideologues," the responses of those never affiliated with a kibbutz will tend to be distributed among all the categories; (2) pro-kibbutz responses will tend to decrease, stress will tend to increase as we move from political left to political right.

I have shown elsewhere that former kibbutz members undergo a greater extent of ideological change regarding the kibbutz ideology than do individuals who are still kibbutz members.[16] Concomitantly, those individuals who have never affiliated with a kibbutz undergo little ideological change; in that sense, those never

---

[16]See Arian, *op. cit.*, Chs. 3, 6.

affiliated with a kibbutz are more similar to kibbutz members than to former kibbutz members. On the other hand, while their extent of ideological change may be similar, present kibbutz members will hold a generally positive evaluation of the ideology while those never affiliated with the kibbutz will tend to be less committed.

The first hypothesis, relating to the differences observed between the civil servants interviewed who are, were or never have been kibbutz members, reflects the supposition that civil servants who formerly were kibbutz members evidenced the most ideological change. Assuming that the kibbutz ideology was the accepted ideology of the past leads to the hypothesis that the former kibbutz members will tend to show a higher percentage of "Realist" sentiment and that present kibbutz members will tend to show a higher percentage of "Ideologue" sentiment.

The hypothesis is partially confirmed by the data presented in Table 3. The small sample cautions against drawing firm conclusions. As pointed out before, the "laboring nation" element produces an unusually high incidence of stress because of the wording of the personal practice statement. This difference shows up graphically when the stress levels for the "laboring nation" element are compared with those generated by the "no difference in possession" element. For the former element, the question concerning personal practice was irrelevant; for the latter, the following question succeeded in discriminating between those who would and would not act to fulfill the principle of equality postulated by the kibbutz ideology: "Given your present position, would you agree to receive the same salary for your work as does the physical laborer with a comparable family situation?"

The "inverting of the pyramid" element produces a high level of stress in all cases. The societal ideology still emphasizes the importance of righting social and economic wrongs and calls for the Jews of the world to aid in creating social justice by personally participating in the venture, no matter the sacrifice. Realistically, many Israelis show contempt for foreign Jewish aid and reluctantly accept the aid only because "we have no choice." The ideology is "doctrinal"; the practice is "developmental."[17] This friction leads to stress.

The other hypothesis to be tested is the relationship between the distribution of response patterns and political tendency. Assuming that the "Marxist left" is closest to the kibbutz ideology, I would

---

[17]Arthur S. Banks and Robert B. Textor, *A Cross-Polity Survey* (Cambridge: M. I. T. Press, 1963), pp. 80-82, Appendix A.

TABLE 3.   RESPONSE PATTERNS FOR THE TEN ELEMENTS OF THE KIBBUTZ IDEOLOGY FOR CIVIL SERVANTS BY KIBBUTZ AFFILIATION (IN PERCENTAGES)

Element	Ideologue		Realist		Consistent		Stress	Unknown
	pro-	anti-	pro-	anti-	pro-	anti-		
1. "To each according . . ."								
Former (N = 30)	23	0	3	17	20	23	13	0
Present (N = 12)	8	0	17	0	58	0	17	0
Never (N = 42)	17	5	2	29	10	19	17	2
2. No difference in possession								
Former	13	0	3	20	7	43	13	0
Present	50	0	0	0	42	0	0	8
Never	12	5	0	7	2	60	10	5
3. Abolition of private ownership								
Former	17	0	0	13	3	50	13	3
Present	25	0	0	25	8	0	33	8
Never	7	2	0	17	2	50	17	5
4. Individual-Society								
Former	3	7	0	37	0	40	10	3
Present	17	0	0	42	0	8	25	8
Never	0	17	2	12	10	17	33	10
5. Laboring nation								
Former	3	0	0	17	33	7	40	0
Present	8	0	0	8	58	0	17	8
Never	10	5	0	12	24	7	41	2

6. Agriculture								
Former	7	3	7	33	13	30	7	0
Present	8	0	17	0	58	0	17	0
Never	14	12	5	26	2	21	14	5
7. Nation not only religion								
Former	0	0	13	0	63	0	23	0
Present	0	0	0	0	67	0	25	8
Never	2	5	2	2	55	0	21	12
8. Immigration								
Former	3	7	0	3	57	7	23	0
Present	8	8	0	8	42	8	25	0
Never	10	14	0	2	29	14	24	7
9. Inverting pyramid								
Former	20	3	0	3	10	30	33	0
Present	25	0	8	8	0	0	42	17
Never	7	2	10	0	17	19	38	7
10. Universal values								
Former	37	0	0	7	3	27	23	3
Present	75	0	0	8	17	0	0	0
Never	24	2	2	12	2	43	12	2

TABLE 4. RESPONSE PATTERNS FOR THE TEN ELEMENTS OF THE KIBBUTZ IDEOLOGY FOR THE KNESSET MEMBER-CIVIL SERVANT SAMPLE BY POLITICAL TENDENCY (IN PERCENTAGES)

Element	Ideologue		Realist		Consistent		Stress	Unknown
	pro-	anti-	pro-	anti-	pro-	anti-		
1. "To each according . . ."								
Center (N=14)	7	0	7	36	7	21	21	0
Moderate left (N=55)	24	2	2	22	16	16	13	5
Marxist left (N=12)	17	0	0	25	50	0	8	0
2. No difference in possession								
Center	0	7	0	14	0	71	7	0
Moderate left	22	0	2	11	13	35	11	7
Marxist left	50	0	0	8	42	0	0	0
3. Abolition of private ownership								
Center	7	7	0	0	0	64	21	0
Moderate left	11	0	0	24	7	35	15	9
Marxist left	50	0	0	17	0	8	25	0
4. Individual-Society								
Center	0	7	7	21	7	14	29	14
Moderate left	5	9	0	22	4	29	25	5
Marxist left	8	0	0	58	8	0	25	0
5. Laboring nation								
Center	0	7	0	36	14	21	21	0
Moderate left	7	2	0	7	27	2	49	5
Marxist left	17	0	0	0	75	0	8	0

	1	2	3	4	5	6	7	8
6. Agriculture								
Center	21	7	0	21	7	36	0	7
Moderate left	11	9	7	27	15	15	13	4
Marxist left	8	0	33	0	25	8	17	8
7. Nation not only religion								
Center	7	0	21	0	50	0	21	0
Moderate left	0	2	2	2	67	0	18	9
Marxist left	0	0	8	0	75	0	17	0
8. Immigration								
Center	7	21	0	7	50	7	7	0
Moderate left	5	4	0	2	42	16	25	7
Marxist left	0	8	0	8	58	8	17	0
9. Inverting pyramid								
Center	7	0	0	0	0	43	50	0
Moderate left	15	0	9	4	16	13	35	9
Marxist left	33	0	8	0	25	8	17	8
10. Universal values								
Center	14	0	7	21	7	29	21	0
Moderate left	45	0	0	7	2	27	13	5
Marxist left	75	0	0	8	0	17	0	0

hypothesize that as we move from political center to extreme left (the right is underrepresented in this sample) pro-kibbutz response will increase and levels of stress will decrease. Table 4 illustrates the results when this hypothesis was studied. In almost every case the predicted relationship held. The fact that stress appears more frequently with the political center (the group farthest from the principles of the kibbutz ideology) fortifies the contention that the kibbutz ideology was the societal ideology. A high rate of anti-kibbutz responses and a low rate of stress would be expected from this group if the kibbutz ideology had not been the societal ideology.

IV

I have shown that changes in the acceptance of the societal ideology are accompanied by stress in public servants. In the case of the kibbutz ideology in Israel, hypothesized reactions to ideological changes were observed: Former kibbutz members tended to be "Realists," and present kibbutz members tended to be "Ideologues"; stress tended to increase and pro-kibbutz responses decreased as we moved from political left to political right.

These two examples indicate the ability of the model to explain ideological change and stress in public servants. In the two examples presented, the possibilities of the model's explanatory powers and its conceptual soundness are demonstrated. The relationships indicated between the dimensions studied are suggestive for students of societal change and developmental administration.

The idea of tapping ideological change by studying stress in public servants has been shown to be a promising road for future analysis. There can be little doubt that the ideological climate in which an administrator works is an important factor in determining his overall effectiveness. Along with further studies of the societal ideology's influence on administrators, empirical work on the nature, formulation, and function of an appropriate ideology are needed. Changes in the public acceptability of an ideology are important features of the process of development and crises management, but the nature and role of ideological change must be more fully understood if our grasp of the process is to be more complete than it is today.

Chapter 10
Ideology and Metropolitan Administration

Charles Press

Department of Political Science
Michigan State University

Iron River is a community in Michigan's relatively depressed Upper Peninsula. In reality, it is five different cities, villages, or townships with a total population of around ten thousand huddled in one relatively compact urbanized area. The depressed economy of this iron-mining community encouraged civic leaders to suggest that these legal units merge to cut costs. Almost immediately the same bitter arguments erupted that are heard when one of America's Great Cities attempts to annex suburbanites. Citizens in the smaller suburban units claimed they were being gobbled up into a big city, what you would hear if Detroit proposed to merge with a few of its small suburbs. Thus, what appears to most outsiders as one social and economic community, and what certainly is for many matters of importance, continues to be splintered among five governments for what seem logical reasons to local residents. Those reasons, which reformers too often have treated as irrelevant or even pathological, are at the heart of the problem of resistance to integration in small as well as large communities. They are primarily rationalizations and idealizations of individual life styles. But they are also buttressed by economic reality; in most urban areas independence is not too expensive for most of suburbia.

Urban administrators acting as fiduciary agents commonly adopt the viewpoints of their political units. Rooted for life as most are, their ideologies have tended to reflect provincial over professional viewpoints; perhaps it is more accurate to say they operate as professionals mainly within a provincial set of assumptions. But a number of trends challenge the appropriateness of the provincial ideology in a metropolis. The urban administrator is receiving more professional training and his mobility rate is growing with the city manager profession setting the style, urban problems are becoming more complex and the need for cooperative action increasingly obvious, and in some instances even the economic feasibility of independence is open to question.

By examining the ideological patterns within Great Cities, one notes that the urban administrator is frequently caught up in what might be described as ideological cross-fire. It is this conflict of ideological loyalties that I will examine in this chapter.

I

A heterogeneity of life styles is the identifying characteristic of a Great City. The larger the metropolitan complex, the greater the smorgasboard of subcultures from which its residents may choose. Nathan Glazer and Daniel P. Moynihan, somewhat overwhelmed by the diversity of living patterns within the legal boundaries of New York City, categorize the result as too complex to still hold in the mind.[1]

Social scientists have only recently begun to devise precise empirical measures for locating and identifying such groupings. Clearly important in setting life styles are those characteristics that limit residential location choices for some residents: Two of these are income as well as ethnic and racial characteristics. The ability to pay for a home and to acquire it without extra hardship because of race or ethnic background are basic factors in determining residential distribution. A third variable of obvious importance also is the composition of a family unit. Those with children desire, if possible, types of housing that are large enough for them and neighborhoods that are safe. Those who are retired or without children may prefer apartment life.

With these three characteristics, Shevky and Bell devised a system of social area analysis and using census reports were able to classify all parts of a metropolitan area into subcultures according to their mixes of these three variables.[2] The economists Hoover and Vernon in their study of the New York City metropolitan area choose similar variables—job type, income level, and age composi-

[1]Nathan Glazer and Daniel Patrick Moynihan, *Beyond the Melting Pot: The Negroes, Puerto Ricans, Jews, Italians, and Irish of New York City* (Cambridge: M. I. T. Press, 1963), pp. 1-23.
[2]Eshref Shevky and Wendell Bell, *Social Area Analysis* (Stanford: Stanford Univ. Press, 1955).

tion of the household—to explain residential choice.[3] They argue that the distinction between blue and white collar workers and the census types within each of these broad classes appear sometimes to differentiate more precisely than income. For Glazer and Moynihan, ethnic background of residents is a major variable that explains the significant subcultures of New York City.[4] They note how social, economic, and political patterns vary among different ethnic groups; how Italians, for example, resist residential invasion by Negroes and Puerto Ricans and continue to live in greater numbers near the center of Manhattan than have other descendents of immigrant groups. They also stress the importance of religion as a differentiator, particularly with groups having parochial schools. Such ethnic groupings, they argue, have not melted into the larger society but rather have developed outlooks somewhat different from both those of natives of their country of origin and those of white Anglo-Saxon protestants.

Other characteristics also lead to differentiation, but these are of secondary importance. A study of the urbanites moving into the farming area on the fringes of Lansing, Michigan, discovered most were blue collar workers in the city's auto plants.[5] But these new settlers had two distinctive characteristics: They wanted some small acreage to cultivate on their own, and four out of five households had a husband or wife who had been raised on a farm. As might be anticipated, these residents tended to view with disfavor the further urbanization of the township. Their specialized subculture was a miniature imitation of a farm community. The metropolis provides living space for other subgroupings with specialized demands as, for example, the Bohemian and the suburban gardener, but these also are subcultures of secondary political significance.

To summarize those characteristics that seem of major importance in forming politically relevant subcultures are race and ethnicity (including in these the factor of religion), occupation (which is closely related to income, educational level, and social status), and family size and age. On this basis most residents of a metropolitan area sort themselves out, and as the result of this sorting out process distinctive life styles evolve.

[3]Edgar Hoover and Raymond Vernon, *Anatomy of a Metropolis: The Changing Distribution of People and Jobs Within the New York Metropolitan Region* (Cambridge: Harvard Univ. Press, 1959), Ch. 7.
[4]Glazer and Moynihan, *op. cit.*
[5]Charles Press and Rodger Rice, *Farmers and Suburbanization* (Washington: United States Government Printing Office, United States Department of Agriculture publication, 1963).

The political importance of such subcultures lies in the distinctive viewpoints that they nourish. Each provides a distinctive set of daily experiences for its residents, and these experiences help shape the political and social outlook. Take, for example, the experience of living in an apartment house as described in Sally Benson's book and play, *Junior Miss*.[6] One study reports that high-cost apartment residents in St. Louis were more likely than home-owners to take what one might describe as a civic viewpoint; that is, they favored governmental reforms even when such reforms cost money, and they voted to improve services even when the benefit affected them very little.[7] The experience of living in or growing up in a Negro slum in a northern city also teaches a lesson in respect to politics. The kinds of political response likely among citizens who are continually affected by patterns of discrimination are ones of suspicious antagonism or apathy.[8]

Citizens beginning with similar social values are profoundly influenced in many of the same ways by their experiences, but experience alone does not determine the political ideology that results. Man's rationality also may influence his views. Different individuals undergoing similar experiences will respond in a variety of ways. But over a period of time, subgroupings form their own distinctive attitudes. Folk ideologies grow just as do folk songs. Such ideologies help individuals to cope with their environment and orient themselves within it. They serve as a shorthand guide that gives people a picture of reality and suggests what should and should not be done.

The elements of such ideologies I see as the valuational, the cognitive, and the emotional. Most important is the valuational because the functional purpose of an ideology is to tell how life ought to be lived, that is, in Plato's terms, what is the just society. The cognitive element is the picture of reality that the ideology conveys. The emotional element is the ideology's symbolic content. Note, for example, how a political ideology of discrimination against a minority group functions. The cognitive content argues that in reality the minority group members are inferior generally both morally and intellectually. The valuational part, thus, suggests

---

[6]Sally Benson, *Junior Miss* (Garden City: Doubleday, 1947).
[7]E. B. Olds and D. W. Salmon, "St. Louis Voting Behavior" (mimeographed by the St. Louis chapter of the American Statistical Association).
[8]James Baldwin, *Notes of a Native Son* (Boston: Beacon Press, 1955), and also *Nobody Knows My Name: More Notes of a Native Son* (New York: Dell, 1961). See also Ralph Ellison, *The Invisible Man* (New York: Random House, 1953).

patterns of avoidance as appropriate and just. Associated with this viewpoint are symbols that will arouse emotional reactions. The weakest part of any ideology is its cognitive element, since this can be challenged by argument or, directly, by experience. Once doubt arises in respect to the picture of reality, the other parts of the ideology are weakened much as the religious beliefs of a freshman on a small college campus might be shaken by scientific questioning of Jonah or some other Bible story. But the breaking down of an ideology is seldom easy or common. Experience may challenge it, but modification rather than obliteration is generally the result.

The ideologies that grow out of the experiences of distinctive subcultures are the elements that have been often overlooked when metropolitan integration has been proposed. Technology and the law have given metropolitan residents the opportunity to create subcultures with independent governmental status, and residents of metropolitan areas have responded to the invitation. The residents of Great Cities have parceled themselves out over the countryside in a variety of subcommunities, living in different life-style patterns designed to appeal to an assortment of specialized tastes. Residents who have chosen the kind of existence they prefer to live and who have met the requirements of membership in such subcultures are loathe to risk change. And the viewpoints that are developed and reinforced in such subcultures accentuate this tendency.

II

But the metropolis also reveals trends of centralization, and these too have led to distinctive ideological viewpoints. Most often it has been the professional concerned with functional rather than unit goals that has embraced such ideologies. We begin by examining the basis for this viewpoint.

On what ground is an urban complex viewed by outsiders as a single entity for which unified adminstrative effort is desirable? The answer commonly given is that this is the case when an urban complex appears to be a single interdependent social and economic community. When an aggregation of people has a focus from which actions are taken that affect all parts of the complex and, in turn, reactions of the parts influence the pattern of decision-making at the center, it is a community. Following the logic of John Dewey one may argue that, when the indirect consequences of acts of others are recognized and it appears desirable that an attempt be made to regulate them, a public comes into existence.[9] Such a public requires a government with an administrative arm so that it can shape its own destiny.

Deciding upon the area within which actions taken at the center of an urban complex have significant effects presents practical problems for administrators and citizens. If communication back and forth is used as the measure, too broad an area is isolated. One would include within the boundaries of the Great City the circulation area of its Sunday newspapers, the broadcast coverage for its major league ball team, or, even, for the largest of America's cities, the readership area of such a journal as *The New Yorker* magazine. In a sense, persons in such outlying areas have their lives affected significantly by communications from the center and to that degree are part of the larger city and have some right to influence decisions made there. But such influence can perhaps most appropriately be channeled through the marketplace or through the national or state rather than local government.

For local government administration, the boundaries of metropolitan areas are more commonly set by transportation patterns — the trip to and from work, shopping or recreation or daily delivery routes of department stores and other local businesses. Even the setting of limits by such measures results in a fuzziness at the fringes since some commuters go far out into the countryside as do the deliveries of some local merchants, and a sizeable minority of residents only come occasionally to the city center. Attempts to improve on the definition have sometimes emphasized natural geographic features as boundaries, population densities, and overlapping memberships of area residents. But no single definition is completely satisfactory, though John Dewey's notions seem to provide a good rough guide: Where decisions made at different parts of an urban complex unexpectedly affect the lives of residents in other parts of that complex in significant ways and where they recognize and wish to control these effects, the conditions for a governmental community are present.

Because definitions like those just discussed are too complex for practical use, the Census Bureau has provided a way out of the difficulty. Their definition of the Standard Metropolitan Statistical Area is also a rough but useful one for delimiting the boundaries of Great Cities. An SMSA includes roughly a city of fifty thousand or more plus the county in which it is located and any other counties

[9]John Dewey, *The Public and Its Problems* (New York: Holt, 1927).

that the Census Bureau determines to be socially and economically integrated with it. The use of county boundaries causes some problems. Thus, 180 miles of largely desert area lying between Los Angeles County and the gambling tables of Las Vegas must be defined as metropolitan.

The 225 SMSA's vary widely in size, and this makes the definition too broad for many purposes. For example, in 1960 the SMSA's varied from 51,850 in Meriden, Connecticut, to 10,694,633 in the New York City metropolitan area, a variation of over 200 per cent. And within the larger SMSA's are many cities which could be SMSA's in their own right if they were as lucky in choosing their location as Pine Bluff, Arkansas; Anderson, Indiana; or Salem, Oregon. But this fact is less important for our purposes, that of delimiting the boundaries of what might logically be considered a local government unit. Each of the SMSA's, large or small, has a center where social and economic decisions are made that affect the whole area in significant and unplanned ways, and reactions suggesting the desirability of control of such decisions occur as well as counterdecisions that influence what actually happens at the center. The recognition of this fact is at the heart of professional ideologies.

III

The previously discussed logic was once commonly applied to the government of metropolitan areas because technical factors made this a necessity. Whether they liked it or not most residents of a Great City lived within the governmental boundaries of one city, even until fairly recent times. To illustrate the history of Grand Rapids, Michigan, can be used. The city was incorporated in 1850 in the shape of a two-miles-by-two-miles square. Seven years later it added a half-mile strip to each of the square's sides to increase the city to roughly a three-miles-by-three-miles square. This annexation was thus ringlike, similar to the way growth rings appear in a log (if you can for the moment imagine a tree with a square trunk). Thirty-four years later, in 1891, another ringlike annexation took place, but for the first time breaks occurred along the boundary. A half-mile strip was added across the top and along the west side. Another strip was added along most of the south and a little over half of the east side. But note, that, even with the breaks, this 1891 annexation again was of the encircling type. At this point a change occurred. In 1916, a small strip was added to the south and between 1924 and 1927 small bits and parcels were added in each direction. And this was the end of annexation of any consequence until 1960.

What had happened between 1891 and 1925, when, following the former pattern, one would again expect another encircling annexation? One clue is that, in 1926, East Grand Rapids, a village since 1891, was incorporated as a wealthy residential suburb independent of the city. The incorporation introduced the age of the automobile. At this stage it was possible only for the wealthy to move away from the fringes of the central city, incorporate a high tax base residential community, and provide a high level of urban services. East Grand Rapids even today has no industry, prides itself on the beauty of its homes, and has always had a first-rate school system.

What was possible for the wealthy in the 1920's became possible for the middle class by the end of the depression and for the lower-middle class after World War II. Technology made it practical to leapfrog settlement to any place in the territory surrounding a city providing it was accessible enough by car to permit commuting. Blacktop roads became the key to urbanization. No longer was it necessary to settle on the city's fringes to receive urban services or be close enough to trolley and bus lines to commute. Other technological advances encouraged this movement: the septic tank, new well drilling techniques, and even the power lawn mower, which made the large lawns of suburbia tolerable for those not quite wealthy enough to employ a yard man.

When urban sprawl became feasible for the middle class, the pattern of government in metropolitan areas changed. Suburban incorporations increased after World War II. In many states such incorporation offered special legal advantages; in Michigan, for example, small suburbs were dramatically overrepresented on County Boards of Supervisors as compared to urbanized townships. The process of incorporation also frequently offered tax advantages if a particularly lucrative plant located in the boundaries of the new city, or, as was sometimes the case, the new city was incorporated around the particularly lucrative plant. In addition, for many of the new middle class, suburbia represented a status leap from ethnic communities and the politics of the big city.

All such factors contributed to the proliferation in government and the rejection of the notion of one government to administer services for a single social and economic community. One should not conclude, however, that all suburban communities have been able to resist merger with the central city. Particularly in recent times, the pressure of economic realities is introducing a new pattern. Between 1950 and 1960, three-quarters of the nation's largest central cities annexed territory, and half of these had annexed more than 10 per cent of their 1960 population in the previous ten-year period.[10] One out of five cities with more than five thousand population annexed territory in 1962 alone. The compilations in the *Municipal Year Book* also reveal that annexations have been on the increase in recent years. The data suggest that economic problems may have blighted dreams of suburban independence for some kinds of communities. For some suburbanites the easiest way out has been return to the central city through annexation. But the dominant trend is still one of suburban proliferation. For every annexation that is successful, several more attempts fail. And seldom does an incorporated suburb merge with the central city or even with another suburb. At this point the battle lines are still drawn with suburb *vs.* suburb and both *vs.* the central city.

IV

Students have recently found that subcultural factors are relevant in explaining why certain administrators in metropolitan areas cooperate with administrators in other units. It appears that this is most likely among units with similar characteristics when the urban service relates to life styles. On the other hand, when services have little effect on community life styles, technical and engineering problems determine patterns of cooperation. Dye found that annexation itself occurred more frequently when the difference in social distance between central city and suburb was small and less frequently when the reverse was true.[11] Similarly, Williams and his colleagues found that cooperation in respect to such value-impregnated services as schools and zoning occurred among communities of similar social-economic status. On the other hand, in respect to traffic control and transportation, sewage treatment and obtaining water supplies, the technical engineering requirements generally determined the patterns of cooperation. Thus, the communities along the river were the obvious location for sewage treatment plants, and suburbs of all status levels cooperated with such

---

[10]Thomas Dye, "Urban Political Integration: Conditions Associated with Annexation in American Cities," *Midwest Journal of Political Science,* VIII (November, 1964), 430-46.
[11]Oliver Williams, Harold Herman, Charles S. Liebman, and Thomas R. Dye, *Suburban Differences and Metropolitan Policies* (Philadelphia: Univ. of Pennsylvania Press, 1965).

communities in establishing an integrated sewage disposal system. Independence is, thus, not a fetish. Cooperation may even occur among differing units when benefits to all are clear, as in matters affecting health and safety or even in cases when substantial economies may be gained. But those mutual arrangements that loosen local control over life style are viewed most suspiciously both by local citizens and administrators.

What are the sensitive services that residents see as influencing the way they live in important respects? Those most important seem to be zoning and housing regulations. Schools also qualify, though sometimes because of school locations mergers may occur without disturbing local arrangements. Through control of these services, residents hope to protect, it appears, what they regard as distinctive ways of life. Residents of a city see these as a variety of subcultures, distinguishable in important ways. Each represents a slightly different view of the way life may be lived. Some are regarded by residents as extremely desirable ways of life, and inhabitants of these communities are those that most jealously guard their independence. It is this notion that preserves five little units of government in Iron River and more than six hundred in the New York SMSA.

V

What then is the probability that metropolitan areas will become more integrated units either through consolidation or cooperation? The answer, I think, depends upon the ideological viewpoints of the urban administrator.

Some observers place their hope in a blurring of divisions that encourage subcultures. That the divisions based on ethnicity are growing less sharp is probably true. Ethnicity is losing some of its hold even though some overoptimistic cliches in respect to the melting pot have proven false. But enough differences will remain for some time to come to encourage division. And the outlook for blurring racial distinctions is considerably less hopeful and that for eliminating class distinctions is equally unlikely. Also it must be remembered that some persons have a stake in exacerbating subcultural divisions within the metropolis. Realtors commonly emphasize the element of race in the sorting out of Negroes within a metropolis. In a few cases primacy may be given to occupation and income, and when this occurs at least some of the tension involved with this subculture is reduced. But residential integration is still only common within high-status communities. Many Negroes themselves also have a stake in preserving subcultural isolation. Some Negro businessmen fit into this category. Also within the next generation or so, a few northern cities may have Negro mayors. In addition, many suburban officials, businessmen, and newspaper editors have an economic stake in preserving governmental independence as means of holding their clientele. Thus, the likelihood that subcultural differences will diminish radically enough in the future to encourage widespread metropolitan integration appears to be unlikely.

Some have hoped for the growth of a common metropolitan-wide viewpoint by citizens. This would be based on the similar experiences of living within the metropolis. The sociologist Louis Wirth in an important essay describes the city as leading to a way of life emphasizing impersonality and interdependence and resulting in a distinctive urban outlook.[12] Others argue that the life of the suburban commuter also leads to a distinctive outlook.[13] I would agree and would also argue that such viewpoints have significant political implications. The basis of the New Deal was, I think, built on experiences of big city residents, as Lubell points out.[14] I also see the more bland politics of today as owing a good deal to the viewpoint and experiences of suburbanites.[15] But the tendency to an area-wide view is not increasing markedly among citizens. First, these viewpoints divide further the large city from suburbia and thus encourage governmental division rather than integration. Second, thus far they seem to have proven more functional for extra-metropolitan rather than intra-metropolitan political relations. They serve to unite metropolitans against nonmetropolitans but less frequently seem to encourage consolidation or administrative cooperation within the metropolis.

But it is likely that force of circumstances will continue to encourage greater governmental integration, and what is becoming clearer to professionals will be clear to citizens. The pressure of state and federal governments interested in an integrated attack on social and engineering problems of Great Cities provides a major

---

[12]Louis Wirth, "Urbanism as a Way of Life," *American Journal of Sociology*, XLIV (July, 1938), 1-24.
[13]Robert C. Wood, *Suburbia: Its People and Their Politics* (Boston: Houghton Mifflin, 1959); and William H. Whyte, Jr., *The Organization Man* (New York: Simon & Schuster, 1956).
[14]Samuel Lubell, *The Future of American Politics* (Garden City: Doubleday, 1952), pp. 29-105.
[15]Charles Press and Charles Adrian, "Why Our State Governments Are Sick," *Antioch Review*, XXIV (Summer, 1964), 149-65.

impetus for cooperative action. In addition, spreading gradually to suburban areas are such social problems as substandard housing, conditions of poverty, crime, and other forms of social disorganization. An efficient expenditure of resources will continue to require greater cooperation and coordination among units and pressure for this will increase. Also the areas experiencing severe service and tax problems are likely to increase as suburban areas age.

In respect to the hopes for complete merger, we may gain some insight from the analysis of the forming of federal states out of separate entities.[16] William Riker demonstrates that the element crucial in bringing about such mergers has not been the growth of a common ideology but a threat that affected all parties. This is not to deny that mergers are more likely between subcultures with similar ideologies, but that a common threat is probably needed even in these cases to bring action.

That such threats will occur in the future in parts of the suburban metropolis seems likely. Technology once permitted a measure of independence, but the day of the septic tank and the individual well is coming to an end, and the trip into town is taking longer. Here mergers may occur. More commonly other solutions will be sought. Integrated governmental effort in the form of massive engineering feats of one or another layer of government will become quite common. And someday, no doubt, the need for metropolitan action in respect to social problems will also become more obvious to citizens and administrators. The solving of such problems may even require the area-wide integration of such sensitive services as zoning and housing. For this reason I regard the consolidation of Great Cities as ultimately desirable and, indeed, in one form or another inevitable.

The form, probably, will be a jerry-built one. Local governmental units will continue to exist even when they no longer make very many significant decisions. The trend is toward larger and larger units taking the significant actions. Some of these units will assume unusual administrative forms. Perhaps the ultimate in providing large-scale services while maintaining a modicum of local independence in respect to zoning is the Lakewood plan of California whereby local units contract for services from other larger units of government. But whatever the particular administrative device the trend will be to larger units making decisions.

---

[16]William H. Riker, *Federalism, Origin, Operation, Significance* (Boston: Little, Brown, 1964), pp. 12-44.

Given the realities of subcultures, citizens of the Great Cities will strive for whatever forms of area-wide governmental integration seem possible. The criticisms of functional integration of separate services are valid. No doubt a multi-purpose federalism like that of Toronto or even of Dade County, Florida, is preferable to a Robert Moses type of operation that acts independently of all other municipal services and grabs off only what is the most financially lucrative. But, nevertheless, action through only partially suitable forms of local government is preferable to stalemate.

What then will be the role of the urban administrators? Some will no doubt continue to emphasize almost exclusively the ideology of the local unit. To the extent that they do so, they and their units will be increasingly bypassed in respect to significant decisions, whether their area of specialty be parks, police, traffic design, libraries, or sewage disposal. These decisions will be made by administrators able to adopt ideologies appropriate to the problems they face.

The recent history of consolidations in respect to schools suggest the crucial role played by such administrators. Schools are among the most socially sensitive of municipal services. School districts with their separate identity and often familiar family names have served as subcultures perhaps to a greater degree than most municipalities. Yet the force of economic circumstance plus the pressures created by a generally united professional group have brought about an integration of educational effort that would have been regarded as visionary a generation ago. State law and educational professionals in the local community have embraced an ideology timely in respect to present conditions.

As municipal officials move to a more professional status, we may see the same change in their guiding ideologies. What will be required of administrators who wish to effectively influence policy will be a blending of unit ideology with the needs of the administrative situation. The metropolis is in the process of change from a unit administered by provincial units to one administered on an area-wide basis. The effective local administrator will have to tailor his viewpoint to this trend. He cannot abandon wholly the ideology of the local unit lest he be politically ineffective locally, but he also cannot overlook the requirements of the administrative condition he faces. Living in two worlds is not easy, but that is what is being required of an urban administrator. His ideology must be one flexible enough to release his skills and energies rather than one that ties his hands.

Chapter 11

The American Administrator in Modern Complex Society

Norton E. Long

Department of Political Science
Brandeis University

Modern society has radically increased the dimensions and relationships of the social and political space in which the administrator has to function. This is so not simply because increases in scale have been accompanied by increasing interdependence. In addition, changes in the cognitive sphere and the realm of accepted values have made life more difficult for administrative Hamlets whose pale cast of thought engenders doubts where previously uncriticized use and wont held sway.

I

We not only know a lot more than we did, we are also far more keenly aware of the immensity of our ignorance. Even had societal scale remained within the limits of the past, our heightened sensitivity to factors now thrust on our consciousness by psychology and the social sciences would have made the relatively simpler problems of an earlier day seem bafflingly complex. This merely underlies the importance of our own definitions for our perception of the objective situation.

We have been taught to see the life around us as complex. The complexity extends from the growing range of variables that scientific research indicates to be critically relevant to informed action to the equally relevant and equally perplexing multiplicity of competing values that confront choice and decision-making.

Thus, the modern administrator is faced with a welter of psychological and sociological theories dealing with crime and delinquency each of which has some supporting evidence and plausibility. From these theories a whole range of competing and often contradictory action programs pose the dilemma of choice between them, or expedient but dubious compromise among them.

Along with the embarrassment of scientific and pseudoscientific riches, choice and decision-making are bedevilled by the uncertain state of the value premises that should direct the course of action. The police officer can no longer be sure of the viciousness of the homosexual, and the welfare agency may be urged to organize the poor to conduct rent strikes and to sue the city for nonfeasance. The stable world of administrative common sense is unhinged. A world in which by and large one could suppose that most of what one thought to be so was, and most of what one believed to be right unquestionably was, has changed into one of endless relativity, grey and full of doubt.

The flux of the older cognitive map, and of the value premises that accompanied it, is associated with and aggravated by the social dynamic straining at the obsolescent inherited political structure. A national policy and a national economy struggle to realize themselves through the limitations of the institutions of a pre-industrial agrarian society. Renewed currents of political modernization are running, bringing marginal populations previously powerless into active participation in political life and bringing the slogans of the Great Society to the test of implementation. Political, social, economic, and ideological change undermines older orthodoxies while as yet providing no new consensus from which the administrative technician can take a safe and sure value orientation.

II

A society that as late as the turn of the century was predominantly agricultural in its self-conception and only somewhat less so in fact has given way to one that is not only urban but becoming overwhelmingly metropolitan. Two-hundred-odd metropolitan areas embrace the bulk of America. This trend seems irreversible and likely to result in growing population concentrations within a fraction of the existing metropolitan areas.

As late as the New Deal the premier department in Washington was agriculture. Today it is the Pentagon with marginal competition from the welfare agencies. World War II and the Cold War have radically shifted though by no means destroyed the New Deal welfare orientation. Despite the substantial sums available for social programs, military and foreign military support programs have sharply reduced the proportion of the national budget available for the Fair Deal and the Great Society from that obtaining at an earlier date. Nevertheless, an overwhelming urban and an increasingly metropolitan society makes inexorably mounting demands for the provision of public goods ranging from housing and education to transport and water resources. These demands are the very stuff of elective and bureaucratic politics, and presidents, Congressmen, and agencies needs must in varying degrees respond to them. The response, however, must work its way through an institutional, constitutional, and normative framework stemming from an agrarian past when state nationalisms had enough reality to provoke a civil war. The nation and the national economy have changed and are changing the political institutions and the beliefs by which tradition has encased them, but the past still dogs the present. Federal standing to deal with emerging urban problems rests in the power to spend money for the general welfare, not on the general responsibility of a national government. The historic result of piecemeal ad hoc intervention has been the creation of vested interests in functional empires with little or no coordination or common purpose.

Federal fiscal competence and federal readiness to respond to particular demands for services have resulted in the development of single-purpose funding agencies. These agencies have built effective clientele support for themselves and along with their state and local counterparts have tended to become so many functional autocracies powerfully resistant to any attempts to subordinate their activities to broader purposes. The Bureau of Public Roads is a prime example. The Urban Renewal Administration, however, has been moved by the logic of its commitment to planning goals to recognize the social costs of its previous project orientation. The continuing and increasing agitation that resulted in a Department of Housing and Urban Development has, at least in large part, been motivated by concern over the waste, duplication, and cross-purposes of piecemeal intervention by functional autocracies. A federal department of urban affairs is, of course, the American analogue to a ministry of local government. Given the traditional commitment to federalism and the limited constitutional path — spending money for the general welfare — it is not surprising that it should have taken this emerging nation so long to follow the practice of other unitary nation-states. Nor is it surprising that, in the course of piecemeal funding, a dense undergrowth of agencies and clienteles should have been created. These facts of history will seriously impede the coordinating efforts of the new ministry, and the local administrator is likely to find the federal dimension of his world more complex before it becomes less so.

The demand for public goods is part and parcel of the shift toward services in a society in which the productivity of agriculture and manufacturing have released vast stores of labor and purchasing power. Many of the objects of desire, such as transport, recreation, environmental control, and even education, are for large categories of the population most readily produced by and consumed through public agencies. Some 40 per cent of the new jobs created within the past few years have been in the public sector and these largely at the local level though frequently with important federal funding. It seems altogether likely that a steeply increasing fraction of the consumption of an affluent society will take the form of public goods.

This trend toward the fully developed welfare state finds us poorly equipped theoretically and institutionally to cope with it. Committed to the slogans of free private enterprise, limited government, and federalism, every new departure in the provision of public service must be treated as an exception to the general rule. This postpones facing up to the need for a more adequate theory describing and interpreting what we are in fact about and where we are heading. It also provides the rationale for piecemeal institutional improvisation since each activity is by way of exceptional and doubtful departure from the general rule. Where some administrative departure from independent agencies occurs, it is likely to take the form of a departmental holding company for largely housekeeping purposes.

The fiscal system that has developed over time makes federal funding the line of least resistance. State legislatures are far more sensitive to the supposed dangers of raising taxes than Congress. Individual members of the legislature feel themselves highly vulnerable. Beyond this there is a genuine, if deluded, fear of adversely affecting the competitive position of the state's economy by upsetting its "business climate." But even where local demands for funds are passed on to Washington, there is a strong insistence that state counterpart agencies stand between the federal government and the local municipalities. While this has been sometimes evaded in the past, the present trend seems increasingly to require at least formal obeisance to the orthodoxies of federalism. For the local administrator, the existence of a state agency may not be an unmixed evil. It is, however, an addition to the governmental complexity and adds to the values and pressures in play.

The limitations of traditional and actual revenue resources of local governments produce a Balkanized competition for fiscal assets and escape from fiscal liabilities that is nearly internecine at the extreme. Given the heavy dependence on the real estate tax, local officials become increasingly in the business of land management to secure highest fiscal returns from potential land use. Quite bluntly this means a struggle to attract highest revenue sources and to avoid or even get rid of low yield, high service cost land-users. The latter tendency is somewhat mitigated by partisan concerns which may not always coincide with promotion of highest yield, lowest service cost land use. Federal urban renewal policy in the past has considerably aided beleaguered municipalities in their efforts to maximize their particular land use revenues at the expense of their neighbors.

Local revenue patterns make almost mandatory a chauvinistic form of municipal nationalism at a time when this dog eat dog and devil take the hindermost approach seems doomed to produce collective frustration even when making individual sense. Local governments suffer from the prisoner problem of economics. Unless they can be sure all will work together, it pays to act selfishly and achieve a larger share of a smaller pie. Regional land use planning may dictate that one suburban community provide the land for parks and another for industry, but unless the resulting differential in revenue is made up the plan remains utopian. To the existing number of competing muncipal entities, we have every reason to expect the future addition of many more. The forecasts of a hundred million increase in population in the next years, almost all of which is expected to settle in metropolitan areas outside the central city, insures this. Given our national predilection for separate municipalities, growth in population of this magnitude coupled with the far more extensive individual land use of present patterns of settlement can only result in a major increase in the number of suburbs. The likelihood is also that this will exhibit widely varying fiscal bases with no close fit to fiscal needs. As Anthony Downs has pointed out, at a time when the density and complexity of our society's pattern of settlement requires more and more capacity for coordination and problem-solving, this capacity at the local level will in all probability be reduced.

III

The increase in the importance of public goods as an aspect of the society's pattern of consumption will reinforce the country's predilection for independent local governments. In the past neighborhood segregation and the acceptance of gross differentials in the levels of neighborhood provision of public services made even the central city a source of widely varied public goods consumption. To an extent this still obtains, but the gap is narrowing. With the equality norm pushing against existing differentials in neighborhood service and tax costs mounting, suburbanization has provided an attractive means for achieving differentiation in levels of public goods comsumption. Indeed a society such as ours that is committed to inequality of income and an equality norm among its citizens is confronted with a serious dilemma in giving effect to each of these values in the comsumption of its public goods.

With the increase of the importance of public goods in consumption, the segregation of this consumption through territorially separate governments is our ready-made answer. Indeed the present vogue of regarding suburban governments as so many rival hotel-keepers catering to different clienteles with the market as their coordinator provides an admirable rationale for the reflection of income inequality in inequality of public goods consumption. And indeed from the neighborhood differential of the central city to the suburban differential, there runs the age-old problem of reconciling equality with diversity. Clearly, income inequality in a period of high public goods consumption will need government institutions to give it effect.

IV

The demand for differentiation in public goods consumption ranging from lot size to schools not only runs into the inability of a patchwork of local government to deal effectively with overall problems of transportation, environmental pollution, water and recreational resources, and the like, but it runs increasingly head-on into the emerging number one national problem of the politics of role redistribution. In the past we have tended to look on the federal government as the main and almost exclusive agency of redistributive politics because of its progressive income taxation and welfare policies. While the redistribution of income is important for role redistribution, it has never been as serious as it has been made out to be. As minorities have made themselves more and more vocal with the Negro revolution, it becomes increasingly clear that what is involved is a change of roles. And this can only happen where the people live and work and go to school. Serious redistribution of roles involves changing where people live, where their children go to school, and what jobs they can hold. While the federal government can do much to affect role redistribution through its leverage on school funds, on housing mortgages, and on governmental suppliers, the guidance of local change is most effectively handled by local leaders. Indeed the current poverty program stemming from a commitment to work through the existing pattern is a striking illustration of federal ineffectiveness and frustration of local government. A program in which each little municipality is expected to set up a committee to solve its poverty within its own borders independently of the metropolitan labor market and the metropolitan housing market seems an exercise in futility unless intended as a reductio ad absurdum of outworn prejudices.

A leadership capable of mobilizing sufficient support to tackle the explosive issues involved in role redistribution and one capable of enlisting that support for the long drawn-out campaign that is required can scarcely be developed in the present fragmented state of local government. As presently constituted few local governments possess the human and financial resources to undertake the task. Indeed, insofar as the fragmentation is designed to achieve segregation in public goods consumption, a major raison d'être of the existing pattern of local government is to inhibit the politics of role redistribution.

V

Each local government constitutes a kind of end system for its officials and for its active citizens. While local government nationalism may have in it an element of the ridiculous, it is nonetheless a reality. It defines the objectives of the local game for players and spectators alike, and it determines the mix and the priority of the values that go into decision-making. To be sure, multiple group membership affects local governments as well as other groups. And, unlike nation-states, local governments possess only limited finality for even their more committed members. However, their resources and constituents can to a large degree determine the purposes of their active members. A planner may feel professionally that planning for the continued survival of a nine-square-mile monstrosity such as Brookline, Massachusetts, is bad planning, but he would feel equally, and indeed much more, compelled professionally to serve his client. No more, and perhaps less, than a doctor would he be prepared to recommend euthanasia to a moribund entity.

Our inherited political culture places major value on territorial loyalty as a means of structuring purposes and achieving integration. The polity, if not possessed of the finality Aristotle ascribes to it, is still felt to convey a higher legitimacy to its proper ends than that possessed by individuals and other associations. Though political theory has scarce condescended to deal with local government, the ideas applying to the city-state have in a vague but real way extended to the municipality. The mediaeval city at any rate has provided a tradition of burgher loyalty and burgher activity that persists though in diluted form and gives some continued meaning to local citizenship. Max Weber's insistence that the city ceased to be when the citizens ceased to man the walls neglected to go into what, if anything, remained.

Clearly some notion of a common good, and some notion of fellow citizen or fellow townsmen, at least for some leaven of the civic lump, persist. Indeed one might well maintain that a rather considerable residue persists — enough to structure a principle of legitimacy and give it some general acceptance in the vocabulary of politics. If this were to be put in behavioral terms, it would predict that as a result of a shared symbolism there would be a marked gradient between attitudes of appropriate concern for members of the municipal association and outsiders. The we and they are the oldest distinctions of politics, and the capacity to mobilize attitudes appropriate to their discrimination is one of the most basic and primitive of politics.

The principle of legitimacy, which endows the local polity with a salient if not absolutely overriding common good, is the core of its status as an entity. It not only bounds the organization by determining legally, habitually, and affectively its membership, but it provides some guiding principle of integration for individual and associational activity within it. As an entity the local government is equally concerned with maintaining external boundaries and internal cohesion. As much a menace to the steady state of the entity as external threats is the constant tendency of institutions and individuals within the entity to lose their subordinated integrated status as members and become independent agents on their own. This ever-present danger is illustrated by the rise of functional autocracies within local governments creating a new feudalism at the expense of the central power and purpose.

Departments and agencies of local governments develop survival interests and autonomy drives, as Sayre and Kaufman have illustrated in their study of New York. The thrust toward self-sufficiency and ingroup security is carried to such extremes as complete reliance on promotion from within. The growing power of constituent institutions of local government is frequently unaccompanied by any corresponding increase in the capacity of overall coordinative power in the political leadership. What Banfield has called the burden of government is mounting while the power to carry the burden is being reduced. In part this results from the very professionalization of the public services, which not only withdraws important elements of patronage from political leadership but also produces an ideology justifying separatism and a constituency and reference group supporting separatist ambitions. In even larger part the burden of leadership becomes staggering through the transformation of citizens into consumers of public goods whose allegiance to the local community resembles that of a customer to a store or a tenant to an apartment house. The input of support may be so limited that the range and intensity of issues that the political leadership can handle is seriously circumscribed. Adrian and Williams have described a local community whose leadership was unable to mobilize enough votes to pass a bond issue as an alternative to floating in its own sewerage. The palsied penuriousness that Vidich and Bensman document in their *Small Town in Mass Society* is almost an ideal type of political degeneration or the atrophy of local government. As local incapacity to deal with a significant range of issues grows, individuals and organizations naturally turn to higher levels of government or to techniques of self-help. The latter device is frequently hailed as a method of market coordination that can do the work of political coordination through a species of consumer sovereignty exercising the sanction of dollar ballots on local governments who needs must complete for desirable residents.

VI

Whether the metropolitan areas in which most of us now live can satisfactorily be left to function as a historically developed ecology of competing and cooperating local governments is perhaps a major question of our domestic politics. The historic interaction of local governments and their departments, state governments and their departments, the federal government and its departments has after all functioned. What Matthew Holden has discussed as the diplomacy of the metropolitan area has achieved levels of cooperation that have not entailed systemic breakdown. The Vernon studies of New York tend to indicate that the metropolitan economy can rock along with piecemeal ad hoc improvisation to deal with area-wide problems. Robert Wood's later speculations would seem to bear out the general conclusion that metropolitan governmental integration is not a precondition to avoid obvious and menacing disaster.

It seems highly likely that the physical problems that metropolitan Toronto confronted and solved can be solved well nigh as well by ad hoc devices. In fact, as metropolitan Toronto has moved from the physical problems on which intermunicipal consensus could be readily mobilized to the politics of redistribution, its success has radically declined. The confederal form of government, though easiest of attainment, has stopped short of creating a new community endowed with the capacity to grow a vital sense of a common good. Gardiner's politically expedient strategy of sticking to the brick and mortar made him in the final reckoning more of a Bob Moses than a local George Washington.

The failure of metropolitan Toronto to deal effectively with the problem posed by the politics of redistribution gives some indication of the amount of political power needing centralization to handle this kind of issue as opposed to those questions of transport and plumbing. Indeed, to treat Toronto's deficiency purely in terms of lack of centralized power is to misstate the problem. The politics of redistribution and even more those of role redistribution require a shared conception of community going beyond a limited purpose commitment to a species of common public works department. Toronto is now in the posture where it is pressed to move toward an enlarged conception of the extent of the metropolitan community's common purpose or perhaps back off from some of the steps already taken.

What really lies at issue is whether the politics of redistribution and role redistribution are to be handled at the local level to an important degree or whether the only governments capable of mobilizing sufficient shared community values to legitimize action in this field are the states and the nation. Some of the states may be able to take effective action, especially where they can to all intents and purposes become metropolitan governments. However, in most cases it seems doubtful that states can muster the leadership and support for facing up to problems state politicians are eager to avoid. Federal legislation and pressure are major factors in furthering social change, but, as the civil rights experience has demonstrated, Washington cannot take the place of local leadership. When the federal government moves beyond its capacity to secure at least local leadership acquiescence, it becomes an army of occupation.

There seems a growing if hesitant awareness in Washington of the need for an effective system of local government that is not met by the present combination of states and existing units. The folly of federal programs designed to deal with housing and poverty but unable to work with any local government competent and concerned over the metropolitan housing and labor markets and hence constrained to operate through status quo-oriented muncipalities while seeking social change is becoming painfully apparent. Tentative steps to encourage metropolitan planning as a way out of the impasse are being made by the Housing and Home Finance Agency whose workable program requirements have proved hopelessly inadequate in scope. That a national government should need an effective system of local government would seem less odd if the existence of the states and their exclusive authority over local government did not distract consideration of functional need into that of constitutional propriety.

When it is recognized that for most purposes the United States has become a nation with a national economy and an emergent national society, it should not seem strange that there should be an emerging national need for a system of local self-government competent to achieve national purposes. Were the states not to exist, the government of the United States might well wish to have a system of local self-government rather than merely a system of localized national administration. The preference for local self-government by a central government relates to the capacity for mobilization of leadership, energies, and participation by that means which administration by itself cannot command. Yet the interest in local self-government on the part of a national government is most closely concerned with the capacity and likelihood of the structure of local self-government entertaining and achieving national ends.

The national government brings into focus support for a program of political modernization embodied in civil rights legislation and the Great Society. The implementation of this program for constitutional reasons requires cooperation by local governments who characteristically reflect different mixes and priorities of values than the national government. Apart from constitutional impediments the sheer magnitude of the task envisioned and the overriding need to use political persuasion rather than coercion makes the mobilization of effective supportive local leaderships with the requisite institutional structure for their action a major requirement for the national program's success.

In administration we have long been familiar with the problem of positioning agencies and bureaus within departments and governments not only to achieve program emphasis but also to achieve a mix of value and fact considerations that will yield a type of decision-making outcome. Local governments too have structures that largely determine what range of values and facts will receive what kind of consideration in their decision-making. The mix of population and resources has major consequences for what officials and political leaders will consider within the range of practical politics. The fragmented mirror of the nation that exists in the segmented jurisdictions of the metropolitan areas breaks and distorts whatever unity the national vision possesses. The myriad parts form far less than a whole, and the generosity of the nation is lost in the parochial egotism and incapacity that afflict its grass roots.

It might seem incredible that there should exist a political program commanding wide national assent that fails to achieve such assent in an operative fashion the closer one gets to where the people live. The phenomenon is accounted for by the values politicians respond to in different political contexts and the resources with which they are equipped. The gerrymandered structure of our metropolitan areas with their segregation of rich and poor, white and colored, and the radically unequal fiscal resources of the governmental units would seem sociologically designed to produce a political culture of Dobuanism in which every suburb would seek its place in the sun and devil take the hindermost. The sociometry of institutionalized hostility, the Balkans, can be produced. In this country it nearly prevented the formation of a nation and nearly wrecked the Union.

From the national point of view, to achieve sympathetic local concern for the furtherance of national social programs, there need to exist local governments responsive to a similar mix of values and forces to that operative through the national government. Such a mix is roughly available in the nation's metropolitan areas in which the variety of problems and populations mirrors those of the nation. In addition these areas possess the fiscal and human resources, if not the political structure to mobilize them, to make a major contribution to effective solution of many problems that now drift upward because of local weakness.

The bulk of the American people live in two-hundred-odd metropolitan areas. There is every reason to believe that soon the overwhelming majority of the American people will be living in metropolitan areas. These areas are becoming homogenized samples of the nation at large. More than most units of government local or state, they reflect the nation's problems and aspirations. The nation's metropolitan areas contain by far the major part of the nation's human talent and wealth. States and nation alike depend upon them. Yet their constituent governmental units are compelled to go, hat in hand, to state capitals and to Washington, seeking the fractional return of their tax dollars. Their human talent, possessing neither a platform from which to develop a metropolitan common interest nor institutions through which such an interest might be given effect, remains immobilized. The divided and devisive structure of local government is increasingly stricken with fiscal anemia and incapable of mobilizing the human resources it presently serves to incapacitate for significant political action.

VII

The present metropolitan trend is to shift leadership and power upward to political arenas more broadly responsive to urgent needs and possessed of fiscal competence. This trend might seem highly likely to continue if the only objective in seeking to provide a political vehicle for a metropolitan common interest were the physical needs of water, sewerage transport, and environmental control. Though it may be costly and wasteful to deal with these needs on an ad hoc basis and though the multiplication of single-purpose agencies increases the difficulty of overall coordination, these are ills that an affluent society may afford. The countertrend that may yet bring about political integration of metropolitan areas is the politics of role redistribution and the need to give this politics an appropriate and potentially responsive local forum. The national government cannot without great strain undertake to carry the whole burden of the political process. It badly needs to devolve the job on a local government structure adequately representative of the parties at interest and fiscally and jurisdictionally competent to make a major contribution to settling the issues. As presently constituted local governments possess neither the power, the competence, nor the need to respond to the parties claiming political redress. The powerless are the wards of Washington. Their integration into the local political process is essential if federal action is to be kept within limits.

Civil rights is only the most salient issue of national policy requiring local action of a major sort for successful implementation. The cities and the metropolitan areas have become the major constituency of the federal government. Their fostering is as much a matter of national interest as the promotion of agriculture was at a time when the nation's population was predominantly agrarian. In the attempt to serve this constituency, the federal government is half-consciously groping for an appropriate local institutional form with which it can cooperate. The land grant colleges and the county agents were among the instrumentalities for reaching the grass roots in the period of agriculture. The search for the urban agent is on.

As the piecemeal intervention of single-purpose federal agencies becomes ever more overtly at odds with overall federal social objectives, the situation that Connery and Leach describe must seem untenable. Federal concern with housing, transportation, jobs, and welfare all point to the metropolitan area as a major focus for effective administrative coordination. The federal carrot and perhaps the federal stick will be called into use to push planning on a metropolitan-wide basis. But planning without power is largely an exercise in futility. In his discussion of urban transportation policy, Lyle Fitch calls for comprehensive land use control. As a former city administrator he should realize what a revolutionary transfer this would amount to. Each federal interest, as the consequence of its pursuit by single-purpose agencies becomes apparent, leads inexorably to consideration of the desirability of local areal coordination for maximum compatible effects. This produces the likelihood that the federal government itself, in the interest of its own effectiveness, will regionalize its administration of programs in urban affairs on a metropolitan basis. And in all likelihood it will — in fact to an extent it now does — seek to develop a local counterpart metropolitan government.

Those local forces that have so far largely failed in producing a metropolitan government beyond the merely partial success of Dade County and the seemingly promising one at Nashville-Davidson will have the powerful assist of federal aid in their endeavor. The lesson of Toronto seems to indicate that a metropolitan government incapable of dealing with the politics of distribution will be found wanting, however great its success in the realm of public works. In fact the uniting of the metropolitan community to deal effectively with the problems of poverty and race through the instrumentalities of housing, education, and employment seems an essential condition for the resolution of these problems by other than federal fiat.

Dean Rose, who has observed Toronto closely from the position of social welfare, has strong doubts of the wisdom of total amalgamation. Indeed anyone who has watched the lifeless neighborhoods of the big city and the powerlessness of many of its people must feel qualms as to a governmental solution that consists merely of a local supergovernment. The desire for differentiation, quality, and individuation is important to retain. We need the yardstick competition of separate locally performed services to avoid the tendency to a dull, complacent, self-protective bureaucratic uniformity. Yet the case for the segregated production of public goods must be made compatible with the public objectives of overcoming poverty and reducing the evils of race prejudice. Local centralization to mobilize the leadership and resources and to provide the leadership with the constituency and goals needed to spark an effective attack on the problems of poverty and race relations should not require the complete destruction of local government differentiation in the production of public goods and their consumption. However, there is no point or hope in evading the issue. Redistribution means redistribution, and role redistributions means access, on a tolerable principle of justice among fellow citizens, to jobs, housing, and education.

The two-hundred-odd metropolitan areas that contain the bulk of America will determine the quality of American life. This is where most of us live and will live. The capacity of these areas for effective, significant self-government will determine the future of local self-government in the United States. The organization of these areas into politically effective governments would for the first time give the nation and the national government a truly national system of local self-government so constituted as to reflect on and respond to national issues. Containing the vast majority of the nation's human talent and material resources, these areas once organized could provide the basis for a richly creative and highly effective new age of cities. They could in doing so give us a new and more meaningful equivalent to the older federalism that has long since served its purpose.

VIII

The organizing of the metropolitan areas, if it comes to pass, would have major consequences for the problems of the administrator. Of all the difficulties he faces in modern complex society, the greatest is the lack of a public philosophy, in Walter Lippman's sense, capable of giving him a value orientation which would give purpose to his technique. The older common goods of the inherited local governments of the past are threadbare, trivial, and hopelessly selfish. The relations of local government to state, to nation, and to commonly accepted purpose are confused. A welter of techniques and a congery of professions provide only so many fragmented claimants inadequate to give general guidance. Administration is the servant of politics and a part of politics. To function responsibly it needs a significant community and a significant community public interest.

Chapter 12
Development for What?
Civilization, Technology, and Democracy

Mulford Q. Sibley

Department of Political Science
University of Minnesota

This chapter examines the significance of development for our moral, social, and political values and asks whether what we usually term democracy is compatible with technological change. Development as used here will be interpreted broadly as the movement from rural life to a highly urbanized and, in modern times, industrialized existence. The term democracy is employed to designate that whole interrelated set of ideals which emphasizes public policy determination by the Many rather than the Few and which stresses such values as equality, freedom of expression, respect for the individual as having ends of his own, and fraternity or the recognition of mutual interdependence.[1]

We shall first attempt to sketch in very broad terms what tends to happen when societies develop from agrarian to urban ways of life. Second, we shall note some of the major political, psychological, and social issues which arise as the development proceeds. Third, we shall ask whether it is possible to control the whole process for democractic ends and, if so, by what means.

---

[1]Although the term is used so widely, democracy as a theory tends to be vague, tentative, and subject to a wide variety of interpretations. There is really no authoritative statement of its principles to which we can point. As background for this paper, however, we might mention Aristotle, *Politics*, iii. 11; John Stuart Mill, *On Liberty Representative Government;* A. D. Lindsay, *Essentials of Democracy* (Philadelphia: Univ. of Pennsylvania Press, 1929), and *The Modern Democratic State* (New York: Oxford Univ. Press, 1962), Vol. I.; J. Roland Pennock, *Liberal Democracy: Its Merits and Prospects* (New York: Holt, 1950); and Henry B. Mayo, *An Introduction to Democratic Theory* (New York: Oxford Univ. Press, 1960).

1. From Simplicity to Complexity

In Book II of Plato's *Republic* we have a graphic ideal-typical—obviously not an historical—portrayal of what happens as societies move from a simple to a highly complex division of labor. In the beginning, economic division of labor is relatively unimportant; in pastoral and even in agricultural societies, trade and commerce are minimal. To be sure, there is always a certain amount of barter, but money is used sparingly, if at all. Village life, moreover, is not conducive to intellectual pursuits, so that education and the arts are sketchy, at best. In this stage of development, man's material wants are few, and he has neither the economic abundance of civilization nor the social and political problems created in part by material affluence. The primitive epoch of development is characterized, too, by what the German sociologists call *gemeinschaft* community relations, that is to say, men are connected with one another more or less directly and are bound together either by the sociological ties of family and clan or by immemorial tradition and custom which tend to reduce conflict between individuality and society.

Plato then went on to trace how these rather primitive conditions break down and give rise to complexity and its major problems. Individuality arises and with it competition for scarce resources. The economic motive, held in check previously by the *folkways* and *mores* and the absence of a money economy, is now given free rein. Men try to get the better of one another, as we say, and their wants appear to be insatiable. But one should note a curious characteristic of economic action: While individuals may freely will it, the results of combined individual economic choices may be directly contrary to the wishes of those involved. Thus if I hear about the allegedly weak position of my bank, my individual choice will be to draw out my deposits. Other individuals will do likewise, and quite understandably so. Yet the social results of our individual economic actions will probably be the failure of the bank and possibly a partial collapse of the economy—consequences which the individuals involved would surely not have willed. In the words of a modern philosopher, "economic action is blind."[2]

Economic action, too, seems to be at war with another aspect of man's nature—his search for fellowship as an end in itself. In economic action, I am engrossing scarce resources, and to the degree that I do so I am depriving my neighbor of those resources.

---

[2]C. E. M. Joad, *Guide to the Philosophy of Morals and Politics* (New York: Random House, n.d.), p. 774.

Yet at the same time I wish to share my joys and sorrows with my neighbor, not for some ulterior end but as a goal in itself. My economic actions, or those of my group acting with equal blindness, may lead directly — as Plato observes — to literal physical war. Yet at the same time I am aware, however dimly, that my fate is bound up with that of my neighbor.

This is the background for the rise of what we call politics. Confronted by the blindness of economic action and by the conflict between economic and social objectives, men seek consciously and deliberately to provide an order within which the desire to gain does not utterly destroy community and with it human personality. Both the economic and the social are essential if man is to become fully man, that is, to develop his latent capacities. Is it possible to discover principles of ordering which, while recognizing both tendencies in man, will make room for them under the aegis of an overall social morality? Plato thought that we can indeed formulate such principles, and the bulk of the *Republic* is devoted to a search for them. Thus what we might call the political philosophy of development is born, and the discussion in the *Republic* establishes a framework which is to be followed by many other thinkers.

Let us now examine the implications of Plato's analysis within the confines of modern history. The several phases of the Industrial Revolution have broken up the world of relatively slow change in an exceedingly drastic way.[3] Men have been induced (or in some instances forced) to leave the countryside and to take up residence in increasingly large urban complexes where it has been most convenient and most economical to locate the machinery so essential for the industrial way of life. This migration from the country began late in the Middle Ages and has not yet ceased.[4] What we are witnessing today in Asia and Africa is basically what occurred in Western Europe during the eighteenth and nineteenth centuries and in the United States and the Soviet Union during the nineteenth and twentieth. In the twentieth century, cities have tended to become what some have called megalopolises — urban clusters vastly more intricate than anything dreamed of before — and the countryside consists increasingly of deserted villages.

---

[3]Many scholars suggest that there have been several "industrial revolutions." See for example Harry Elmer Barnes, *An Economic History of the Western World* (New York: Harcourt, 1937). W. W. Rostow, *The Stages of Economic Growth* (Cambridge: Harvard Univ. Press, 1960), discerns five "stages" of economic growth from "traditional" society to highly developed industrial society.

[4]Never before in history have cities grown so rapidly as during the past hundred years. And from a purely economic point of view, many economists maintain, half the farmers of the United States are even today "redundant."

As this process continues, division of labor becomes progressively more minute. The tendency to emphasize economic "efficiency" as a value leads us to disregard all other values and to make reduction of per-unit cost in monetary terms the sine qua non of "progress." But reduction of unit cost of production inevitably involves still more specialization which in turn means that each person tends to be regarded simply as an economic man and not as a personality transcending his productive role. The material result of all this, of course, has been utterly fantastic. Estimated gross national product of the United States in the mid-1960's is about $650 billion and promises to soar far beyond this figure by the end of the century. Few can question the magnificent achievements of industrialism when measured by the standard of material goods produced. Indeed, Karl Marx himself paid a glowing tribute to what machine economies did and can do for the Western world, suggesting that the productivity of the industrial middle classes dwarfed all the efforts of ancient times.[5]

But, as Plato stressed long ago, this very economic development through division of labor entails certain inevitable corollaries. For one thing, labor that has been divided must be co-ordinated if it is to be of any utility. Initially, this co-ordination was accomplished in considerable degree by the "market," that is, the bargaining of buyer and seller helped make such basic economic decisions as what should be produced, how it should be distributed, and what proportion of the gross national product should be reserved for replenishment and expansion of capital.[6] The market still plays an important co-ordinating role in advanced industrial societies. But the very competition of the marketplace tended to destroy the market as a method of co-ordination. The economies of mass production and the necessity for large pools of capital led to the development of the limited liability corporation, and with the growth in size of corporations the elements of bureaucartic co-ordination—always present, obviously, in the organization of the factory—became increasingly great. Wherever we look in highly industrialized societies, bureaucratic co-ordination and administration—through hierarchies of company officials and civil servants and contractual arrangements between sets of corporation officers—have vastly expanded as price and other forms of competition have declined. Whether co-ordination is by civil servants or by highly structured "private" corporations makes relatively little difference,

---

[5]The *Communist Manifesto* praises the achievements of early industrial capitalism.
[6]For a careful examination of the nature and functions of economic organization, see Frank H. Knight, *The Economic Organization* (Chicago: Augustus M. Kelley, 1951).

for both schemes involve certain characteristics of bureaucracy. Bureaucracy tends to be impersonal, to "rationalize" life and development, and to be suspicious of spontaneity.[7] Planned co-ordination becomes the order of the day, whether in a privately owned industrial system or in arrangements of the State.

Actually, as we move from agricultural modes of existence to urbanized schemes of life, everything becomes increasingly politicized. Broadly speaking, by politicized we imply that, whereas in more primitive and less complex societies social order is largely the fruit of custom and rather rigidly defined and unconsciously established folkways, in a complex and particularly in an industrialized society, it tends more and more to be the result of deliberate formulation, implementation, and evaluation of what we call policy. Where social change is relatively slow, as in agrarian-oriented communities, new customs more or less unconsciously and gradually arise to absorb and order the changes and relate them to the past. But where the dynamics of life move to the forefront and technology injects constant change, there is no time to develop a gradual re-ordering: We either re-order consciously and therefore politically, or we allow a kind of hodge-podge order to arise which is the fruit of the clash of special interests, force, or economic dictation.

In a sense, what Plato and others were saying is that, once we enter complex, urbanized societies, it becomes almost impossible to reverse the tendency and restore simple, nonurban communities. In urban-dominated societies, we either legislate consciously, that is, try to order the various elements of life according to some overall scheme of values deliberately arrived at, or we allow events to legislate for us by what Plato called "accident"[8] and what we might term happenstance. The choice would seem to be one between, on the one hand, fully accepting the challenge of complexity by attempting deliberately to control the process and, on the other hand, rejecting the challenge and hoping that the gods, or luck, or some fortunate concatenation of forces will perform the task for us.

---

[7]Max Weber has examined the implications and characteristics of bureaucracy. See, for example, his *Theory of Social and Economic Organization* (Glencoe, Ill.: The Free Press, 1957). See also H. H. Gerth and C. Wright Mills, trans. and eds., *From Max Weber: Essays in Sociology* (New York: Oxford Univ. Press, 1946). Another sociologist, Alvin W. Gouldner, has dealt with bureaucracy in industrial organization. See his *Patterns of Industrial Bureaucracy* (Glencoe, Ill.: The Free Press, 1954).

[8]Plato, *Laws* iv. Putting the case in extreme form, the Athenian in the dialogue says: "I was going to say that man never legislates, but accidents of all sorts, which legislate for us in all sorts of ways. The violence of war and the hard necessity of poverty are constantly overturning governments and changing laws." Jowett's translation; the Random House edition of *The Dialogues of Plato*, II, 480.

Put in another way, the challenge of the political is the issue of whether or not men can or wish to be rational in their conduct of collective affairs.

There is a perennial conflict within human consciousness about this problem, as the history of political thought reveals. On the one hand, human beings are fearful of the complexity engendered by the division of labor and the bureaucratic co-ordination which ensues; they dread the loss of face-to-face relations and of the small-community fellowship associated with the nonbureaucratic way of life; they also fear that they will become the victims of their own creations and cannot control what they brought into being. We see this horror of complexity and urbanization throughout almost every stage of human development: in the yearning of many ancient Hebrews for the tribalism which preceded the establishment of the monarchy,[9] in the cults of withdrawal so common in almost every epoch,[10] in the idealization of the primitive stressed by thinkers like Rousseau,[11] and in the belief of Marxists that many of the presumed benefits of the pre-civilized state will be restored in the "final stage" of communism.[12]

It is also true, however, that the history of thought expresses a contradictory tendency. Along with the dread of civilization, urbanization, and politicizing (and the three accompany one another) goes a very strong tendency to think of development as "natural" to man. Even in periods of relatively little change—during the early Middle Ages, for example—men's social dynamics are preparing the way for urban culture, and the very intellectuals who often suggest that the process of human development is relatively uncontrollable are themselves products of the development. As Plato emphasized, moreover, there is usually a strong tendency to wish to improve the material conditions of life, and this very quest for economic progress leads to the social and political which, with one side of our being, we dread.

---

[9]Note the story of the foundation of the monarchy in which Samuel warns the people of the consequences of kingly rule: The monarch will introduce rigorous military conscription, set up a highly organized bureaucracy, establish high taxes, and virtually enslave the people. I Samuel, 8: 11-18.

[10]The Essenes, for example, sought to restore communal simplicity in the years immediately preceding New Testament times; the monks of the Middle Ages thought that life could be more virtuous outside the larger society; and in our day groups like the Bruderhof and Hutterite communities earnestly attempt to perpetuate the withdrawal ethic.

[11]In his Dijon Academy prize essay on inequality, for example.

[12]In a truly Communist society, Marxist doctrine holds, the benefits of development—material abundance and the culture which that makes possible—will be present without the bureaucracy, State institutions, alienation, and violence which in the past have accompanied development.

We wish the fruits of complex division of labor, in other words, but we fear the price that may be involved. To cite an example familiar to Americans: We desire the cheap goods that can be produced by machinery and mass production, yet we hope against hope that we can gain this objective without destroying the competition of yesteryear. To preserve competition, we pass anti-trust legislation, but to make sure that we also achieve the fruits of mass production and large-scale organization, we then refuse, by and large, to enforce the very legislation we have passed.[13]

Most men dream of a day when the social and the economic can somehow be reconciled, when we can be brothers, experiencing genuine fraternity, and, at the same time, have an abundance of material goods. Such has been the ideal of much of Judaism and Christianity as well as of other high religions. In some instances, as with the Marxists, we seek to show how the very process of producing an abundance of material goods will destroy the ancient conflict between our urge to get the better of our fellow human being through engrossing scarce resources and our equally great desire to treat him as if he were truly a member of the family.

In broad outline, then, this is what happens as we move from simplicity to complexity. Let us now show a bit more explicitly, keeping in mind the rough sketch, how major political, psychological, and social issues arise in the very process of development. We call attention to the apparent conflict between many of the values we profess, on the one hand, and the imperatives which seem to be set up, on the other, by the process itself: It is this conflict which constitutes the heart of the issues about which we shall speak.

2. Human Valuations and the Imperatives of Developed Societies

Highly developed societies tend to give rise to certain common problems, whatever the cultural context. Thus whether the background be Russian, American, or Chinese, industrialism will pose for man an implicit series of questions; he will be compelled to relate the attributes of the industrial order to his own value

---

[13]This has been the general history of antitrust legislation in the United States with only a few interruptions. According to former Senator Paul H. Douglas, not only has concentration of economic power as a whole increased enormously since World War II, but competition has begun to be stifled even in those industries which used to be most competitive — textiles, clothing, leather, boots and shoes, lumbering, furniture, and food. Paul H. Douglas, "The Central Problem of Economic Giantism," in *Problems of United States Economic Development* (New York: Committee for Economic Development, 1958), p. 99.

schemes and his own potentialities. His creatures — division of labor, bureaucratic co-ordination, machines — will tend to demand certain things of him which he may be reluctant to give. As we have noted earlier, this is an old observation, but it becomes particularly acute in modern times when on the eve of a cybernated culture we confront the implications of complexity in a form so extreme that we are virtually without any even approximate precedent to guide us. The gist of these problems was, indeed, recognized by Plato and other thinkers, but they could not and did not envision the issues in a context precisely like that of our age. Here we identify three of those issues.

Occupation, Alienation, and Class

In an ultra-complex industrialized society, the minute division of labor involved tends to separate men from one another not merely in terms of their work but also psychologically and socially. A specialist in one field develops a whole way of life and even a means of communication which set him apart from other men. His outlook is colored enormously by the factors involved in his method of earning a livelihood. Although he continues to have many things in common with other men — the need for food, shelter, love, and so on — the way he apprehends these needs and his approach to them will still constitute a barrier between him and other men. Carpenters will have their own peculiar perspective on things and tend to associate primarily with men of similar status and outlook; physicians will find themselves moving in circles which, generally speaking, will exclude carpenters. The highly educated will and do regard the world quite differently from those of little formal education.[14]

Income differentiations, moreover, which are often accentuated through economic development, tend to create other lines of separation, the basis of which is not merely economic but also social.[15]

[14]In attitudes to sex, for example, as the Kinsey studies seem to show, there is a marked difference between highly educated professional groups and relatively unskilled and uneducated segments of the population. On the whole, too, those with greater formal education tend to be more liberal than the uneducated with respect to such matters as freedom of expression.

[15]The newly rich may not have social status, but, if their families manage to hold on to their wealth, their children or grandchildren will almost certainly possess it. The way in which income has been distributed has not changed substantially during the past two generations or more. Currently, the upper 10 per cent of all income recipients in the United States receive about 28 per cent of the income, after taxes; the lower 10 per cent get approximately 1 per cent. See Gabriel Kolko, *Wealth and Power in America* (New York: Praeger, 1962).

Economic class lines heighten and extend divisions among men and help add to the many tensions characteristic of highly complex societies.

But if men tend to be increasingly separated from one another, what becomes of the possibility of community, which, according to political thinkers, is essential for full development of human personality and, indeed, for a peaceful political life? How can men communicate with one another across gulfs of psychological and social separation? There have been studies which seem to conclude, for example, that, when members of lower-income groups become mentally ill, their types of sickness are quite different from those of upper-income groups. Moreover, it is almost impossible for psychologists, psychiatrists, and psychoanalysts to treat the lower classes because, being generally of the upper strata themselves, they cannot communicate with manual workers, artisans, and small tradesmen.[16] In the absence of communication and the presence of rather widely differing ways of life, it would appear that democratic political consensus will be increasingly difficult.

To be sure, separation of men by classes and occupations has been with us from the dawn of recorded history, and slave and serf-ridden cultures have been ubiquitous. We should never make the mistake of thinking that there has ever been a time when community and communication have not been problems. But under modern conditions, the accentuation of occupational separation and the tendency, for example, to dissolve primary groups, like the family, have added a new dimension.

It is important, too, that we keep in mind the international ramifications of these observations. Men are not only separated from one another within economically developed societies but find themselves divided by the vast gulf which exists between so-called underdeveloped and highly industrialized societies. The average native of India, with an income of perhaps $75 a year confronts the average American who receives possibly $3,000. The underdeveloped nations find themselves increasingly alienated from the third of mankind who live, on the average, in relative abundance. This means that there is often a sharp tension, frequently reflected in politics, between that part of the human race where technology is primitive and those regions where it has made great inroads. Inhabitants of the underdeveloped areas aspire to greater material

---

[16]See August B. Hollingshead and Frederick C. Redlich, *Social Class and Mental Illness* (New York: Wiley, 1958).

wealth, but the process of attaining it seems excruciatingly slow to them, particularly when they note that the gulf between developed and underdeveloped regions is growing larger rather than smaller.[17] Poverty used to be accepted as inevitable; but, when millions see that it may be possible to eliminate it, they no longer remain passive and tend rather to become militant, often resorting to self-defeating violence as a way out. The whole theme of men's alienation from one another is an important theme in modern novels and other literature. As many writers see it, the breakdown of community—whether within nations or between them—is one of the most significant facts of modern culture.[18]

Imperatives of Technology

A central thread in the movement from pre-industrial to industrial society is the role played by the tools of production. In pre-industrial societies man is, in a sense, the slave of Nature and of the unconsciously developed folkways and mores. The weather and the habits and needs of animals impose their imperatives upon him. He is governed, too, by long-entrenched customs which in extreme cases are regarded as little less than laws of God. The path away from pre-industrial cultures tends to emancipate him from Nature and the folkways, and he is confronted by the political challenge, as we have suggested before. At the same time, his complex tools impose their own imperatives, and he runs the risk of finding his recently won relative freedom from Nature more than counteracted through a new enslavement to the machine.

The impact of complex technology involves man in the acceptance of what is little less than a revolution. For the first time in human experience, it makes possible such material abundance that the spectre of hunger can be completely banished. Properly used,

---

[17]On problems of development and underdevelopment, see the various publications of the Department of Economic Affairs of the United Nations. A brief analysis, from an American "liberal" viewpoint, will be found in *Economic Development Abroad and the Role of American Foreign Investment* (New York: Research and Policy Committee of the Committee for Economic Development, 1956). For a Marxist analysis, see Paul Baran, *The Political Economy of Growth* (New York: Monthly Review Press, 1957). The tendency is for private investors to provide capital for areas that are already heavily capitalized and to look with suspicion of investing in the areas which need it most—countries that by and large have a high incidence of political instability.

[18]One might mention, for example, the novels of Albert Camus and James Baldwin. Some, too, would cite such names as Beckett, Salinger, Agee, Golding, and Orwell.

machines could free men from the age-old fear of want and thus release them for the pursuit of those ends which most civilizations regard as final—beauty and goodness and truth. It is also true, however, that the cost of technological development may under certain circumstances be enormous and could in some contexts be more than man is willing to or should pay. Once a culture embarks on technological development, it tends to have its future choices restricted by increasingly involved demands and can only with difficulty alter its course. As we have suggested before, economic action divorced from overall social decisions tends to be blind and to result in social consequences which we might have repudiated had we anticipated them. Introduction of complex technology is a prime example of this generalization.

Thus we freely introduce automobiles and find in the end that we do not know what to do with them: Their parking needs often absorb our best land, their sheer number in traffic sometimes slows the speed of transport to what it was in horse-and-buggy days, and their notorious mechanical inefficiency absorbs a substantial proportion of the much-vaunted increase in national income. Although the automobile purported to be simply a new mode of transport, its social impact has revolutionized many areas of life, including even courting customs and the structure of the family.[19]

To take another illustration, the needs of all technology force us to place much greater emphasis than in most pre-industrial societies on exact timing of our lives. We must become, as the Victorians used to put it, as regular as clockwork. The whole rhythm of existence must be altered to fit the needs of precision machinery. Regardless of the psychological effects on human beings of this slavery to the clock, the machine must be served.

The machine becomes so ubiquitous that it impresses itself on all aspects of life. Men think and act mechanically. They reduce music to mechanical reproductions. Education itself tends to take on the characteristics of the factory system—that scheme of production developed primarily to cater to the needs of the machine. Bachelors of Arts and even Doctors of Philosophy are turned out on an assembly line, their teachers often having little personal acquaintanceship with them; like animal carcasses stamped with the approval of the Department of Agriculture, they have degrees imprinted on them as they rush by on an educational conveyor belt. Teachers, too, are engulfed in the imperatives of the machine: Recently this writer was called by the Dean's secretary, who said

---

[19]Cf. Michael Harrington, *The Accidental Century* (New York: Macmillan, 1965).

very solemnly, "I hope your grades will be in by Tuesday. The machines are waiting."[20]

To be sure, man always expects to gain more from the machine than he gives. But the question has often been raised—as in Mary Shelley's *Frankenstein*, for example—as to whether this net advantage necessarily results; whether, in the long run, and particularly with respect to some types of technology, human beings do not give away far more than they gain. Although complex technology is usually defended on the ground that it enables us to produce more material goods at a lower per unit cost, even this proposition may be questioned in some instances. Some have even asked whether a mechanized culture—at least in the context we know best in the West—has resulted in as much leisure as is usually thought.[21] And if we take into account the social, psychological, and political dimensions of technology, the question of overall cost of technological development becomes still more serious. Thus the speeding up of social change may profoundly affect the mental, emotional, and spiritual life of man in ways we do not yet fully understand and would not, if we did understand, deem to be in accordance with our overall value system.

About a century ago, the great social satirist Samuel Butler put some of these doubts into very emphatic words in the "Book of the Machines," where at one point he observes:

> From a low materialistic point of view, it would seem that those thrive best who use machinery wherever its use is possible with profit; but this is the art of the machines—they serve that they may rule. They bear no malice towards man for destroying a whole race of them provided he creates a better instead; on the contrary, they reward him liberally for having hastened their development.

> Machines will only serve on condition of being served, and that too upon their own terms; the moment their terms are not complied with, they jib, and either smash both themselves and all whom they can reach, or turn churlish and refuse to work at all. How many men at this hour are living in a state of bondage to the machines?

[20]It is as if man were hypnotized by his own inventions and rendered helpless by their power over him. Ironically, it was the University of Chicago, a center of humanistic studies, which played the important role in developing the atomic bomb, and with only a few exceptions scientists and engineers were able to rationalize the construction of nuclear weapons.

[21]Sebastian de Grazia, *Time, Work, and Leisure* (New York: Twentieth Century, 1962), helps support the thesis that the extent of increase in leisure has been exaggerated.

How many spend their whole lives, from the cradle to the grave, in tending them by night and day? Is it not plain that the machines are gaining ground upon us, when we reflect on the increasing number of those who are bound down to them as slaves, and of those who devote their whole souls to the advancement of the mechanical kingdom?[22]

Although we should always remember that for the bulk of mankind the problem is still one of how to produce enough material goods for a bare existence, in the developed societies the issue of weighing the benefits of technology against its enormous demands and costs takes on greater centrality with the onset of cybernation. Although automation may have the effect of saving much human labor and increasing the demand for more skilled workers, it may well be asked whether this is necessarily good. If the increased leisure gained is primarily used, let us say, for spectator sports, playing the races, or consuming dubious products in response to the manipulations of advertisers, is this truly a better situation — either socially or individually — than spending extra hours at work?

Is all economic progress necessarily good? Suppose for the moment that we could prove that men are happier living in less developed economies than in highly industrialized ones, should this not immediately lead us to question the desirability of further economic development? Perhaps there is a point somewhere between ideal-type primitive society, on the one hand, and extremely developed society, on the other, where men, on the whole, feel most at home and are happiest. If this could be shown to be true — and thus far it has neither been proven nor disproven — would it not be quite evident that we should halt economic development at that precise point? In a sense, both Plato and Aristotle believed exactly this; they thought that men can become most truly men (defined as creatures seeking comtemplation as an end) if they deliberately (politically) limit material resources and do not allow all possible material wants to be satisfied. In our day, Gandhi appeared to take a similar position, arguing that even an underdeveloped nation like India should limit the kinds of machinery it introduced. Thus he was willing to accept the sewing machine, for example, but insisted that many forms of complex machinery ought to be barred.[23]

---

[22]Samuel Butler, *Erewhon*, Ch. 24.

[23]Gandhi maintained that some complex technology was inevitable but that where it was admitted, ownership should be vested in the public. For a more detailed discussion of Gandhi's attitudes to technology and the control of technology, see Mahadeva Prasad, *The Social Philosophy of Mahatma Gandhi* (Gorakhpur: Ishwavidyalaya Prakashan, 1958). Even those not taking Gandhi's position have often warned against "unbalanced" development.

Whatever we may feel about questions of this nature, they are central to any political thinking which endeavors to get beyond the superficial. And they are particularly relevant for those who would inquire into the goals of development. Many, including this writer, would contend that they are far more basic than the supposed issues involved in the ideological struggle turning on the existence of communism.

Knowledge, Forecasting, and Politicizing

Urbanized and industrialized societies, as we have said, give rise to situations where larger and larger segments of life are opened to the possibilities, indeed the imperatives, of politicizing. Personal freedom and consciousness of individuality are enlarged as immemorial folkways disintegrate. With freedom and individuality come many possibilities of conflicts and the need for re-ordering through deliberate means rather than through unconsciously generated habits. Even decisions *not* to plan are political, in the sense that they are more or less deliberate and involve the group rather than merely individuals.

But in order to politicize we must forecast. We must, that is to say, make some judgment as to the probable consequences of different policies or the absence of policies. Forecasting, however, is notoriously difficult. In one sense, we may say that civilized man is compelled to make predictions yet cannot. He must act as if he were a god when it is all too evident that he lacks the prescience of the gods. It is out of this very awkward situation that some of the most acute conflicts of politics emerge; they turn on differences over measuring the consequences of given decisions in a complex where the results of many choices must be evaluated as a whole. Under such circumstances, it is unavoidable that disagreements will arise. Yet we cannot refuse to make judgment about the future if we are to act as rationally as possible, and, if we repudiate the quest for rationality, we automatically subject ourselves, as noted earlier, to legislation by accident. We either attempt to control the historical process within which we find ourselves or we give up the attempt and allow the process — with all its uncertainties and its clashes of interests — to control us. We either make it the object of our manipulations or permit it to make us the object of its happenstance directions.

Although forecasting and rationality — and therefore political ordering — are extremely difficult, we are not without some assistance, for the very process which develops the problems also gives birth to the scientific, philosophical, and historical knowledge and wisdom which are so essential if we are to make forecasts and rational decisions. With the aid of science, history, and philosophy we can at least provide relatively more educated guesses about the future than we might otherwise make.

Even at their best, however, the kinds of forecasts upon which the legislator (or the administrator) must build can never be more than rough in nature. Man is forever taking pride in his limited knowledge or claiming more knowledge than he really possesses, and this is the point, or at least one point, of such Biblical stories as those of the Fall of Man, the Tower of Babel, and Noah and the Flood.[24] Man makes pretences to knowledge at his peril, for knowledge can be used to destroy, and alleged knowledge to delude him. His moral knowledge, moreover, which must ultimately be grounded on intuitions or revelations, appears to be less clear and more confused than his technical understanding, and his social insights—thus far, at least, in developed societies—tend to lag behind his material achievements. He builds Towers of Babel before thoroughly considering *why* he wishes to reach the sky or whether he can do so. Similarly, he engages in races to the moon and constructs larger and larger bombs.

It is this problem of the necessity for prediction combined with our awareness of the limits to our capacity which becomes a central theme in many political philosophies that touch on issues of human development. Generally speaking, the "conservative" tends to stress human limitations and to be dubious about rationally planned orderings of human affairs. For guidance, the conservative would attempt to rely on such traditions and customs as remain extant and, for the rest, trust to legislation having only limited objectives. The "liberal," by contrast—and even more so the "radical"—aspires to a rationally ordered society and with this aspiration goes a considerable confidence in the capacity of human beings to make predictions and evaluate consequences. The conservative is most at home where there is a strong undergirding of custom and where technological change is slow; he is less certain where detailed guidance through custom declines and where technological changes press inexorably for ordering by political methods. Under these circumstances he either succumbs in part to the liberal temper or seems to become irrelevant. The liberal, by contrast, is

---

[24]Genesis 3; Genesis 11: 4-9; Genesis 6-8. Medieval thought, too, tends to think of pride—and particularly pride of intellect—as the central of the seven deadly sins.

characteristically associated with conditions where guidance through tradition has become uncertain and where the problems of freedom from mere want are matched by the equally great questions involved in a deliberate ordering of public affairs.[25]

In our day, the ends of development are widely subsumed under the term democracy. Whether in the West or in the East, it is a word held in highest repute, although its precise meaning may differ from culture to culture. Because it has become so much the hallmark of all political ideologies, we turn in the last section to a consideration of how its propositions might affect our judgments of the goals which we seek or ought to seek and of the means most appropriate for those objectives.

3. Development and Democracy: Ends and Means

As political methods of developing social order come more and more to take on added importance, the question immediately arises as to what groups in the community should make the decisions. Should it be the One, the Few, or the Many? Democratic theory argues for the latter, maintaining that in anything which affects all, it is only reasonable that all should be consulted. At the very least, democracy demands that public policy should not be made without the positive consent of the Many.[26]

But democracy also implies principles beyond this. Under what conditions *can* the Many most freely express their consent to or rejection of a proposed policy? The answer to this question can be very complex, and there is no unanimity among democratic theorists concerning it. At a minimum, however, democratic methods would seem to imply full freedom of expression, for without it the rationally arrived at consensus suggested by the democratic outlook would seem to be impossible of attainment. Democratic policy-makers must thus build into their value structure the idea that they ought not to limit freedom of expression in any way.

It will also be contended by many exponents of democratic theory, this writer among them, that democracy implies an account of human personality which does not reduce the individual to the

---

[25]In the period of classical Greek political thought, Aristophanes may be thought of as a conservative and Plato as a radical. In the late eighteenth century, Burke epitomizes the spirit of modern conservatism, while men like Thomas Paine, William Godwin, and Richard Price reflect a radical outlook.

[26]In one sense, of course, all government reposes on consent. Even despotism must have at least the passive acquiescence of most. But passive acquiescence is to be sharply differentiated from active and freely expressed consent.

status of a mere social product. No biological individual, to be sure, can become a human personality without the group; but this does not mean that the person can have no ends outside those of the group or groups to which he may belong. Society is a necessary but not a sufficient condition to account for what we call personality. The horizontal or social dimension of personality is enormously important; but the vertical dimension, in which the individual transcends the group out of which he arises, is equally significant. The person, in fact, is more than the sum total of all the biological, social, psychological, and other "parts" which are thought of as his constituent units; he is also a whole which shapes the parts. Democratic theory seeks in its political philosophy to recognize both the horizontal and the vertical poles, even though at points they appear to be incompatible with each other. Thus in the ideal democratic society the political decisions of the Many would be freely arrived at and would not be out of harmony with individual judgments of what public policy ought to be. There would be no minorities seemingly requiring coercion, for a freely arrived at general will would have been attained.

Now it should be obvious that no actual society in the twentieth century even approximates these methods and goals, although some, no doubt, are closer than others. The gulf between the actual and the ideal, we may suggest, is so great that by comparison the very real differences between and among existing societies pale into insignificance. The ideal, for the most part, remains to be achieved, whether in "communist" or in "capitalist" societies and whatever the stage of development.

What bearing does development have on attainment of the ideal and all the corollaries associated with it? What tendencies in development appear to facilitate the goal? In what sense do certain characteristics of development seem to make the task more difficult? What principles and devices can be discovered which will help to control development for the ends suggested? To these questions we now turn.

Relation of Development to the Ideal

Development is related to the ideal in a number of ways. In the first place, a certain stage of development must have been reached before men even speculate about ideals. In an ideal-type primitive society, what was must ever be. Only with the rise of individuality and consciousness of the person as in some sense apart from the group does the necessity for social and political ideals arise.

Second, one does not have to be a technological or economic determinist to recognize the ways in which the mode of production during any given age will at least condition the contents of social and political ideals. In a pastoral stage of existence, sheep-raising experiences will permeate the ideologies through which men express their goals, as, for example, in many Biblical statements. Or again, John Locke's theory of property was very much affected and limited by the preponderant forms of property relations existing during an era of commercial capitalism.

Third, and more specifically in relation to democratic ideals, it is important to note that modern democracy arose in the pre-industrial era and that many of its formulations remain colored by the limitations of that age. Although there have been many attempts to adapt those formulations to the period of industrialism—democratic socialism, for example, is such an effort—the full implications of democratic doctrine have never been worked out for the framework of an industrialist or automated culture. In fact, one of our problems is whether the imperatives of automated industrialism are compatible with democratic ideals.

Finally, as development proceeds, the question must be asked as to whether it will dominate or be subjected to man. Thus far we have not demonstrated that the technological process can be effectively subordinated to social goals outside those which it may dictate. Hence we hear it said very often today that man's essential task is to "adjust" to the "coming age of automation." The era of automation is a kind of sacred object in the shadow of which men are asked to change drastically their places of abode, their occupations, their politics, their economic order, their methods of rearing children, their educational systems, and even their sex life. Few ask how the epoch of automation can be "adjusted" to what may be man's social and political ideals.

What Tendencies in Development Facilitate Achievement?

Although there is a cult of democratic primitivism in every age, it would seem clear that many tendencies in development can be highly favorable for the attainment of democratic objectives. First of all, there is little doubt that widespread use of complex technology can solve the problem of material needs. This is still the central issue, in general, for most of mankind. It is also one of prime importance for the development of democratic institutions for it is clear that without a basic minimum of material goods, men are likely to be subject to frequent gusts of irrationality and to lack of concern for such democratic values as civil liberties, freedom of expression, suspicion of the military, and respect for personality. A hungry man is not a rational being and cannot even communicate effectively with his fellow-citizens.

Second, if an explicit or implicit goal of democracy is an enlarged consciousness of oneself and of the world, then the urbanization associated with development would appear to be essential. Whatever the demerits of cities, in some form they are the indispensable condition for high art, for culture, and for awareness. They afford opportunities for freer associations than do rural villages and the very anonymity of the city, which on some grounds may be criticized, helps provide the context for growth of that private world which we said it was the ideal of democracy to recognize and even encourage.

The struggles and tensions of humanity are to be interpreted in some degree as efforts to develop the qualities that set apart homo sapiens from other levels of creation. These qualities classically have included imagination, sensitivity, and rationality. Cities, more than an agricultural or a pastoral existence, help stimulate these characteristics. Democracy has as one of its values the drawing out of these distinctively human qualities in all men, rather than in merely a few.

The Impediments of Development

But development also brings with it certain impediments to the achievement of democratic ideals and even to those more general objectives which have been associated with a substantial segment of Western thought. As Plato pointed out in the passage we cited earlier, movement from relative simplicity to complexity, while it may stimulate man's intellect, also brings with it a series of new problems.

First of all, the very abundance potentially connected with complex technology carries its own perils. Although experienced by very few up to now, great material possessions, accumulated beyond a certain point, can produce a kind of complacency hardly conducive to intellectual or spiritual growth. Sometimes the possession of economic goods – particularly in certain social contexts—will simply suggest the inadequacy of primarily material goals for human fulfillment, and those disillusioned, knowing no other ideals, will tend blindly to revolt, as with many modern juvenile delinquents coming from upper middle-class homes. Although material goods in themselves cannot, of course, produce these results, their acquisition in periods of rapid development is often associated with other phenomena which do just that. Thus rapid urbanization is linked with dissolution of primary groups, like the family, and, at the very time when material standards are rising, a sense of purpose or goal is often lost.

Second, development in itself is likely to enhance economic inequalities, unless strenuous efforts are made to counteract these tendencies. Large stores of capital come under the control of the few, the gulf between highest and lowest incomes either increases or is not diminished, and old taboos on the acquisition of wealth fall into disuse. With these phenomena, means of communication come to be controlled by relatively small groups, politics is sometimes dominated by the handful who own capital, and social class distinctions follow the economic demarcations. To be sure, sharp economic and social divisions also exist in less developed societies but the point is that economic development in itself does little if anything to alter the situation, which is incompatible with democratic ideals whether in pre-industrial or industrial societies. The democratic ideal would seem to entail only minimal economic inequalities, whereas development—other things being equal—often moves in the reverse direction.

Third, the alienation of men from one another, even at the very time they become more and more interdependent economically, makes for difficult communication and hence increases the obstacles to community. But a high degree of community is indispensable for making and implementing democratic decisions. Another way to put it is to say that specialization tends to reduce men to mere segments of themselves, whereas democracy requires whole men.

Fourth, the imperatives of technology which help shape what human beings become make it easy psychologically to forget that machines should be mere tools and not ends. Machines, although created by man, become his idols. But any form of idolatry is antagonistic to democratic ideals, which require a constant critical re-assessment of ends and means by the Many.

Fifth, as men become more and more dependent on one another economically, they are likely to reflect a desire to subordinate themselves to those who control their livelihoods. But subordination in one area may affect all of a person's actions; he no longer feels free to speak or express himself generally for fear that he might offend his employer or his customers or his government. This was the factor which led Jefferson to distrust the development of cities, for he saw in them the element that would undermine the fearlessness and independence of outlook so important for demo-cratic institutions.

Sixth, great acquisition of knowledge is a two-edged sword, as we have seen. Knowledge can be used to wipe out the very civilization which produced it and the more complex the civilization, on the whole, the greater are the potentialities for destruction. Men may have the same passions in developed as in undeveloped societies, but in the former the release of these passions tends to be fraught with more universal destructive consequences.

Finally, the phenomena connected with complex organization of any type constitute serious impediments to attainment of demo-cratic ideals. The tendencies to bureaucracy, oligarchy, and the manipulation of men simply as means are ubiquitous. Complexity, war, and rapidity of social change place a premium on quick decisions, which in practice mean executive decisions, and thus legislative bodies lose either the capacity or the will to control a proliferated bureaucracy and the course of events.[27]

Control of Development for Democratic Ends

From the viewpoint of democratic means and ends, the central problem is how to assure the maximum benefits of development while reducing its impediments to the lowest possible point. Are there principles and devices which can do this? One tendency in thought would answer in the negative and argue in effect that development must always be basically antagonistic to community and to democratic values. If one accepts this answer, two alterna-tives would confront the world: We could (1) attempt deliberately to restore a less industrialized culture in the hope that this would enable us to preserve and extend the democratic features against

[27]And a sense of helplessness tends to pervade the masses, who feel more and more powerless to cope with situations in which the leaders allegedly know the answers. Thus in a condition of war or near-war, the executive can almost always manipulate news in such a way as to gain his own ends—even in an ostensibly democratic nation. Some of the problems of leadership in the supposedly democratic process are dealt with in Chester I. Barnard, *The Dilemmas of Leadership in the Democratic Process* (Princeton: Herbert L. Baker Foundation, 1939). See also Walter Lippmann's classical study *Public Opinion* (New York: Harcourt, 1922).

which development works; or (2) frankly accept more or less unlimited development and surrender any expectation that it might be reconciled with democratic objectives.[28]

But we must reject this position along with its alternative courses of action. Development can bring with it too many features conducive to achievement of democratic ideals for us to say that its admitted impedimenta must necessarily outweigh its potential benefits. Even if one accepts the view that control of development is a hopeless task, deindustrialization would appear to be equally hopeless and, if tried, fraught with serious consequences. To deindustrialize would itself require large-scale planning and involve many of the difficulties which the extreme critic sees in development. We might well ask, too, how we could support even a fraction of the world's present population without a large measure of industrialism.[29] As for the second alternative, we might observe that we have hardly begun to apply the principles which might make development compatible with democracy. Surely we should not surrender without much greater effort than in the past to subdue man's creations and make them subservient to human ideals.

We must, then, suggest lines along which the world might indeed check those tendencies in development which work against democratic values and take full advantage of those that assist us to fulfill our ends. Due to space limitations, our discussion can be only a sketch.

First of all, our conception of the units of control requires a rather fundamental overhauling. On the one hand, we need greater attention to overall world planning of resources and, on the other, a marked geographical and functional decentralization in planning for details. Basic allocation of the world's resources should be the task of a world organization — perhaps an adaptation of present UN structures. Within this fundamental framework of allocation, there should be not a little legislative and administrative decentralization. Although this decentralizing process should take account of present nations — since nations, after all, represent one aspect of humanity's cherished and supportable values — within each nation present units might have to be revised. Democracy requires participation by workers in the control of their individual factories, for

---

[28]Among those who seem to adopt the first alternative in rather extreme form, we might mention Wilhelm Roepke. See his *Civitas Humana,* trans. Cyril S. Fox (London: William Hodge, 1948). And writers like James Burnham appear to argue that the possibilities for democracy are very remote.

[29]Even if the rate of increase declines, the projected population figures for the year 2000 would be huge.

example, within the broad scheme of overall planning. Public ownership and administration of all land and natural resources would facilitate this combination of centralized and decentralized controls, for private control of land today often impedes the rational and democratic planning of cities.

Experimentation should be the key principle in developing units of control. Today we often cling to old units when they are obviously irrelevant in terms of encouraging democratic values and enhancing human ends. Thus our schemes for controlling urban areas are nineteenth century in inspiration. Short-run economic interests, socially blind as they are, tend to overshadow the goals implicit in democratic ideals. Instead of legislation by deliberation, we have legislation by accident.

Second, the machinery of control requires a fundamental reordering in many respects. Often it is ill-equipped to subject the complex factors of technological development to effective planning by the community. Generally speaking, it would seem that legislative bodies (at whatever level) should be unicameral to make for clearer lines of responsibility, should be elected by schemes of proportional representation to assure expression of minority views, and should control the executive directly through the power of appointment and removal to promote accountability and keep irrelevant bickering between legislature and executive at a low level. Tendencies to monarchy—such as reflected in the presidency of the United States—must be counteracted in every feasible way, possibly through the device of a plural executive with a short-term rotating chairman. These principles would apply from the world legislative body down to factory, school, professional, and other control groups.

Democratic values dictate re-ordering, too, in the administrative area, possibly at the expense of efficiency in the narrow sense of that term. The problem of controlling bureaucracy is a never-ending one. Among the devices which ought to be considered are greater legislative oversight; adequate machinery for quick redress of grievances against administrators (like the Scandinavian ombudsman scheme); a provision that after a limited term—possibly four or five years—in a senior administrative position, an official would return to a subordinate post, whether in government or industry; a fairly frequent and regular shifting of personnel from one department to another; and much greater administrative decentralization.

Third, we need to ask what should be controlled in a society which, by reason of a fairly high level of development, becomes increasingly politicized. We must also inquire about devices for control. Broadly speaking, democratic values would seem to require that any enterprise or service which affects all or a substantial part of the community should be directed and guided by methods in which all have a voice and should be accountable to the whole community rather than to a segment of it. To specify details here would take us too far afield, but surely this principle would command us to subject the introduction of all complex technology to the general political process. If it is important to subordinate the post office department to deliberate direction by the legislative body, it is of even greater urgency to adopt a similar principle with respect to acceptance of the machine tools which can literally revolutionize our lives. While we have rejected the alternative of deindustrialization, the introduction of new machinery is too earth-shaking to be left any longer to private profit-motivated individuals and private corporations. Modern technology is of enormous public concern and should be treated accordingly. Its adoption should depend on deliberate political decisions governed by public discussion in accordance with the overall value system of the community. In some instances, this might result in the rejection of certain technology but, if so, the decisions would not necessarily be less intelligent than those of private profit-seeking entrepreneurs today. Indeed, they would probably be far more sensible from a social point of view.

Overall allocation of world resources would entail, too, deliberate planning for economic development in regions where it is most needed rather than where it is most immediately profitable. Possibly 5 per cent of the gross national product of highly developed areas might be devoted to planned growth of the underdeveloped part of the world and to training of personnel. This would have to continue until conditions among regions were roughly equalized.

Similar controls would be established within each nation with respect to distribution of income. Ceilings as well as floors on personal income would be established, with the greatest gap between incomes restricted to a ratio of perhaps four or five to one. Free services would also be expanded as first-order priorities. Thus bread might well be distributed without intermediation of a price system, just as we distribute parks and schools today without charging fees. In general, both market and nonmarket controls would be used in segments of the economy not involving direct distribution of goods and services. Thus within the overall scheme of allocations, a price system would continue, prices being adjusted frequently by planning boards in accordance with supply and demand as indicated on the market.[30]

Fourth, the population and density of cities should be limited to make them comprehensible and governable. Where at all possible, they should be replanned, priorities being given to adequate space for human beings rather than greatest convenience for industries.[31] Beyond a certain size, urban complexes tend to be uncontrollable without developing extremely cumbrous administrative machinery which is itself undesirable. Generally speaking, we should regard a quarter of a million people as perhaps the maximum permissible population of a city, and largely unoccupied tracts of considerable minimum breadth between cities should be made mandatory. Within the cities, the basic living area should be the neighborhood group of possibly not more than 350 persons arranged in houses around a common green and including all age groups. This neighborhood group would be the fundamental unit of co-operation and would include such institutions as a nursery school, meeting hall, and recreation center. Hopefully, it could help establish on a regular basis those face-to-face relationships so essential for building a democratic political structure. It would be the primary unit of decision-making.

An urban scheme of this nature would entail a gradual decline of the automobile industry and a great expansion of swift public transportation. Even in cities of limited size, there is not room for both a good private and a first-rate public transport system. Public transportation would be much more efficient than use of the automobile and could be made more convenient as well. Limited natural resources should be devoted to products more worthwhile than indefinitely increasing numbers of automobiles.

Fifth, an extension of the rule of law is indispensable, whether at the world level — where the need is obvious — or in employee-employer relations. Arbitrary decisions must be excluded wherever possible. This becomes particularly important in highly developed societies where economic interdependence is pushed to extremes.

Finally, the role of education, in the broadest sense of the term, cannot be overemphasized. Education must absorb a vastly increased percentage of the gross world product if enlarged and deepened consciousness of the universe is to be brought about and men are to be able to control their own creations socially. The heightened awareness which education can help accomplish

---

[30]See Benjamin E. Lippincott, ed., *On the Economic Theory of Socialism: Essays by Fred Taylor and Oscar Lange* (Minneapolis: Univ. of Minnesota Press, 1928).
[31]Cf. Edward Higbee, *The Squeeze: Cities Without Space* (London: Cassell, 1961).

should not be regarded as merely instrumental but as an end in itself. Broadened sensitivity to the universe and to other human beings is one of the distinctively human qualities which we should regard as a sine qua non of civilized life. Economic activity can be justified only in terms of noneconomic ends.

Here we suggest, with John Stuart Mill[32] and many others, that the human being who most distinctively represents the ideal of humanity is one whose consciousness is expanding continuously through life; whose ultimate ends are those of spiritual, intellectual, aesthetic, and ethical growth and fulfillment; whose interests in material things are only incidental and not central; who is an active rather than merely a passive personality; and who accepts responsibility for the life of the community as well as for his own personal concerns. Personalities having these qualities constitute the goal. Any desideratum short of this elevates means into ends and makes a mockery of development itself.

But development as such will not ensure this goal. The ideal will not be achieved automatically, nor will the gods make its attainment certain. Only deliberate and informed human action guided by clearly articulated principles and ready, if necessary, to limit as well as encourage technological development can bring us measurably nearer the objective.

---

[32]In Mill, *Representative Government* as well as in Mill, *Utilitarianism.*

Author Index

Subject Index